Brutalism as Found

Brutalism as Found

Housing, Form and Crisis at Robin Hood Gardens

Nicholas Thoburn

Goldsmiths Press

For Runa, Noah and Ilan

First published in 2022 by Goldsmiths Press

Goldsmiths, University of London, New Cross
London SE14 6NW

Printed and bound by Versa Press, USA
Distribution by the MIT Press
Cambridge, Massachusetts, USA and London, England

A CIP record for this book is available from the British Library

ISBN 978-1-913380-04-5 (hbk)
ISBN 978-1-913380-03-8 (ebk)

www.brutalismasfound.co.uk

Goldsmiths
UNIVERSITY OF LONDON

For the book's images in colour and more of Kois Miah's portraits of Robin Hood Gardens' residents, visit www.brutalismasfound.co.uk

Contents

1

Introduction: For a Critical Brutalism

It is the lack of transcendence, the permanent uncertainty of any resolution, which propels brutalism back into the world as a form of ethical realism.

Ben Highmore, *The Art of Brutalism*

In England the key problem is that of the council house.

Alison and Peter Smithson, *Ordinariness and Light*

Robin Hood Gardens, the East London council estate designed by New Brutalist architects Alison and Peter Smithson, sat on the fault line of class and inequality that courses through the city. More than a cleavage between rich and poor, this fault line is a destructive force of redevelopment that bore down on the estate and culminated in its demolition. Cleared for a £600-million redevelopment named Blackwall Reach, demolition commenced in 2017 with one of the estate's paired buildings, the other to be dispatched in 2022. But the fault line had long been visible, on the one hand, in the estate's physical disrepair, readied for demolition by local-authority neglect and disinvestment, and, on the other, in the logo-topped towers of the international banks at Canary Wharf, looming ominously on the estate's near horizon (Figure 1.1).

These gleaming towers sited on London's former docks are both instance and icon of the "revanchist city", to invoke geographer Neil Smith's term for the renewed and vengeful calibration of the urban terrain to profit, rent and speculation – the city remade by and for global finance.[1] It is a social assault with a pronounced aesthetic dimension. *Social*, because the demolition of Robin Hood Gardens is one instance of the increasing ejection of working-class populations from inner London, and from housing affordability, security and safety, a process that goes by the dissimulating term

Figure 1.1 Robin Hood Gardens, seven-storey west block and green, Canary Wharf in the background, as seen from the roof of the east block. (Kois Miah, November 2015)

regeneration. *Aesthetic*, because this social assault is commonly cloaked and lent motive force in its repackaging by government and media as a liberating "blitz" on the "concrete monstrosities" of Brutalist and other post-war council estates, of which Robin Hood Gardens has routinely figured as a preeminent example.[2]

The aesthetics of demolition are nothing if not complex, however. The moment the stigmatizing symbolism of the concrete monstrosity had fulfilled its promise in the destruction of Robin Hood Gardens, it was joined by an apparently opposing aesthetic evaluation, when London's Victoria and Albert Museum (V&A) stepped in to salvage a three-storey section of the estate. Destined for installation in the culture-industries quarter of another London regeneration, part of the V&A's acquisition was first exhibited at the 2018 Venice Architecture Biennale. Here a curious transformation took place. What had long been maligned and condemned when it served as working-class housing was in Venice championed as a "small segment of a masterpiece", now that it provided middle-class cultural consumption in the circuit of global art and culture.[3]

Such are the social and aesthetic forces that have taken hold of Robin Hood Gardens in recent years. They also illustrate the public prominence of the estate. Since 2007 and the first of two high-profile campaigns to gain it heritage listing, Robin Hood Gardens has been the subject of colloquia, design competitions, artists' projects, documentary films, television features, a stage play, photography exhibitions, folk songs and a vinyl record, journalism, academic articles, books and now the V&A work of salvage.[4] Some of these have been more critically adequate to their object than others, and valuable for that. But Ang Li, in an essay about the listing dispute, is right, I think, that Robin Hood Gardens has become something of a "concrete marionette", a malleable symbol for shifting representations, opinions and political stakes, in which "the architecture is silenced into mere iconography".[5]

I make this observation, I hasten to add, not as preamble to a book that would cut through representation and politics to rediscover an architectural object cleansed of incrustation. Representation and politics are integral to architecture and prominent in these pages. The claim I make for this book, rather, is that it recentres Robin Hood Gardens in its own story and in our time. This is not to integrate the estate or plot it in narrative, but to be *immersed* in it, to grasp it in its architectural and social complexity and originality, to encounter it as it confronts and provokes us in the crisis conditions of today. Robin Hood Gardens takes shape here in its architectural forms, materials, atmospheres, images, concepts and myths, in its lived experience, demolition and afterlife, as it courses with the conflictual conditions of the present. In turn, Robin Hood Gardens *intervenes* in these conditions, where its social and architectural forms interrogate and challenge the Brutalist revival and the politics and aesthetics of council housing in its present crisis.

This is what it means to engage the estate "as found", as in the title of this book. The as found, one of the many neologisms coined by Alison and Peter Smithson in the course of their practice, is a Brutalist *sensibility*, even a *method*. Against the imposition of predetermined built form, it names an immanent relation to materials, sites and social conditions, their flux and crises brought to light as integral to architectural expression. An architecture – and a *criticism* – that is as found is *flush with the world*, and all the more awkward, unfinished, experimental and critical for it.

Brutalism as Class Architecture

Recent years have seen a significant political challenge to the social violence and inequity of estate regeneration and the privatization of social housing, from residents' groups and housing movements in London and across the globe.[6] For those states with histories of social housing, this movement is aptly characterized by the slogan of East London's Focus E15 Campaign: *Social Housing Not Social Cleansing!* There's a definite aesthetic dimension here, a struggle over the public image of social housing. Questions of architecture feature too. But the focus on pressing housing need is such that architectural questions have not been prominent, and the revival of architectural interest in Brutalism has been either inadequate to these crisis conditions or has itself served the forces of privatization, as I consider below. There is space, then, for a *critical* Brutalism, a theory of Brutalism adequate to the crisis of social housing today. That is one of the central tasks of this book, in its theory of Brutalism as *class architecture*, as pursued through the architectural forms and lived experience of Robin Hood Gardens.

As with much of the book, I take the impetus for this critical approach from the Smithsons. Brutalism is a term with a wide ambit, including examples that bear little or no relation to the Smithsons' theory and practice, or to the social aims of public housing.[7] I should underscore, then, that the Brutalism of this book is the *Smithsons'* Brutalism, including the constellation of ideas, practices, artists and architects from which they drew, and which Robin Hood Gardens manifests, complicates and extends. At the same time, this book *critically appropriates* the Smithsons' Brutalism, driven by problems that confront housing and architecture today. Hence I sometimes extend the Smithsons' ideas in ways only latent in their work, or in directions they left untravelled, and on occasion I twist their ideas against themselves, for there are definite elements to their writing that are far closer to liberal and neoliberal thinking than to the critical perspectives that inform this book.

If there is a social rationale for this critical appropriation, provoked by contemporary problems, there are also good grounds for it *internal* to the Smithsons' Brutalism. One of the meanings of their awkward and jarring word, and not the most well-known, is that of a *brute* injunction to social relevance. Writing in 1957, they encapsulate Brutalism as "an attempt to be objective about 'reality'", its aim to "drag a rough poetry out of the confused and powerful forces which are at work".[8] They see this as an *ethical* injunction, against which, no less, Brutalism *stands or falls*. As Peter Smithson remarks in a 1959 interview, "We are interested in expressing not ourselves, but what is going on and building which denies what is going on is just the opposite of brutalism – it is chi-chi, which is a sort of evasion."[9] To recover the meaning of this injunction to Brutalism, a central aim of this book, requires a close reading of the place of the social in the Smithsons' architecture, but this is not only an historical endeavour. To avoid – or to *challenge* – an evasive, chi-chi Brutalism necessitates that this ethical injunction *be applied to Brutalist architecture today*, grounded in social problems that present themselves to our present moment. To do so, I argue, is to draw out and develop the *class* dimensions of architecture – in both the Smithsons' work and in Brutalism today – through the concept of class architecture.

In this concept, the working class is not *identity*, as it is all too often misunderstood, but *crisis*. It is a fraught and unstable social condition, a condition of dispossession, exploitation, insecurity and conflict, ever buffeted and pulled out of shape by the tangle of social relations of which it is comprised. At the same time, it is in this *non-identity* of the working class, its lack of fit with society, wherein resides the wrenching force of critical interrogation and social transformation that is the class standpoint – "its restlessness within its very self", in Marx's phrase.[10] For, *without a place of its own*, without an achieved and satisfied identity accommodated to society, class politics must of necessity push out *into the social realm as a whole*, critically engaging the gamut of social relations that cleave and buffet each particular working-class experience. As for how this understanding of class is manifest in *architecture*, it has two interrelated aspects which run throughout the book's appraisal of Robin Hood Gardens.

First, class architecture names and critically pursues *the crisis conditions of working-class housing* – the social and aesthetic forces, agents and forms that coursed through Robin Hood Gardens and culminated in its demolition. Second, class architecture is concerned with how the fraught conditions of class society were *modulated in the architecture* of Robin Hood Gardens, a process that was at once internal to the estate and pushed out into site and society. For this second aspect there is scant critical precedent. Class architecture is not a question of the *representation* of the working class, the architectural modelling of superficial or clichéd impressions. My focus, rather, is on how the estate interrogated and grappled with social and material features of the working-class condition, fashioning forms that strained to both protect from and restructure the hostile social forces of class society. In this way, class architecture bears the non-identity of the working class into built form, crisis confronted but unresolved – the experimental condition of Robin Hood Gardens.

Robin Hood Gardens features in these pages less, then, as an historical architecture besieged by crisis than as an architecture that *speaks to and confronts our present* in its handling of crisis in built form. I will say more about how this manifests in the focus and structure of the book, but first it is high time I introduced the estate.

Robin Hood Gardens and Its Times

Robin Hood Gardens was built between 1968 and 1972 in Poplar, in the London Borough of Tower Hamlets. It comprised 214 maisonettes and single-storey flats in two sculptured and dramatic mid-rise, concrete slab-blocks of seven and ten storeys (I refer to these, respectively, as the west and east blocks).[11] Bent at plan as the paired structures followed the bordering roads, they nurtured between them a large, tranquil garden and artificial mound, significant features of the architecture, as we will see (Figure 1.2). The scheme was characterized by deck-access "streets in the sky" – aerial walkways that ran like impressed bands along its exterior sides at every third floor – and protruding mullions, asymmetrical fin-like structures that vertically strode its raw-concrete façades. To channel cars away from the residential and garden areas, an open-air "moat" of garages ran the exterior length of each building at basement level, accessed by a ramp at one end of each moat and by internal stairwells.

Robin Hood Gardens was the Smithsons' only mass-housing scheme, though mass housing and associated issues of habitat and urbanism were a central focus of their writing and discussions in Team 10, where the Smithsons were leading figures. I do not consider Team 10 in depth in this book (even less so the Smithsons' other groups, MARS and the Independent Group) but it indicates the significance of the Smithsons' critical dialogue with modernism that the formation of this group of architects in 1953 precipitated the demise of the International Congress of Modern Architecture

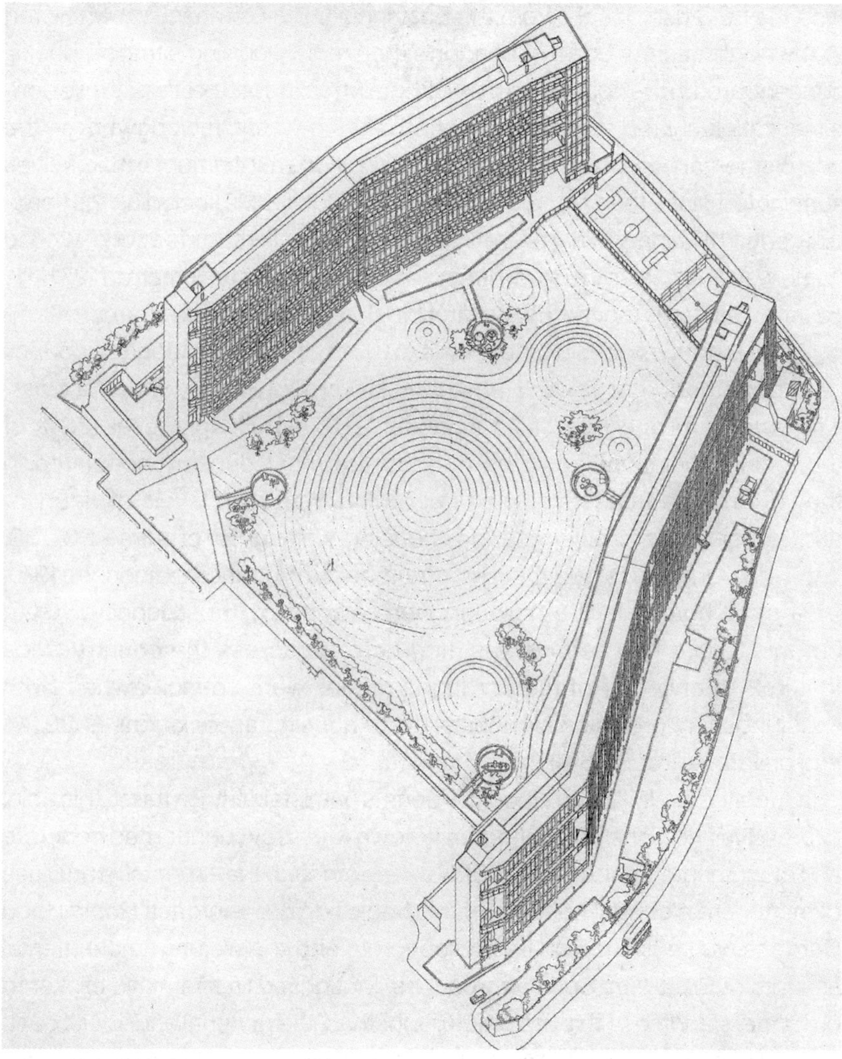

Figure 1.2 Robin Hood Gardens, axonometric from the north-west. (Kenny Baker, 1968. Smithson Family Collection)

(CIAM), which had set the intellectual agenda of modernist architecture and planning since 1928, under Le Corbusier's direction.[12]

Robin Hood Gardens was commissioned by the London County Council (LCC), succeeded in 1965 by the Greater London Council (GLC), on land the LCC had bought from the East India Dock Company.[13] It was sited at the north-eastern edge of London's then rapidly closing shipping docks, concentrated in the adjacent peninsula known as the Isle of Dogs. While containerization shifted shipping away to the deep-water dock downriver, the complementary capitalist trend of financialization saw the docks themselves supplanted, since the early 1980s, by London Docklands (including the financial centre of Canary Wharf), an initially tax-exempt "enterprise zone" whose name was first used by a government-commissioned study team in 1971, the year the residents moved into the first block of Robin Good Gardens.[14]

The estate's wider locale, Poplar, a ward in the borough (or council or local authority) of Tower Hamlets, is still predominantly working class, with a large proportion of its inhabitants British Bangladeshi (32% of the local population).[15] The borough is the most densely populated in the UK and the fastest-growing in London, with high levels of deprivation, housing overcrowding and a housing waiting list of some 20,000. Yet it has dramatically diminishing numbers of council homes. In 1981, 97% of all homes in the borough were owned by the council or GLC, but this tenure has been devastated here, as across the country, such that in 2011 only 12% of the borough's homes were council-owned (with social-housing provision by quasi-private housing associations at 22.3% and private rent at 32.6%).[16]

Architecturally, Robin Hood Gardens is unmistakably Brutalist, this bold, expressive and visceral architecture known for its raw, unadorned concrete and monumental scale (Figure 1.3). However, though the expressive qualities of matter are a central concern of this book, I do not approach Robin Hood Gardens with a fixation on its raw concrete and the weighty, monumental aspects of Brutalism. Such approaches, though significant, have blinkered our understanding of this architecture. Instead, the material and social qualities of Brutalism and Robin Hood Gardens are considered here through the question of *form*. My contention is that the scheme modulates class society through a set of socio-architectural forms – what I call *forms in process* or *deforming forms*, so as to emphasize their dynamic and processual nature. Robin Hood Gardens did not have a coherent architectural identity. It was loosened from overbearing formal integration, and was instead an "assemblage" of forms – forms that were at once distinct, overlapping and folded

Figure 1.3 Robin Hood Gardens, garden façade of the ten-storey east block. (Kois Miah, June 2015)

into and out of each other, held together in their difference.[17] And these forms took shape through interrogating their own social and material conditions. Robin Hood Gardens, then, was an assemblage of forms in the process of deforming themselves, and their site and society with them.

This is what the Smithsons called a "non-Euclidean" architecture.[18] Rayner Banham, in his movement-defining essay "The New Brutalism", called it "topological" or "aformal", where topology, as a discipline, concerns the coexistence of form and deformation, continuity and change.[19] Yet the topological qualities of Brutalism have played little role in its critical appreciation, and even less in the appraisal of Robin Hood Gardens. With topology on the horizon of the critical humanities again, this is another reason to find the contemporary in Robin Hood Gardens.

It may seem curious, even perverse, to talk of the contemporaneity of this estate, for it has no *fit* with the social relations of today. Indeed, this was characteristic of its lifespan as a whole. Loosened from internal integration, the estate was also out of joint *with its times*. Built at the very end of the post-war boom in council housing, it is commonly seen to be a late – or *too* late – expression of the welfare state in housing, any social fit it may have expected immediately lost, as state priorities, ideologies and finances veered away.[20] Robin Hood Gardens was completed, after all, the very year that the architectural critic Charles Jencks declared modern architecture to have died, indexed for him to demolition of the Pruitt Igoe public-housing projects in St Louis, Missouri. By the time demolition came to Robin Hood Gardens, it had long been an anathema to the neoliberal consensus of housing speculation, state-promoted home ownership and private rent, and welfare retrenchment, as pursued by national and local governments of all political shades.

Yet this lack of fit with its times is no reason to appraise the estate unfavourably – unless, of course, one accords with the political economy of these times, which I do not. The demolition of Robin Hood Gardens and other council estates is not evidence of their anachronism. It is evidence of the *contemporary* state of working-class housing, where government, media and the house-building industry advance demolition by *producing* the cultural impression of estate anachronism, thus masking and consolidating the ongoing class assault on housing. The point I wish to make now, though, is slightly different. In cleaving to social complexities and contradictions, modulating them in architectural form, Robin Hood Gardens was in significant ways *necessarily* out of joint with its times, with *any* times. And this awkward quality, the estate's lack of fit, integral to its class architecture, is what makes it *most* contemporary. Its significance is not as an image of past welfare-state harmony to hold up against revanchist urbanism – however much council housing, its past and present, stands as an indictment of the dire state of housing today. Its contemporary significance, rather, is as an experimental housing estate fashioned as a confrontation with society, an understanding that is unfurled through the course of this book.

Concrete Monstrosity and the Crisis of Housing Affordability

Brutalism is an architectural style of today, in that it is much in the eye of government, developers and opponents and enthusiasts of modernism. It appears to us in two dominant symbolic frames or discourses, where Brutalist structures are either turned against themselves in the stigmatizing symbolism of the *concrete monstrosity*, or refashioned as class-cleansed modernist masterpieces, the symbolism of *beautiful Brutalism*, I will call it.

Both are key to understanding the recent fate of Robin Hood Gardens and other post-war estates, hence I take time here to unpack them, along with their associated social conditions, policies and consequences.

To start with the first of these discourses, Brutalist council estates like Robin Hood Gardens have long been subject to a discursive barrage of stigmatizing tropes and representations. The assault takes place in policy pronouncements from local and national governments, reports by think tanks and property companies, tabloids and broadsheets, television dramas and feature films. These tropes and representations have causality and consequence, as Tom Slater has shown of the *sink estate*, what he calls "a semantic battering ram in the ideological assault on social housing".[21] They do not work all by themselves and are complex, without unitary effect, but they play a leading part in distributing and stoking social moods that support and propel agendas in social and economic policy. Not least of these agendas is the UK governmental programme of council-estate demolition and regeneration, currently supercharged but in play as a dominant governmental approach to council estates since the New Labour administrations of Tony Blair, from 1997. If the sink estate is the leading stigmatizing trope here, it shares features and is often partnered and sometimes substituted with that of the concrete monstrosity, as was the case at Robin Hood Gardens.

In the earliest incarnations of Blackwall Reach, Robin Hood Gardens' replacement, the forces of speculative development took architectural shape in pastel-shade promotional images of the scheme's anodyne, featureless buildings. Their polite and insubstantial nature befitted the abiding narrative of change, which aimed to rid the Poplar locale of its hulking concrete monstrosity. As John Grindrod observes, the trope of the concrete monstrosity, this "potent and irresistible cliché", is the default government and media descriptor of post-war modernism.[22] It snags on the collective imagination ("Postwar buildings are *concrete monstrosities* in the same way that political correctness is always *going mad*") and is capacious in its application to council estates, not limited to those of Brutalist style.[23] At core, it turns against the favoured material of Brutalism and trades on a claimed sympathy with working-class residents, who are understood to be the voiceless victims of the hubris of middle-class architects and planners. There is also a dose of populism to it, and nativism too, the notion of an "elite out to smash the decent British way of doing things, to crush the life out of it beneath *concrete monstrosities*".[24]

Such is apparent in the following remark by Margaret Hodge, who as minister at the Department for Digital, Culture, Media and Sport ruled against the first attempt to list Robin Hood Gardens: "Anyone who wants to list that place should try living there. It is simply not fit for purpose and I cannot believe that anyone is trying to list it. They should try living in it or raising a family there."[25] The journalist Simon Jenkins in *The Guardian* provided a variation on the theme, again regarding Robin Hood Gardens, though now the metaphoric role of concrete, as violence, is made plain: "Never have the rich been robbed to dump so much concrete ugliness on the heads of the poor."[26]

The violent party is not Robin Hood Gardens, however, but the trope of the concrete monstrosity itself. Despite the claimed inter-class solidarities, the vehemence of the condemnation and its formidable effects of "territorial stigmatization" suggest that the real object of hostility is not a building material and architectural style but the *social form and visibility of council estates as such*.[27] In this trope, middle-class contempt for the working class is disguised and disavowed, making the concrete monstrosity a little different from the "national abjects", as Imogen Tyler characterizes them, of *single mother*, *benefits cheat* and *chav*.[28] But it has a strong family resemblance and serves the same function, wherein the welfare retrenchment and housing dispossession that render working-class lives ever more precarious are obscured and refashioned as solutions to unsightly and pathogenic moral failing.

In readying estates for demolition, the symbolic assault of the concrete monstrosity also serves the global market in real estate. As is well documented, in liberal democracies across the world the state is in retreat from the provision of public housing, while capital shifts from the circuit of production, with its declining profitability, to finance, insurance and real estate. Here housing is an investment asset with which to speculate, extract rents, park surpluses, launder money and facilitate new financial instruments. It results in soaring house prices and the demolition of buildings that drag on the prized "value uplift" – in the UK, council estates foremost among them.[29] Tens of thousands of London council homes have been razed to date. Since 1997, a staggering 54,263 units have either been demolished or are slated for demolition on estates of more than 100 units, according to Loretta Lees and Hannah White, with a conservative estimate of 135,658 households displaced.[30] Another recent estimate has 31,000 Londoners currently facing the loss of their homes due to estate demolition and regeneration, and the Estate Watch project identifies over 100 London estates under threat.[31] In consequence, as Josephine Berry encapsulates the stakes, "housing – an essential structure of care – has become the site of bitter social conflict and class cleansing".[32]

Is this what is called *the housing crisis*? For all that this phrase – ubiquitous in pronouncements by politicians, broadcast media and the property lobby – appears to identify the dire state of UK housing, it has a duplicitous dimension. As Simon Elmer and Geraldine Dening have argued, in conveying the sense of an extraordinary and unmanageable situation, the phrase obscures that the crisis is *actively produced*.[33] For David Madden and Peter Marcuse, the "housing crisis stems from [and reproduces] the inequalities and antagonisms of class society", of housing as a commodity and vehicle of accumulation against housing as a need. "Housing crisis is not a result of the system breaking down but of the system working as it is intended."[34] It is produced in legislation and practice by a plethora of actors – national and local governments, institutional and individual speculative investors, construction and maintenance firms, housing developers, estate agencies and consultancies, global accountancy companies, mortgage lenders, housing associations, private and corporate landlords – who are dependent upon and reap vast rewards from what is a *booming* housing economy, worth in London £2.4 trillion.[35] For example, Berkeley Homes, one of the top ten UK building companies, reported six-monthly profits of £533 million in 2017 (a year in which it completed 3,536 homes at the far-from-affordable average price of £715,000) and a total of £2.9 billion profit in the seven years up to 2018 – while maintaining, in 93% of its London developments, that local-authority affordable-housing targets were economically unviable.[36] And Berkeley Homes is not alone; between 2010 and 2015, the end-of-year profits of the five biggest UK housebuilders rose from £372 million to over £2 billion, an increase of over 480%.[37]

Not only does the trope of the housing crisis obscure its manufactured nature, it also *exacerbates* it. Successive governments and the "finance-housebuilding complex", as Bob Colenutt calls the nexus of property actors, have constructed the housing crisis "quite deliberately as a crisis of numbers", for which private housebuilding is the vaunted solution.[38] This empowers the causes of the problem it claims to name, for the crisis is not one of supply but of housing affordability, security and safety, a crisis made *worse* by the conditions and consequences of private development.

A signal instance is the influential 2015 Institute for Public Policy Research (IPPR) report *City Villages: More Homes, Better Communities*, by Andrew Adonis, Labour Member of the House of Lords. Adonis proffers new-build "solutions" to the housing crisis, couched in the comforting language of community, village and street, which actually entail the destruction of London's council estates – estates he revealingly describes as sitting "on some of the most expensive land in the world", whose "sheer number and size ... is far larger than commonly appreciated".[39] On the same track, though more directly integrated into policy, are the estate-demolition proposals contained in *Create Streets*, the 2013 report by the right-wing think tank Policy Exchange, and *Completing London's Streets*, the 2016 government-commissioned report by the global real-estate company Savills.[40] These supplied the rhetoric and spurious evidence for David Cameron's 2016 announcement to "blitz" poverty by demolishing 100 of the UK's "worst 'sink estates'". A triumphal, new-year announcement by the then prime minister, it epitomized the coarticulation of the trope of concrete monstrosity with estate demolition, and the leading role therein of government and the property industry, working hand-in-glove. Here Cameron identified council estates as the cause of a welter of social ills, where "blocked opportunity, poor parenting, addiction and mental health problems" are allowed to "fester and grow unseen" – until they erupt in social unrest.[41] For it is "not a coincidence", in his illogic, that the "riots of 2011 didn't emerge from within terraced streets or low-rise apartment buildings". Once again, concrete and allusions to Brutalism carried the burden of persuasion. "Step outside in the worst estates", he continued with his scene of horror, "and you're confronted by concrete slabs dropped from on high, brutal high-rise towers and dark alleyways that are a gift to criminals and drug dealers. The police often talk about the importance of designing out crime, but these estates actually designed it in."

Even when new build is not premised on estate demolition, increased private supply does nothing to reduce prices and tends actually to inflate them, contrary to the commonplace of "supply and demand" duplicitously spread by the property lobby. This is because private new build raises the potential land values of adjacent property – it creates a *rent gap* – putting further pressure on private-sector rents and incentivizing the demolition or privatization of council homes. New private developments also feed the ever-growing market in price-inflating mortgage lending (now the majority of UK loans, following the deregulation and liberalization of the credit market in the 1970s and 1980s) and the near unlimited demand from domestic and overseas speculative investors, who are attracted, not repelled, by house-price inflation, "since rising prices are always a sign of high potential investment yields".[42]

Demolition and rent gaps do not work alone, of course. Council estates and tenures have been undermined and pulled apart in a more capillary fashion by a barrage of punitive and exploitative neoliberal social policies in housing, planning, regulation and welfare. I refer readers to others who have researched these policies and their devastating personal and social consequences in exhaustive detail, and will instead note only some of the most notorious.[43] Most damaging of all is the decimation of council stock brought through Right to Buy privatization and stock transfer. A provision of the 1980 Housing Act, Right to Buy gave council tenants the right to purchase their homes at huge discounts (the maximum discount started at 50% and reached 70% by 1989) and compelled councils to return 75% of the receipts to central government, preventing their use for new council building.[44] The first of Margaret Thatcher's public-sector privatizations, the policy has been vigorously pursued ever since. Between 1981 and 2014, 1.8 million council homes were sold this way, and sales continue apace, at an average of 12,000 per year between 2012 and 2018.[45] Thus withdrawn from council provision, at great cost to state finances, a large proportion of Right to Buy homes are subsequently rented again, only now in the private sector – in London, 42% of them, in Tower Hamlets, more than half – with the attendant fall in security, conditions and regulation, and hikes in rent levels (private-sector rents are on average 2.3 times those of social rents).[46] This enforced shift of householders with the highest need from council tenancies into the private-rented sector has also created sky-rocketing levels of Housing Benefit, where state finance is used to line the pockets of private and corporate landlords rather than to build council housing, amounting to some £22 billion a year.[47]

Complementing these mass sales of individual units, from the mid-1980s Thatcher's council-housing privatization proceeded also through the stock transfer of *whole estates* to ownership by quasi-private housing associations, a process known as the *demunicipalization* of social housing. By 1997, around 300,000 council units had been sold to this increasingly deregulated and commercialized sector, now a leading actor in the development industry. The policy was recharged by Tony Blair's Decent Homes Programme from

2000, which also included measures to encourage council-estate transfers to arms-length management organisations (ALMOs), owned by councils but run on a commercial basis (Tower Hamlets Homes, for example, which took over management of the borough's remaining council housing, including Robin Hood Gardens).[48] In turn, housing associations have become major agents in estate demolition and rebuild, combining new social housing with build for private sale. Swann Housing, the developer of Blackwall Reach, is a prime example, which first advertised this development to the global real-estate market in Hong Kong, in October 2017, with two-bed apartments priced from £565,000[49] (Figure 1.4).

In consequence of these forces of demolition, privatization and demunicipalization, the number of council homes has been cut nationally from 6.5 million in 1980 to just 2 million in 2018.[50] Save for a tiny smattering of new council homes, for which demolition-happy councils are far too quick to pat themselves on the back, the building of social housing is now exclusively the preserve of housing associations, at numbers vastly diminished compared to previous council builds. And these are concentrated in the new and

Figure 1.4 Advertising Blackwall Reach with an image of Canary Wharf, Robin Hood Gardens in the background. (Nicholas Thoburn, March 2017)

dissimulating category of affordable rent, set at up to 80% of market rents, the focus of social-housing subsidy since the 2010 Conservative–Liberal coalition government.

Those who continue as council tenants in this residualized sector are subject to a barrage of punitive measures. These include provisions of the 2011 Localism Act, which removed the obligation for local authorities to provide the unintentionally homeless with social housing, while permitting that the remaining requirement to provide temporary accommodation be discharged by placing people in private accommodation in distant towns and cities, uprooting them from support networks, schools and jobs. The same legislation resulted in hundreds of thousands being cut from housing waiting lists as local authorities used their powers to tighten eligibility criteria. Council tenants are subject also to the "bedroom tax", introduced by the 2012 Welfare Reform Act, which hits them with a reduction in Housing Benefit if they're deemed to be under-occupying, despite the chronic lack of options to downsize. The 2016 Housing and Planning Act mandates local authorities to grant only fixed-term tenancies, of two to ten years, although this has yet to be fully implemented, and requires the sale of "higher-value" vacant council homes, with receipts remitted to the Treasury to fund the extension of the Right to Buy to housing associations.

Meanwhile, savage cuts to welfare and housing support between 2010 and 2021 total £27 billion a year, and funding for local authorities has fallen by one third in the poorest boroughs (and one quarter in the wealthier ones).[51] This puts further pressure on stretched maintenance budgets and encourages more transfer of land and council stock to private developers.[52] But the enthusiasm by which local authorities in London have pursued such privatization – Labour administrations in particular, such as Southwark, Lambeth, Newham, Haringey and Tower Hamlets – and the revolving door between local-authority planning departments and the firms who make extraordinary profits from these developments show local authorities and their officers to be willing partners.[53] The party line is that this is the only available means to finance social housing, where in exchange for the land developers commit to providing a proportion of the new units at affordable and social rents. But in addition to the destructive social consequences of this private build, developers are adept at using "viability assessments", cloaked in commercial confidentiality clauses, to slash the unit numbers of these Section 106 obligations.[54]

Given this symbolic and policy context, it should be no surprise that as Robin Hood Gardens was dispatched from Poplar, it took its council housing with it, with no objection from those who trade in the stigmatizing trope of monstrosity. Whatever proportion of social-rent tenures Blackwall Reach eventually includes, there will be no council homes.[55] The estate's Tenants' and Residents' Association (TRA) campaigned hard to retain the rights of tenants' secure tenancies in transfer to the new development, with some success, but these will not be provided to new and subsequent tenants.[56] And with the Right to Buy now applied also to housing associations, it is a safe assumption that social-rent tenures in Blackwall Reach will steadily decline over time.

Beautiful Brutalism at Balfron Tower

Persistent though it is, the trope of the concrete monstrosity is not the only discursive framing of Brutalism today. As would be hard to miss, recent years have seen it rivalled by a renewed enthusiasm for Brutalism, as middle-class tastes for modernism, hitherto tethered to the glass-fronted white boxes of the pre-war International Style, have come to embrace the monumentality and raw concrete of this post-war architecture.[57] On the terrain of architectural taste, this discursive framework of beautiful Brutalism positions itself as saviour of the maligned and endangered, late arriving and under conditions of heritage emergency, but in time to provide a positive reappraisal of Brutalism that may at least prevent further demolition. It is not the boon to Brutalist public housing that it might seem, however. For it is too often just as interested in separating council residents from their homes as is the trope of the concrete monstrosity. This time, though, it is not the residents who are to be saved from Brutalism, but *Brutalism that is to be saved from council residents*.

In saving, it appropriates, for beautiful Brutalism is approximately indexed to the move of middle-class homebuyers into ex-council properties, a market resultant of the resale of Right to Buy purchases and the ballooning property prices that have put traditional middle-class housing stock increasingly out of reach. For this class, fearful of council estates and anxious about downward social mobility, beautiful Brutalism serves to cleanse the architecture of its working-class associations, or translate and modify these associations into palatable forms, and thus eases the transition into the new market. Indeed, in some instances beautiful Brutalism stridently *drives* the transition, as in the private redevelopment of Sheffield's Park Hill (1957–1961) and, to which I turn shortly, East London's Balfron Tower (1965–1967), ex-council estates heavily marketed on their Brutalist aesthetic. In these latter cases, beautiful Brutalism takes an infrastructural form, where what was first encouraged and codified by the cultural intermediaries of books, blogs and Instagram is now celebrated and commercially leveraged by developers, design agencies, the museum industry – even Airbnb.[58]

Though ultimately unsuccessful, this middle-class Brutalism had a presence in the campaign to save Robin Hood Gardens. High-profile champions of the architecture had a tendency to place fault for its perceived failings at the feet of those for whom it was built. Richard Rogers, for example, though rightly highlighting the destructive legacy of local-authority neglect, described the estate, in comparison to the Smithsons' upmarket Central London office scheme, like this: "Whilst the Economist Building has been maintained and upgraded, Robin Hood Gardens has been appallingly neglected and, from the beginning, has been used as a sink estate to house those least capable of looking after themselves – much less their environment."[59] Laying cause for the bad public impression and condition of the estate on council residents, stigmatizing them in the process, the implication is that this modernist masterpiece would be better served by a different class of residents – students, as it was sometimes touted in the campaign to save the estate, or private owners.[60]

It was, though, at a different Brutalist estate in Poplar where this route of private ownership was pursued: Balfron Tower, the 26-storey council block designed by Ernő Goldfinger, Grade II-listed in 1996 (Figure 1.5). Less than half-a-mile north of Robin Hood Gardens and clearly visible from the estate's mound, Balfron Tower had long shared with it the stigmatizing trope of the concrete monstrosity, the estate and its architecture subject to extraordinarily aggressive cultural representations.[61] At a certain point, however, the trajectories and representations of the two estates markedly diverged.

In 2007, ownership of Balfron Tower was transferred from Tower Hamlets council to Poplar HARCA (Housing and Regeneration Community Association) at a cost of £1, on condition of refurbishment. Yet in February

Figure 1.5 Balfron Tower. (Sebastian F., 2008. Creative Commons Attribution – Share Alike 3.0)

2015, having initially decanted residents with the promise of a right to return, Poplar HARCA revealed a plan that residents and critics had long suspected: to sell all the apartments into the private sector. In the course of the maturation of this plan, the trope of the concrete monstrosity was overlaid and then displaced by the symbolism of beautiful Brutalism, which developed numerous facets as it accompanied the progress of the estate's image cleanse, marketing and sale. To draw from Bev Skeggs' research on middle-class appropriation of working-class cultural forms, one sees in this episode how beautiful Brutalism serves to translate, legitimize, modify and codify the former council estate for middle-class consumption – first as alienable artefact of cultural consumption and then as purchasable property.[62] The process bears consideration in some depth.

Different agencies played a part, including Poplar HARCA, Bow Arts (a local public-arts body), the National Trust and the Olympic public-arts vehicle Legacy List. In the case of Robin Hood Gardens, English Heritage (now named Historic England) sided in no uncertain terms against the estate. It "fails as a place for human beings to live – and did so from the start" was its verdict in 2008, so startlingly damning and at odds with architectural opinion as to suggest political influence.[63] With Balfron Tower, however, the heritage industry took the alternate route, the National Trust serving beautiful

Brutalism with sell-out tours to a top-floor apartment, once briefly inhabited by Goldfinger, and kitted out for the occasion by Hemingway Design in vintage 1960s interior furnishings.[64] This was one of numerous cultural events on site, in what *The Guardian*'s Oliver Wainwright aptly dubbed a "gentrification jamboree".

> As residents have battled their displacement [at Balfron Tower], their plight has been framed against a backdrop of arts events, in a kind of live gentrification jamboree. There have been pop-up galleries and impromptu supper clubs, 24-hour theatre performances and a weekend branded as a "vertical carnival", concluding with an architectural symposium on the roof – from which one artist also proposed to hurl a piano, before her plan was damned as an act of crass lunacy. All the usual actors of regeneration have been paraded through the building, the artist-tenants performing their valiant role as the kamikaze agents of real estate "value uplift", enjoying a last hurrah on the deck of the brutalist Titanic.[65]

Much could be said about each of these cultural events, but to focus on the Hemingway-furnished apartment, there was a particular *temporality* at play, which I want to tease out in relation to the temporality within which council housing is today near invariably positioned.

As Steph Lawler shows, the working class tends to be discursively shaped by government and media as an "anachronistic space", deemed to be "suffering from a political, social and cultural atavism: *in* the present, but not *of* it".[66] The effect, of course, *is* in the present, as the lived class experience of crisis and precarity – the intrinsic non-identity of the working class, its out-of-joint quality – is discursively refashioned as the result of collapsed and outmoded social and cultural forms and identities. It is a move that both cloaks and justifies the *production* of that crisis in the present.

The post-war council estate is an exemplary instance. Here the discourse of anachronism has long held a seemingly unshakeable hold, vital to the claimed necessity of estate demolition and regeneration, when in fact the dismantling of council tenures and estates is a leading *cause* of housing crisis. Under sway of beautiful Brutalism, however, the temporality of anachronism has, in some estates like Balfron Tower, started to fall away, unevenly replaced by temporal frames that help refashion the cultural associations of council housing in terms more conducive to middle-class aspiration. At Balfron Tower, this temporality took a *retro-futurist* quality.

In the National Trust partnership with Hemingway Design, the temporality had a somewhat kitsch form, the apartment looking "like some supercharged Austin Powers film set".[67] To the extent that this Brutalist tower can be identified with one show flat, its long-maligned style was in this way redeemed to the present by accentuating its difference to today, along the lines of the it's-so-bad-it's-good variety of taste for 1960s consumer aesthetics. In the move towards the private sale of the apartments, however, the estate's retro-futurist aesthetic became less gaudy plastic, more "mid-century modern", and was associated not with one flat but the building as a whole. This was evident around the same time as the Hemingway makeover, in a test promotional film for the sale by the architectural firm Hawkins\Brown.[68] Over the course of two-and-a-half minutes the film animates a series of still images and text to rewrite the history of the building as a class-cleansed design icon and archetype of the Swinging Sixties. Commencing with reference to Le Corbusier and Goldfinger's ideas of high-rise living, it strings together Op Art dresses, Lambretta scooters, James Bond and so forth to the sound of Mel Tormé's *Comin' Home Baby* – a social and aesthetic scene diligently stripped of signifiers of the scheme's true heritage as a council estate. Thus cleansed, the film's retro image is then sutured to today's urban creatives and young professionals, codified by their satchels, MacBooks and sharp suits, the sale's idealized market.

In the later stages of marketing, this mid-century palette became more sophisticated still, with sales brochures sketching the history of Brutalism and the building's design qualities, emphasizing the renovation's attention to detail and its sensitive modernization and flattering its would-be purchasers' taste ("It has taken a new generation of design aficionados to recognize the innate charm and generosity of Brutalist design").[69] Of this, a promotional piece in the design magazine *Wallpaper* is exemplary, as beautiful Brutalism takes its next step, integrated in private development.

> For decades, the bold concrete visions of the 1960s and 1970s were for aficionados only. In recent years, brutalism has been celebrated in crisp black and white photography and rendered in seductive graphics, yet all too often the reality lagged far behind. A chronic lack of maintenance, plus the experimental nature of concrete construction, might have given these rain-streaked monoliths a certain raw edginess, but up close, only the true fetishist could get excited. Finally, though, the rehabilitation is getting structural.[70]

Again, markedly absent in this account of how the estate is being "brought back to life" is the place in this process of its working-class former residents. They are not voided entirely, however. The *Wallpaper* article mentions the social displacement of the regeneration (albeit in a confused manner, that "the block's original quota of affordable housing would be gone forever") and Ab Rogers, whose firm collaborated with Studio Egret West in the refurbishment, gestures to the same problem. With Rogers, though, there appears to be an aspiration to square the circle.

> Doing Balfron, I think we've learned about trying to encourage a diverse community where people from different worlds can come together. For us, projects go a lot further than the aesthetics of the architecture: good design is about creating communities and making sure no one is siloed. So, if when Balfron Tower opens it feels like a gated community, then we've really failed as designers. If it becomes a part of expanding, without gentrifying, the area then I think we've exceeded at getting people to live together in different ways.[71]

It is difficult to put one's finger on it, but beautiful Brutalism has here gained an additional feature, something "further than the aesthetics of the architecture" – a certain *togetherness* or *community*, where housing which was aggressively class-cleansed in actuality is imagined and marketed as a revived idyll of cross-class harmony. It works in two steps. First, community is presented as a positive value loosely associated with the social aims of the design in its time. As the marketing brochure puts it, "the new Balfron Tower retains a strong commitment to the local community, continuing Ernő Goldfinger's acclaimed legacy", the refurbishment "designed to revive this sense of togetherness. The designer Ab Rogers speaks of Balfron's new occupiers becoming part of a well-established community".[72] Second, though this community is posited against neoliberal urbanism (against "gated communities" and "expanding, without gentrifying, the area"), it is actually a quality to be consumed *in one's private purchase*, that is, *as* an artefact of neoliberal urbanism. Community here articulates not a critique of inequality, but a feel-good image of organic wholeness with which class realities are obscured and the development marketed, to be experienced as a set of private community features ("a communal kitchen and dining room for events that can't be held in a two-bedroom flat, together with a workshop, cinema, library, gym and yoga room, as well as a generous communal roof terrace") framed as the ethos of Goldfinger's design.[73]

The refurbished Balfron Tower, then, takes on board something of the commonly assumed community values of Brutalism, 1960s democratic sociality revived, but in order to consolidate a neoliberal, middle-class enclave from which the working class is excised. One even gets the impression at times that the new inhabitants of such ex-council regenerations are imagined, and imagine themselves, to be the *true* subjects of these homes, the promise of Brutalism realized. Now the working class, having been discursively framed as hating the concrete monstrosities of their sink estates, suffer a new "indignity", "the implication that they never saw the potential".[74]

Structure of the Book

Having considered the class conditions that buffet and tear at working-class housing, and the centrality of class in understanding Brutalism today – that is, the first aspect of class architecture – I pick up now the second aspect, the modulation of class society in the estate's architecture, for this provides the book's structure.

The deforming forms of Robin Hood Gardens emerged not pristine from the minds of its architects, but through identifying and interrogating social and architectural *problems*. Problems *intrude* on thought and solicit form. I consider the estate to have been fashioned of four problem-mediating forms, each of which is given a chapter of the book. For shorthand, we can call these forms *street*, *home*, *mass* and *landscape*. But in the process of identifying, teasing out and modulating problems into form, the Smithsons developed a repertoire of concepts and phrases with which to name them – *affective* concepts, Christine Boyer calls them, so as to convey their galvanizing and figurative quality.[75] Hence we can step on from the shorthand to name the problem-mediating forms more precisely, using the Smithsons' phraseology, and with these sketch the content of the book's four chapters on the estate's deforming forms.

Chapter 3 explores the problem-form of *streets in the sky*, as it was developed by the Smithsons in response to the crisis of the working-class street. The chapter tracks the features of the streets in the sky at Robin Hood Gardens through the theme of play and against the functional urbanism of

CIAM, including the alternate model of territory that this entails. Chapter 4 engages the affective concept of *ordinariness and light* in order to explore the problem of home in its codetermination with the *unhomely*. Anti-Brutalists wield the homely *against* Brutalism, whereas this chapter contends that the homely is integral to Brutalism, the carving out of a little liveable space from hostile conditions. It is a *classed* home, dialed into the unhomely, rather different to the domestic little England that is monotonously ventriloquized as the tastes of the working class. Chapter 6 takes up the problem of mass, through the concept of *repetition and difference* (it is Gilles Deleuze who supplies the phrase in this instance, not the Smithsons directly), as it pertains to the estate's system-built concrete and the expressive qualities of the buildings' surfaces, freed up from the modernist requirement to reflect interior form. Chapter 7 considers the classed form of landscape and the mound at Robin Hood Gardens through the concept of the *charged void*, an inchoate spatial and affective state produced of the relation between architecture and its surround, where a building "is only interesting ... if it charges the space around it with connective possibilities".[76]

Each of these four chapters interrogates its particular problem-mediating form, seeking to express the contours, qualities and complexities of the form, as it is articulated in the architecture, in residents' experience of the estate and in the Smithsons' writing. The chapters also engage other theoretical work, architectural criticism and associated problems and themes when these offer insight and means to develop the form in question. I draw in particular on the aberrant materialist philosophy of Gilles Deleuze and Félix Guattari – it is most unlikely the Smithsons read this broadly contemporary work, having shown little interest in French intellectual culture, but there is a remarkable consonance on a number of themes.[77]

Brutalism as Found contains three chapters that work tangentially to the four on the estate's problem-mediating forms. Chapter 2 is a critical appropriation of the Smithsons' Brutalism from the perspective of class architecture, developing their engagement with materials as found, social relations and topology. A number of ideas I have sketched in this introduction are developed in more depth in this chapter. This is the one chapter that does not engage directly with Robin Hood Gardens, but the ideas pursued here were provoked by my experience of the estate and are threaded through and developed in subsequent chapters.

Chapter 5 explores the Smithsons' diagrams. The Smithsons grappled with problems and forms not only with affective concepts but also *visually*, with drawings, collages and diagrams. Such paper architecture is integral to the discipline, naturally, but the Smithsons developed a Brutalist approach, what I call *diagrammatic Brutalism*, and this warrants a chapter of its own. The chapter title, "an active line on a walk", is taken from Paul Klee, whose graphic practice greatly influenced the Smithsons in this respect. Despite not addressing a problem-form of the estate, I have placed this chapter in the middle of the four chapters on the estate's forms, because I understand this diagrammatic work to be integral to the architecture – preceding it, accompanying it and bearing something of its forms after demolition. If the placement of this chapter disrupts the book's movement through the estate's forms, this is no bad thing. For I have sought to carry into these five chapters the processual or topological qualities of the estate, where each is at once distinct, overlapping and folding into and out of each other, and through which the reader, I hope, gains a sense of passage in and around the estate's deforming forms. In this sense and others, the *book* is a *building* – a beguiling notion of the Smithsons that I take up in the Epilogue. That these five chapters are rather short might give an awkwardness to the shape of the book, but such is the nature of Brutalist structures.

Chapter 8 turns to the strange afterlife of Robin Hood Gardens in the V&A's salvaged fragment of the estate. As I complete this book, in March 2022, one of the estate's paired buildings is still inhabited. Living in limbo, it will in all likelihood be demolished by the time of publication, but its living presence has left me uneasy about my choice of the past tense in referring to Robin Hood Gardens, all the more so since ushering council housing out of the conflictual present and into the past is a key function of the prevalent cultural notion of class anachronism. It is a function performed by the V&A's fragment. As this chapter shows, the V&A's fragment is a fraught and class-ridden artefact, implicated in the dispossession and demolition of working-class housing. It confounds this interpretation, however, for its destructive valence is bound up with its capacity to appear *not* so, but rather as a seamless artefact of modern architectural heritage. The chapter pursues this through the fragment's *museum effects* – of cultural history, the public, neutrality and civic exchange – which obscure and contain the crisis of social housing, and tracks how the fragment bears the regeneration aesthetic of *council-house art*.

Residents, Methods and Expressive Voice

I close this chapter with a key question for the book: the place here of the estate's residents. This invites an account of the book's research and methods, and the nature of its expressive voice, which differs from the common tendency in books about Brutalism to take autobiographical form.

If Robin Hood Gardens was a work of architectural rough poetry, awkward and out of joint with its times, this is not to say that it was a difficult or unpleasant place to live – far from it. The weight of government and media discourse condemned the estate as a self-evident horror, and did so typically by ventriloquizing residents' supposedly universal and unmitigated hostility – that much is evident in the quotations from Hodge and Jenkins above. But that is not what will be found in this book, which presents a multifaceted picture of residents' typically *enthusiastic* experiences of the estate's social and architectural forms.

For Kim, who lived at Robin Hood Gardens for 15 years from 1971, when the east block first opened, "there have always been some people that like it and some who don't, but when we moved in [age 12] it was like a palace and, well, I couldn't get enough of it".[78] Of a later generation, Motiur Rahman, whose family lived on the estate between 1988 and 2011, was impressed by its "vastness" when he arrived, aged nine, recalling that "It felt like it was a community. There was everything nearby, shops, school. If you wanted greenery it was there on your doorstep, if you wanted your mates they were there on your doorstep. Holidays were amazing. I loved growing up there."[79] Another resident, Rani Begum, who moved into the east block in 2000 with her baby son, remarked: "I always said that I loved living there."[80] I asked residents why the estate was being demolished. "To get people out of the area, to get us out of the area, people who haven't got lots of money to live or to spend here. We are going to get priced out of everything", replied Darren Pauling.[81] Kim called it, simply, "social cleansing".[82]

I encountered these and many other residents' accounts in the course of a research and photography project about the estate, a collaboration between Kois Miah, Runa Khalique, Aklima Begum and myself. Kois and I established the project in dismay that residents of Robin Hood Gardens were almost entirely absent from the prominent public debate about its merits, failings and impending demolition. Whether celebrated as a masterpiece of modernist mass housing or reviled as a concrete monstrosity, residents' presence here was at best occasional and tokenistic, where clichés and stigmatizing portrayals abound. With Kois' photographic portraits of residents and interviews conducted by Aklima, Runa and myself, in Bengali and English, we sought to challenge this situation and place residents' experiences and narratives at the centre of the living architecture of Robin Hood Gardens.

We interviewed 38 residents and two caretakers, in qualitative interviews lasting between ten minutes and two-and-a-half hours, and photographed approximately 30 families or individuals.[83] Semi-structured and often wide-ranging, the interviews focused on residents' social, emotional and sensory experiences of living on the estate, and their views about its architectural forms, demolition, regeneration, public image and council housing. Six interviews were conducted wholly or in part while walking around the estate, our conversations attentive to the architectural forms and spaces we passed through. One interview was held at an open-air café at nearby Chrisp Street Market, another at a community centre and two online due to the Covid-19 pandemic, though most were conducted in residents' homes.[84] The portraits were taken in residents' homes and in other parts of the estate, typically while following them in their routines – preparing food, passing time on a street deck, getting ready for church, packing and moving out of their home, playing in the garden. Often the interviews and photography were conducted on the same visit, alternating between the two activities.

Part-funded by the British Academy and Leverhulme Trust and the University of Manchester School of Social Sciences, the research and photography were conducted between August 2014 and July 2017, with two late interviews and some photography in October 2020.[85] We partnered with two local charities, South Poplar and Limehouse Action for Secure Housing (SPLASH) and Docklands Outreach.[86] The directors of these charities, Sister Christine Frost and Runa Khalique, respectively, made our first introductions and Runa conducted interviews. We met and recruited other participants through word of mouth, striking up conversation while taking photographs and passing time on the estate, leafletting each apartment and knocking on doors. Some residents preferred to be interviewed but not photographed; for others it was the reverse. Most chose to have their words identified by their first or full names, while some opted to use a pseudonym chosen by themselves. Names are typically pseudonymized in social-science research, often with good reason, but it furthered our aim of centering residents' lived experiences that they are named parties in the visual and textual representations when that was their preference.

The photographs from the project have been twice exhibited, under the title *Lived Brutalism: Portraits at Robin Hood Gardens*, where they were captioned with text drawn from the interviews and reflections on the estate's architecture, social life and demolition. The first of these exhibitions, in 2016, was hosted close to the estate at St Matthias Community Centre. The second, in 2019, was held at Four Corners, a gallery with a history of supporting local and political photography located in London's Bethnal Green, close to a number of council estates (including the Cranbrook Estate, Berthold Lubetkin's last major work) and in an area photographed by the Smithsons' fellow Brutalist Nigel Henderson. An online exhibition accompanies this book, where a large selection of the project's photographs can be seen in high resolution and colour.[87]

In addition to our ethical concern to foreground residents' experiences, the project was driven by a political commitment to council housing as a tenure under threat. For both reasons, it was important for us that the exhibitions were an opportunity to host public events critical of estate demolition, with talks by housing-movement groups and estate campaigns against demolition: Focus E15 Campaign, Southwark Notes, Architects for Social Housing, Achilles St Campaign and Save Cressingham Gardens. It was a source of pleasure for us that the exhibitions were well attended by residents of Robin Hood Gardens, especially those who featured in the portraits. One visit was a particular delight. Shortly after we had finished installing a super-size poster of Moyna Miah and two of his grandchildren in the street-display window of Four Corners, a young woman leapt off a bus to photograph the poster and inform Kois that Mr Miah was a relative of hers (Figure 1.6). Since we had lost contact after his move, she offered to inform him of the exhibition, and on its last day he visited with 12 members of his family, clearly moved by the occasion.

Though this project's representation of residents had ethical and political aims, we were conscious of the ambivalences, risks and pitfalls entailed in the representation of working-class and racially minoritized populations, three of which this book seeks to avoid in particular. First, though residents were largely excluded from public representations of the estate – representations that had consequence for the estate's future – they were fully present to its

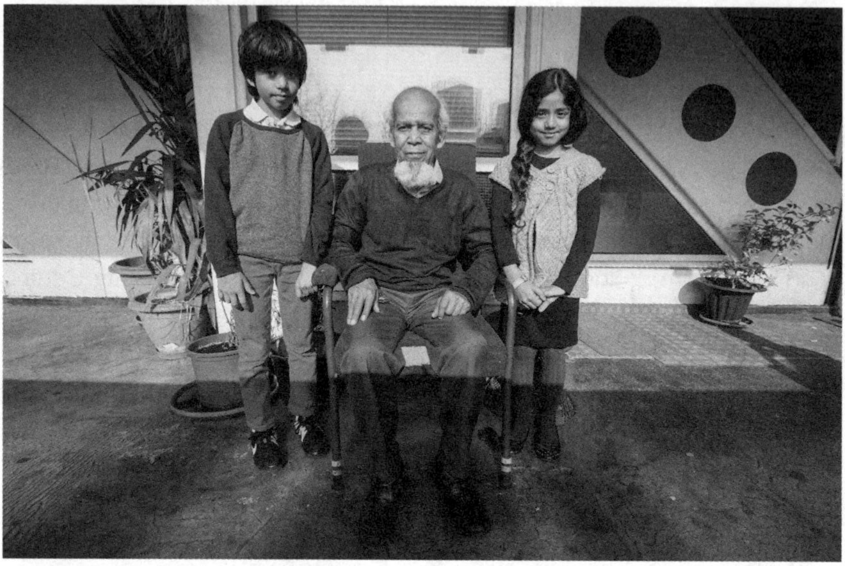

Figure 1.6 Moyna Miah and grandchildren on the street deck outside their west-block maisonette. (Kois Miah, April 2015)

social reality, including to local dispute about its regeneration. Hence this book is not conceived of, paternalistically, as *giving voice* to an otherwise silent population. Rather, the purpose of the portraits and interviews here is to contribute towards a critical understanding of the estate, its architecture and lived experience, as an intervention in the present moment of estate demolition and Brutalist revival. Second, to the extent that this book does bear residents' voices into a discursive space from which they have been largely absent, this is not so as to correct the imbalance with a more inclusive and representative civic conversation. As I consider in Chapter 8, the presupposition and consequence of such civic exchange is a representation of the social as cohesive and unified, as a *public* – a representation which substitutes for the reality of society *cleaved* by class, racialization, gender and other structural oppressions. It is in society in this latter sense wherein this book seeks to contribute, where critical conversation is critical too of the *grounds* of conversation, and painfully aware of its inadequacy without accompanying practical intervention.

Third, we were determined to avoid transforming the estate, its residents and its demolition "into a source of aesthetic pleasure", a "consumer sensation", as Christoph Lindner puts it, regarding today's visual aesthetics of ruins, slums and Brutalism – so many "superficial, sensational, hype-driven supplement[s]" to the corporate imagery of neoliberal speculative development and gentrification.[88] The book's portraits are not images of *poverty*, or *culture*, or even of *class*, complex and fraught social formations that photography tends to reify and spectacularize. Neither can the emotional textures and complexities of the portraits be reduced to mourning the estate's passing, even less the passing of a way of life, as is a common and problematic tendency in the long history of photographing working-class populations.[89] Instead, they are images of inhabitation, images of the estate's lived experience, where residents are placed firmly at its centre – not secondary to the architecture, but agents of the scene, as they inhabit and vitalize the architectural forms in the period of the estate's impending demolition. Hence, in some of the portraits the architecture is barely evident, while in others particular architectural forms or qualities are picked out through the activity or passage of the photograph's subject. In one of my favourite photographs, for example, a boy peers into the distance over a street deck balustrade; the spatial qualities of the deck's expansive view, its sense of elevation in the sky and the expressive texture of the estate's concrete are all vitalized by the poise and expression of his young face (Figure 1.7).

Figure 1.7 Boy on a street in the sky. (Kois Miah, October 2015)

In photographs interspersed through the chapters, the estate's residents *populate* the book. This is more so in the accompanying online exhibition, where some of the portraits can be seen in series, as individuals and families move through the estate's different spaces. The residents also *participate in the presentation and analysis* of the estate's forms, through their words integrated in the chapters, sometimes attentive to more biographical features of life at Robin Hood Gardens. Here residents become part-players, along with the Smithsons' writings, architectural and cultural theory, diagrams and architectural photographs, and my site observations and analysis, through which is constructed a particular kind of expressive voice. This book is not autobiographical, in contrast to a common and often problematic tendency in books about Brutalism, a criticism I make briefly in Chapter 2. Instead, the book's various, overlapping and divergent contributing parts comprise a *collective assemblage of enunciation*.[90] No unitary or integrated collective voice, this is the expressivity of lived experience, social relations and ideas, but also of built structures, materials, objects, atmospheres and landscapes, the deforming forms of Robin Hood Gardens coming into expression.

It is rare enough to find a book devoted to a single building that it is reasonable to ask: why write a book about *this* building? Answers to that question are threaded through this introduction and can be restated here. Robin Hood Gardens is a prominent instance of the social violence that is estate demolition, of the stigmatization of post-war council estates, of dispute over the merits of Brutalism – it is, in these various contexts, a preoccupation of our present. It is the first Brutalist ruin to be salvaged as national heritage, opening an afterlife that reveals new and disturbing dimensions in the politics and economics of museums and state- and culture-led regeneration. Robin Hood Gardens is the Smithsons' only mass-housing scheme, the architects who gave us the term Brutalism and much of the thinking that comprises this architectural ethic and aesthetic, and yet its particular articulation of and contribution to Brutalism has been insufficiently understood. The estate provokes and facilitates a critical reappraisal of Brutalism, pulling it away from the fixation on raw concrete and towards its social and architectural forms, confronting the class and social-cleansing dynamics of the Brutalist revival. Finally, Robin Hood Gardens bears the non-identity of class into architectural form, rendering it contemporary to the crises of the present, contemporary because of its confrontation, not its fit, with its times.[91]

Notes

1 Neil Smith, *The New Urban Frontier: Gentrification and the Revanchist City* (London: Routledge, 1996).

2 Caroline Davies, "David Cameron Vows to 'Blitz' Poverty by Demolishing UK's worst Sink Estates", *The Guardian*, 10 January 2016, www.theguardian.com/society/2016/jan/09/david-cameron-vows-to-blitz-poverty-by-demolishing-uks-worst-sink-estates.

3 Christopher Turner, "A Small Segment of a Masterpiece", *V&A Blog*, 6 March 2018, www.vam.ac.uk/blog/museum-life/a-small-segment-of-a-masterpiece-2.

4 A brief history of the two listing campaigns is as follows. The Twentieth Century Society proposed the building for listing for special architectural interest in November 2007, with the journal *Building Design* mounting a campaign and petition to save the estate in the following February. The campaign was supported by prominent architects, including Zaha Hadid, Richard Rogers, Norman Foster, Sunand Prasad (the then head of the RIBA) and former heritage minister Alan Howarth. In July 2008, Margaret Hodge, minister at the Department for Digital, Culture, Media and Sport, ruled against the listing request, declaring the estate "not fit for purpose", and in May 2009 Andy Burnham, Secretary of State for Culture, Media and Sport, granted a five-year Certificate of Immunity from Listing. The Twentieth Century Society's second attempt to have the building listed, though high-profile, was soon rejected by Historic England, in August 2015. For the timeline of the first, four-month campaign, see "Timeline of BD's Campaign to List the Estate", *Building Design*, 4 July 2008, 3. Hodge's decision, and responses from leading figures in the campaign, is included in "EH Fails to Support Robin Hood Gardens", *Building Design* 1818, 9 May 2008, 1. Earlier, in 1995, Peter Smithson had himself called for the estate to be listed, at the time the council tendered, without consulting him, to fit concierge extensions to each block. Peter was eventually involved and the extensions were fitted but no listing application was made. Peter Popham, "Brutalist, Original, but a Slum", *The Independent,* 1 October 1995, www.independent.co.uk/arts-entertainment/art/news/brutalist-original-but-a-slum-1575542.html; David Taylor, "Smithson Excluded from Work on Estate he Designed", *Architects' Journal,* 10 August 1995, 7; "Council Drafts in Smithson", *Building Design* 1239, 20 October 1995, 3.

5 Ang Li, "Raised by Association: Robin Hood Gardens and its Interpretations", *Thresholds* 43 (2015): 110–119 and 292–299, 299, 298.

6 For a comprehensive critique of the features and effects of estate demolition and rebuild, focused on 14 estates, see Paul Watt's impressive book *Estate Regeneration and Its Discontents: Public Housing, Place and Inequality in London* (London: Policy Press, 2021) and the vital housing-movement blogs Southwark Notes, https://southwarknotes.wordpress.co and 56% Campaign, www.35percent.org. Key resources for the history and present of housing struggles are Neil Gray (ed.), *Rent and Its Discontents: A Century of Housing Struggles* (London: Rowman and Littlefield, 2018) and, with a global focus, the open-access *Radical Housing Journal*, https://radicalhousingjournal.org.

7 For instance, the Brutalist style was also perfectly amenable to corporate, banking and establishment institutions, as Barnabas Calder, Adrian Forty and Owen Hatherley have all noted. In Forty's words, "the best clients of brutalism tended to belong to the Establishment – the City of London Corporation, Oxford and Cambridge Colleges, etc.; for all its seeming radicalism and devil-may-care attitudes, somehow brutalism seemed to serve these patrons' relatively conservative interests surprisingly well, providing them with

a cover of progressivism". Adrian Forty, "Paean to Brutalism", *RIBA Journal*, 8 August 2016, www.ribaj.com/culture/the-beauty-of-brutalism.

8 Alison and Peter Smithson, "The New Brutalism: Alison and Peter Smithson Answer the Criticisms on the Opposite Page", *Architectural Design,* April 1957, 113.

9 Alison Smithson, Peter Smithson, Jane B. Drew and E. Maxwell Fry, "Conversation on Brutalism", *October* 136 (2011 [orig. 1959]): 38–46, 42–3.

10 Karl Marx and Friedrich Engels, "The Holy Family; or Critique of Critical Criticism", in *Collected Works*, vol. 4 (London: Lawrence and Wishart, 1975), 36.

11 During the design and construction of the estate, the two were known as the Blackwall Tunnel South (BTS) Block and Cotton Street (CS) Block. One of the 214 apartments, on the ground floor of the west block, was given over to the estate's caretakers' office. Thirty-eight were ground-floor flats designed for elderly people and the rest were maisonettes, in the following sizes and numbers: two-person = 26 units; three-person = 26; four-person = 60; five-person = 54; six-person = 10. The largest maisonettes had four bedrooms. In administrative terms, the estate also included Anderson House (22 flats) and Mackrow Walk (15 houses), which pre-existed Robin Hood Gardens on the northern edge of the green. These are not discussed in this book, but they explain why the total number of units on the estate is sometimes given as 252 rather than 214. At the time of the estate's demolition, 24 of the 214 Robin Hood Gardens units had been sold to residents under the Right to Buy; the rest were council-owned.

12 Annie Pedret, *Team 10: An Archival History* (London and New York: Routledge, 2013).

13 Alan Powers, "A Critical Narrative", in *Robin Hood Gardens: Re-Visions*, ed. Alan Powers (London: Twentieth Century Society, 2010). Powers records the total cost of the build as £1,845,585. The area of the estate was 4.922 acres, built at a density of 141.8 persons per acre, for a site population of 698 persons. Alison and Peter Smithson, *Ordinariness and Light: Urban Theories 1952–1960 and their Application in a Building Project 1963–1970* (London: Faber and Faber, 1970), 193.

14 London Dockland Study Team, *Docklands Redevelopment Proposal for East London* (London: Department of the Environment, 1973). The east block of the estate opened in 1971, while its partner was being completed.

15 Tower Hamlets, *Borough Profile 2020: Chapter 1. Population*, 2010, www.towerhamlets.gov.uk/lgnl/community_and_living/borough_statistics/Borough_profile.aspx.

16 Fairness Commission, *Who Lives in Tower Hamlets? Where Do They Live? Communities and Housing Evidence Pack*, no date, www.towerhamlets.gov.uk/Documents/One-TH/Communities-and-Housing-Evidence-Pack.pdf; Watt, *Estate Regeneration and its Discontents*, 92.

17 *Assemblage* is a famed term of Deleuze and Guattari's, the meaning of which is broadly as I use it here, though I am drawing from the Smithsons' description of Robert Stephenson's Rocket (which they contrast to the integrated modern locomotive) as "*assembled*: with pieces of things which also remained themselves". On the following page, though now less in the sense in which I am using the term, they call New Brutalism an "assemblage-of-the-bare-necessities technique". Alison and Peter Smithson, *Without Rhetoric: An Architectural Aesthetic 1955–1972* (London: Latimer, 1973), 63, 64.

18 Smithson and Smithson, *Ordinariness and Light*, 130.

19 *Ibid.*, 86; Rayner Banham, "The New Brutalism", *October* 136 (2011 [orig. December 1955]): 19–28, 27.

20 Miles Glendinning, *Mass Housing: Modern Architecture and State Power – A Global History* (London: Bloomsbury, 2021).

21 Tom Slater, "The Invention of the 'Sink Estate': Consequential Categorisation and the UK Housing Crisis", *The Sociological Review Monographs* 66 no. 4 (2018): 877–897, 877.

22 John Grindrod, *Concretopia: A Journey around the Rebuilding of Postwar Britain* (London: Old Street Publishing, 2014), 15.

23 *Ibid.*

24 *Ibid.*

25 Margaret Hodge, cited in David Rogers, "Hodge Scoffs at Latest Attempt to List Robin Hood Gardens", *Building Design*, 18 March 2015, www.bdonline.co.uk/hodge-scoffs-at-latest-attempt-to-list-robin-hood-gardens/5074417. This remark was made in 2015; Hodge's ruling was on 1 July 2008.

26 Simon Jenkins, "This Icon of 60s New Brutalism has Its Champions. So Let them Restore It", *The Guardian*, 20 June 2008, www.theguardian.com/commentisfree/2008/jun/20/architecture.

27 Loïc Wacquant, "Territorial Stigmatization in the Age of Advanced Marginality", *Thesis Eleven* 91 no. 1 (2007): 66–77; Hamish Kallin and Tom Slater, "Activating Territorial Stigma: Gentrifying Marginality on Edinburgh's Periphery", *Environment and Planning A* 46 (2014): 1351–1368.

28 Imogen Tyler, "Classificatory Struggles: Class, Culture and Inequality in Neoliberal Times", *The Sociological Review* 63 no. 2 (2015): 493–511.

29 Land "value uplift" is "the difference between the purchase price of the land and the value of the land with the new development on it". Bob Colenutt, *The Property Lobby: The Hidden Reality Behind the Housing Crisis* (Bristol: Policy Press, 2020), 34. Though financialization intensifies this process and gives it new and powerful features, it is a dynamic intrinsic to capitalist urbanism, as noted by Engels in 1872: "The growth of the big modern cities gives the land in certain areas, particularly in those which are centrally situated, an artificial and often colossally increasing value; the buildings erected on these areas depress this value, instead of increasing it, because they no longer correspond to the changed circumstances. They are pulled down and replaced by others. This takes place above all with workers' houses." Frederick Engels, *The Housing Question* (London: Lawrence and Wishart Ltd, 1942), 19.

30 Loretta Lees and Hannah White, "The Social Cleansing of London Council Estates: Everyday Experiences of 'Accumulative Dispossession'", *Housing Studies* 35 no. 10 (2020): 1701–1722.

31 Joe Mellor, "Over 31,000 London Residents Losing Homes as Council Estates to be Demolished", *The London Economic*, 3 September 2018, www.thelondoneconomic.com/news/over-31000-london-residents-losing-homes-as-council-estates-to-be-demolished/03/09/. Estate Watch, www.estatewatch.london.

32 Josephine Berry, *Art and (Bare) Life: A Biopolitical Inquiry* (Berlin: Sternberg Press, 2018), 305.

33 Simon Elmer and Geraldine Dening, "The London Clearances", *City* 20 no. 2 (2016): 271–277, 275.

34 David Madden and Peter Marcuse, *In Defense of Housing: The Politics of Crisis* (London and New York: Verso, 2016), 4, 10.

35 *Ibid.*; Elmer and Dening, "The London Clearances"; Anna Minton, *Big Capital: Who Is London For?* (London: Penguin, 2017); Andrew Michael and Laura Howard, "UK House

Prices – Latest News", *Forbes Advisor*, 1 December 2021, www.forbes.com/uk/advisor/personal-finance/2021/12/01/house-prices-updates/.

36 Colenutt, *The Property Lobby*, 14.

37 Minton, *Big Capital*, 41–42; Tom Archer and Ian Cole, *Profits before Volume? Major Housebuilders and the Crisis of Housing Supply*, October 2016, www4.shu.ac.uk/research/cresr/sites/shu.ac.uk/files/profits-before-volume-housebuilders-crisis-housing-supply.pdf.

38 Colenutt, *The Property Lobby*, 13.

39 Andrew Adonis and Bill Davies (eds.), *City Villages: More Homes, Better Communities* (London: Institute for Public Policy Research, 2015), 9; Elmer and Dening, "The London Clearances".

40 Nicholas Boys Smith and Alex Morton, *Create Streets* (London: Policy Exchange, 2013) www.ippr.org/publications/city-villages-more-homes-better-communities; Savills, *Completing London's Streets: Savills Research Report to the Cabinet Office*, 7 January 2016, https://pdf.euro.savills.co.uk/uk/residential---other/completing-london-s-streets-080116.pdf. For a compelling critique of the driving role of Policy Exchange and Savills in the housing policies of the Conservative–Liberal coalition, see Slater, "The Invention of the 'Sink Estate'".

41 David Cameron, "I've Put the Bulldozing of Sink Estates at the Heart of Turnaround Britain", *The Times*, 10 January 2016, www.thetimes.co.uk/article/ive-put-the-bulldozing-of-sink-estates-at-the-heart-of-turnaround-britain-rtcgg2gnb6h.

42 Daniel Rossall Valentine, *Housing Crisis: An Analysis of the Investment Demand Behind the UK's Housing Affordability Crisis* (The Bow Group, 2015), 37, https://paperzz.com/doc/9214114/daniel-rossall-valentine; see also Alice Martin and Josh Ryan-Collins, "The Financialisation of UK Homes", *New Economics Foundation: The Housing Crisis, Land and the Banks*, 21 April 2016, https://neweconomics.org/2016/04/the-financialisation-of-uk-homes.

43 See especially Dan Bulley, Jenny Edkins and Nadine El-Enany (eds.), *After Grenfell: Violence, Resistance and Response* (London: Pluto Press, 2019); Colenutt, *The Property Lobby*; Stuart Hodkinson, *Safe as Houses: Private Greed, Political Negligence and Housing Policy after Grenfell* (Manchester: University of Manchester Press, 2019); Minton, *Big Capital*; Watt, *Estate Regeneration*.

44 This provision had actually existed on a discretionary basis since 1936, resulting in some 271,000 sales by the end of the 1970s. Watt, *Estate Regeneration*, 61.

45 Colenutt, *The Property Lobby*, 15.

46 Tom Copley, "Right to Buy: Wrong for London", London Labour Assembly, January 2019, www.london.gov.uk/sites/default/files/rtb_report_feb_update.pdf. *Social rent*, regulated by the National Rent Regime, is determined largely in relation to local average income, in contrast to *affordable rent*, set at up to 80% of local market rents.

47 Colenutt, *The Property Lobby*, 16.

48 Hodkinson, *Safe as Houses*, 31.

49 Anna Minton, "Setting the Scene: Thirty Years of Regeneration in East London", in *Regeneration Songs: Sounds of Investment and Loss from East London*, ed. Alberto Duman, Anna Minton, Dan Hancox and Malcolm James (London: Repeater Books, 2018), 50.

50 Colenutt, *The Property Lobby*, 15.

51 Hodkinson, *Safe as Houses*.

52 Felicity Lawrence, Niamh McIntyre and Patrick Butler, "Labour Councils in England Hit Harder by Austerity than Tory Areas", *The Guardian*, 21 June 2020, www.theguardian.com/business/2020/jun/21/exclusive-labour-councils-in-england-hit-harder-by-austerity-than-tory-areas.

53 Anna Minton found that, while in office, just under 20% of Southwark's 63 councillors also worked as lobbyists associated with the development industry. As an example of the revolving door, former leader Jeremy Fraser went on to found the lobbying firm Four Communications, one arm of which advertises itself as having "an enviable track-record in securing political and community support for planning applications for developments across London and other regions of the United Kingdom". Anna Minton, *Scaring the Living Daylights out of People: The Local Lobby and the Failure of Democracy*, Spinwatch, March 2013, 10.

54 For a critical account of the "viability assessment", a 2012 planning provision of the Conservative–Liberal coalition government, see Colenett, *The Property Lobby*, 92–97.

55 The council has stated that 561 units, 35.6% of the total, will be social rent – a tenure comparable to council rent, though not as affordable or secure. If this transpires on completion, it will be a significantly greater proportion than is typical on new developments, though for reasons I give above it is likely to decline steadily over time. *The London Borough of Tower Hamlets (Blackwall Reach) Compulsory Purchase Order 2013: Statement of Reasons* (London: London Borough of Tower Hamlets, 2013), 20. That one should be circumspect about such figures is proven from research by the 35% Campaign which shows, in the London Borough of Southwark, a marked difference between the *claims* the council and developers make about the number of new social-rent and affordable-rent units achieved and the numbers in reality. 35% Campaign, "Social Rent or Affordable Rent?", 16 January 2021, www.35percent.org/affordable-housing-monitoring-15000-homes/.

56 An account of the TRA's role in the consultation is in order. In the early days of the consultation, which commenced in 2007, the TRA was split between pro-demolition and pro-refurbishment members. Having become dysfunctional, around 2009–2010, Musa and Abul Hasnath (both interviewed for this book) took on the roles of chair and vice-chair, joining Darren Pauling (also interviewed), who had campaigned for refurbishment from the start. By then, demolition had been set in train. The new TRA had a struggle getting the council to appoint for their representation an independent tenants' and leaseholders' liaison officer (ITLA), paid for by the council and Swann Housing, who the residents' later fired, finding the officer not to be adequately representing their interests. The TRA's hard-fought campaign achieved for tenants an "assured shorthold tenancy with preserved rights", less secure but comparable to the "secure tenancy" they were losing, though they soon encountered problems – favourably resolved through collective pressure – over the transfer of residents' parking permits and family rights of succession. For leaseholders, the TRA demanded a like-for-like swap, but had to settle for a lesser agreement, where some had to enter shared-ownership tenancies, purchasing only a proportion of their new home and paying the rest in rent. The TRA gained also a freeze in rents for seven years. To compare the rent levels for one family, their four-bedroom maisonette at Robin Hood Gardens was £498 per month in 2015, rising to £698 for their five-bedroom in the first phase of the Blackwall Reach development.

57 As a rough-and-ready means of dating this revived enthusiasm, Google's Ngram Viewer shows a steady rise in book references to Brutalism from the early 1990s, but the steep uptick starts as recently as 2010. The pattern is similar for references to Robin Hood Gardens, Park Hill estate and Balfron Tower. For Trellick Tower, the first of the council estates to receive the attention of the Brutalist revival, the uptick starts from the early 1990s, with a dip between 2005 and 2010.

58 With Airbnb rentals now marketed as concrete chic ("This 1-bedroom flat is exquisitely wrapped in modern brutalist sophistication", etc.), as Christoph Lindner observes, beautiful Brutalism serves also the *rental* market, in the form of middle-class urban transience and tourism that has its own significant role in displacing working-class residents from inner cities. Christoph Lindner, "Brutalism, Ruins, and the Urban Imaginary of Gentrification", in *The Routledge Companion to Urban Imaginaries*, ed. Christoph Lindner and Miriam Meissner (London: Routledge, 2018), 285. The quotation is from an Airbnb listing in Manila.

59 Richard Rogers in a letter to Andy Burnham, cited in "Architecture Save Our Scheme... Architects Turn to Public", *The Irish Times*, 15 May 2008, www.irishtimes.com/life-and-style/homes-and-property/architecture-save-our-scheme-architects-turn-to-public-1.1264941.

60 Jonathan Glancey, "This Frog Could Become a Prince", *Building Design*, 29 February 2008, 32.

61 In making a compelling case for examining not the failure of post-war estates but their cultural *construction* as such, David Roberts collates an assortment of extraordinarily violent representations of Balfron Tower, including another hellish vision from Simon Jenkins, in *The Times* in 2000: "Balfron Tower ... gives Poplar a final mugging. Its footings are a no-go area for humanity. Trash, chicken-wire and graffiti abound. The tower is without charm or visual diversion. It makes Wormwood Scrubs seem like the Petit Trianon." David Roberts, "Making Public: Performing Public Housing in Ernő Goldfinger's Balfron Tower", *The Journal of Architecture* 22 no. 1 (2017): 123–150, 126.

62 Of the many important features of Skeggs' analysis of this extractive cultural process, her formulation helps us to appreciate how a single cultural form, Brutalism in our case, can be both denigrated/damaging and valued/enabling at one and the same time, depending on the class with which it is associated in each instance. Beverley Skeggs, *Class, Self, Culture* (London and New York: Routledge, 2004).

63 English Heritage's statement, by chairman Lord Sandy Bruce-Lockhart, is included in Rory Olcayto, "Robin Hood Gardens Will Not Be Listed", *Building Design*, 1 July 2008, https://architexturez.net/pst/az-cf-31331-1214927181. Simon Smithson, the architects' son, suggested that the report was "leaned on" by politicians and "hastily rewritten" to justify the decision. Simon Smithson, "The Brutal Truth about the Destruction of Robin Hood Lane", in Jessica Mairs, "Robin Hood Gardens Demolition is an 'Act of Vandalism' Says Simon Smithson", *Dezeen*, 10 August 2017, www.dezeen.com/2017/08/10/robin-hood-gardens-demolition-simon-alison-peter-smithson-post-war-housing-estate-london-uk-news/. This is supported by the fact, leaked at the time, that the English Heritage commissioners had overruled their own advisory committee, which had recommended the estate be listed at Grade II. The view of the Twentieth Century Society was that English Heritage's decision "will be seen as an example of a beleaguered quango seeking to curry favour with its

paymasters". "Hodge Refusal to List Snubs Profession", *Building Design*, 4 July 2008, 3; "EH Fails to Support Robin Hood Gardens", *Building Design*, 9 May 2008, 1.

64 The apartment was open for two weeks in October 2014, for which 600 tickets sold out in less than 48 hours, and a further 400 soon after. The admission fee was £12.

65 Oliver Wainwright, "Wayne Hemingway's 'Pop Up' Plan Sounds the Death Knell for the Legendary Balfron Tower", *The Guardian*, 26 September 2014, www.theguardian.com/artanddesign/architecture-design-blog/2014/sep/26/wayne-hemingways-pop-up-plan-sounds-the-death-knell-for-the-legendary-balfron-tower.

66 Steph Lawler, "White Like Them: Whiteness and Anachronistic Space in Representations of the English White Working Class", *Ethnicities* 12 no. 4 (2012): 409–426, 418.

67 Wainwright, "Wayne Hemingway's 'Pop Up' Plan".

68 The film was not used, but was saved by the campaigning blog Balfron Social Club. Balfron Social Club, "Balfron Tower Redevelopment Video by Hawkins\Brown (July 2014)", 20 July 2015, http://balfronsocialclub.org/2015/07/20/balfron-tower-redevelopment-video-by-hawkinsbrown/.

69 Londonewcastle, *Balfron Tower*, 2019, 19, https://londonewcastle.com/content/4-for-sale/balfron-tower/balfron-tower-brochure.pdf.

70 Jonathan Bell, "London's Brutalist Balfron Tower Is Brought Back to Life", *Wallpaper*, 2 July 2018, www.wallpaper.com/architecture/balfron-tower-brutalism-london-londonewcastle-studio-egret-west-brody-associates.

71 Ab Rogers, in "A to Z of Modern Living: Ab Robers on Balfron Tower, Sensitive Architecture and Community-Focused Design", *The Modern House Journal*, 15 October 2019, www.themodernhouse.com/journal/ab-rogers-design-balfron/.

72 Londonewcastle, *Balfron Tower*, 5, 41.

73 Bell, "London's Brutalist Balfron Tower Is Brought Back to Life". For discussion of the communal facilities of the original scheme, and Ernő and Ursula Goldfinger's research into this and other aspects of the lived experience of the estate while living in one of the apartments for two months, see Roberts, "Making Public".

74 James Meek, *Private Island: Why Britain Now Belongs to Someone Else* (London: Verso, 2015), 202.

75 M. Christine Boyer, *Not Quite Architecture: Writing around Alison and Peter Smithson* (Cambridge, MA and London: MIT Press, 2017).

76 Smithson and Smithson, *Without Rhetoric*, 34.

77 This approach, based on found points of connection and the potential for critical interference, as against direct intellectual influence, is itself a point of relation between the Smithsons and Deleuze and Guattari, where the "picking up" and "putting with" (the Smithsons) and the "pick up" or "and" (Deleuze and Guattari) of heterogeneous elements is crucial to the creative and critical process. It is a sensibility that Deleuze characterizes as his own "art brut", referring to his particular approach to philosophy's "raw materials" and external encounters. Gilles Deleuze, *Negotiations 1972–1990* (New York: Columbia University Press, 1995), 89. In this connection I am not at all suggesting a shared intellectual project in the broader sense between the Smithsons and Deleuze and Guattari.

78 Kim, interview, 28 August 2015.

79 Motiur Rahman, interview, 4 December 2015.

80 Rani Begum, interview, 10 September 2014.

81 Darren Pauling, interview, 5 September 2015.

82 Kim, interview, 28 August 2015.

83 Some broad data about the participants is as follows. Two-thirds were men and one-third women. The majority were aged 25 to 59 at the time of the interviews; four were in their 60s; four were over 70. Of the interviewees, 22 were Bangladeshi, first- and second-generation British; 8 were white British; 5 were Black British, of Caribbean and African heritage; 1 was Egyptian, second-generation; 1 was South American, first-generation; 1 was Pakistani, first-generation. By tenure, 28 interviewees were council tenants; 7 were leaseholders, purchased through Right to Buy; 3 held temporary council tenancies. Approximately half of the interviews were recorded and transcribed; for the other half notes were taken during the interviews. Translations from Bengali were made by Aklima and Runa. Informed consent was taken for all interviews and portraits.

84 For the merits and limitations of both walk-along and sit-down interviews in researching embodied experience of place, see Vanessa May and Camilla Lewis, "Researching Embodied Relationships with Place: Rehabilitating the Sit-Down Interview", *Qualitative Research* 20 no. 2 (2020): 127–142.

85 British Academy/Leverhulme Small Grant, number SG141268, "Concrete Dreams and the Demolition of Robin Hood Gardens", £9,996. The project's photography exhibitions, talks events and the accompanying online exhibition were supported by a Small Grant, a Social Responsibility Award and a Research Support Grant, all from the School of Social Sciences, University of Manchester.

86 This campaigning charity, SPLASH, is not to be confused with the developer Urban Splash, responsible for the private regeneration of Sheffield's Park Hill estate, among other developments.

87 See www.brutalismasfound.co.uk.

88 Lindner, "Brutalism, Ruins, and the Urban Imaginary of Gentrification", 280. It is a certain "accidental brutalism" that Lindner has in mind here, where Brutalism's rough aesthetic is rediscovered and aestheticized in moments of interruption and breakdown in neoliberal urbanism, such as cultural representations of the temporarily squatted shell of the Torre David tower in Caracas, Venezuela.

89 For continuities and changing discursive frames in the photographic representation of the working class, see Darren Newbury, "Photography and the Visualization of Working Class Lives in Britain", *Visual Anthropology Review* 15 no. 1 (Spring–Summer 1999): 21–44; Derrick Price, "Photographing the Poor and the Working Class", *Framework: The Journal of Cinema and Media* 22/23 (Autumn 1983): 20–25.

90 *Collective assemblage of enunciation* is Deleuze and Guattari's term, which I appropriate here in the spirit if not the detail of their formulation. See Gilles Deleuze and Félix Guattari, *A Thousand Plateaus: Capitalism and Schizophrenia Volume 2*, trans. Brian Massumi (Minneapolis: University of Minnesota Press, 1987).

91 Awkwardness pertains also to the estate's place in the Brutalist canon and its literature, which, if not in itself a reason to study Robin Hood Gardens, does mean that the various rationales for this book tend not to draw on received wisdom about the estate. Though Zaha Hadid called it her favourite London building, it has not been especially popular among aficionados of Brutalism and post-war council housing. For John Bouton, Robin Hood Gardens was a less-than-successfully-achieved response to the constraints of the site. John Boughton, *Municipal Dreams: The Rise and Fall of Council Housing* (London: Verso,

2018). Owen Hatherley has positive things to say about the street decks, use of concrete and other features, and has an essay about the estate, but considers it "far less tectonically or socially convincing" than Sheffield's Park Hill, comparing its "clumsy, fortress-like enclosure" unfavourably to Balfron Tower. Owen Hatherley, *A New Kind of Bleak: Journeys through Urban Britain* (London: Verso, 2012), 27; Owen Hatherley, "Not the Same as Building for the Socialist State: Robin Hood Gardens in and Against the Architecture of the Welfare State", in Jessie Brennan, *Regeneration! Conversations, Drawings, Archives and Photographs from Robin Hood Gardens* (London: Silent Grid, 2015). Even the campaign to save the estate began without great enthusiasm for the architecture itself, the launch article describing it as "not an easy place to love". Amanda Baillieu, "To the Rescue of Robin Hood", *Building Design*, 22 February 2008, 2. Needless to say, these less-favourable views of the architecture all issued from within the camp firmly opposed to the demolition.

2

Architecture "as Found": Matter and Society in Brutalist Form

Brutalism tries to face up to a mass-production society, and drag a rough poetry out of the confused and powerful forces which are at work.

Alison and Peter Smithson, "The New Brutalism"

We are involved in mass housing not as reformers but as form givers.

Alison and Peter Smithson, *Ordinariness and Light*

Alison and Peter Smithson first used the term New Brutalism in print in December 1953, where it describes aesthetic qualities of the legibility and display of structural elements and materials in the couple's unrealized House in Soho.[1] But in April 1957 they added to this aesthetic an *ethical* dimension, where Brutalism is fashioned through a critical engagement with society. In this short text, titled "The New Brutalism", the movement gained a crystalline definition.

> Any discussion of Brutalism will miss the point if it does not take into account Brutalism's attempt to be objective about "reality" – the cultural objectives of society, its urges, and so on. Brutalism tries to face up to a mass-production society, and drag a rough poetry out of the confused and powerful forces which are at work.
>
> Up to now Brutalism has been discussed stylistically, whereas its essence is ethical.[2]

It is reasonably clear in this 1957 statement that the aesthetic and the ethic of Brutalist "rough poetry" are entangled. Yet in the literature on Brutalism, this entanglement is often passed by in favour of the aesthetic. Or when the social does hold a prominent place in studies of the movement, it tends to be taken simply as a commitment to post-war, social-democratic values, with little critical reflection or sense of its impact on Brutalist form. In this chapter I depart from these trends. My contention is that the originality of the Smithsons' architecture arises from the co-determination of the aesthetic and the ethic, the material and the social. I follow the lead here of Ben Highmore and Mark Crinson, for whom the awkward, raw, critical and experimental qualities of Brutalism reside in its encounter with conflictual social forces, Brutalism "shaped by forces alive in the world", "refusing to ... placate social antagonisms", as Highmore has it, against the tendencies, noted above, to absorb the movement into conventional categories of beauty and the canonical, on one side, and narratives of post-war class settlement, on the other, in Crinson's framing.[3]

To be more precise, this chapter contends that Brutalist architecture *courses with social relations*, relations that *intrude upon, inflect and are wrought by its forms*. And these social relations are *classed*. It is in this chapter that I build out the book's guiding theory that the Smithsons' Brutalism is a *class* architecture, bearing the non-identity of the working class into architectural form, a crisis condition of life out of joint. What does it mean to drag architectural form out of the confusion of social relations, for architecture to work with, to interrogate, to yield to and to modulate society as crisis? That is the problem the Smithsons face up to, and which this chapter reconstructs, prompted to do so, and shaped by, the set of problems that confront and configure Brutalist council housing today.

To this end, the chapter centres the Smithsons' method of the "as found", a method that favours not the imposition of predetermined architectural form, but an *immanent* relation to the "confused and powerful forces" of the socio-material world – the world as it is encountered, with all its rough edges, awkward, complex and unfinished. I begin by showing the significance of class to the Brutalist critical revival, where the working class is either disavowed and cleansed from Brutalism or reified as an achieved identity of welfare-state modernism. Against this, the chapter proposes its theory of class architecture in dialogue with the Marxist architecture critic Manfredo Tafuri. Reading the Smithsons' Brutalism through the lens of class architecture, the chapter then explores their approach to matter and society as found, and how these come together in Brutalism's *topological* understanding of form – *deforming form* or *form in process* – where form is intuited and provoked through the architectural interrogation of *problems*, problem-forms that transform themselves and their site and society too.

The account of Brutalism in this chapter provides a broad conceptual and methodological apparatus for the reading in subsequent chapters of the particular socio-architectural forms of Robin Hood Gardens. Yet, to reverse the order of presentation, this reconstruction of the Smithsons' Brutalism has itself been provoked by the living architecture and crisis of Robin Hood Gardens over its last years, and by the recent career of Brutalism, such that the reconstruction is also an *appropriation* – a Brutalism for the crisis conditions of today.

Critique of Class in the Brutalist Revival

It is commonly appreciated that *class* is a significant dimension of Brutalist architecture, for class is integral to the socio-architectural form with which Brutalism in the UK is most associated: the post-war council estate. Yet in the two main trends of the Brutalist critical revival, the place and features of class are disavowed or inadequately grasped.

Leading one of these trends, and demarcating the terms of division, is Barnabas Calder's high-profile book *Raw Concrete: The Beauty of Brutalism*, published in 2016. At the book's heart, Calder identifies and upholds a fissure in Brutalism's fan base between *aesthetic* and *social* concerns, "between those who are fundamentally above all else enthusiasts for the concrete, and those who prioritise more highly the social ideals of the Welfare State".[4] For Calder, only the first of these trends is fully adequate to Brutalism; the other takes architecture as a "proxy" for social agendas, where it is "used to embody the optimism and ambition of Britain's social-democratic past" in the critique of neoliberal urbanism.[5] Society thus placed at a distance, Calder's "concrete" is to be assessed in conventional aesthetic terms – for its *beauty*, as his book's subtitle forewarns.

From the perspective of the Smithsons' 1957 definition, Calder's separation of the social and the aesthetic makes little sense. But more than this, the way that the social is *excised* from Calder's formulation actually facilitates the *damaging social effects* of the Brutalist revival. Championing Brutalist aesthetics may sound harmless enough, even necessary, given the opprobrium long levelled at this architecture, so much of which has been demolished or is in peril. But through this a-social beauty, whether by intent or default, beautiful Brutalism all too easily becomes an active participant in regeneration, as working-class residents are socially cleansed from housing estates once decried as concrete monstrosities but now refashioned for middle-class inhabitation as modernist gems. This function becomes evident if we read Calder's aesthetic directly on the terrain of council housing.

When attending to the design, history and recent experience of Brutalist council housing, Calder's separation between social and aesthetic form is not readily apparent – indeed, his book has to *produce* it. Here the social form of the working-class estate features as a *spectre* to be named and exorcized, thus facilitating the extraction, cleansing and revaluing of the Brutalist aesthetic for its newfound middle-class constituency. In a framing passage that was significant enough for the book's author and assumed readership to merit the third paragraph, he writes: "Growing up in the 1980s and '90s, in a comfortable Edwardian suburb of London, concrete architecture represented everything which was frightening and other."[6] His point is underscored with a list of horrors that culminates "above all" in council estates, "on whose raised walkways and deserts of patchy grass nameless but horrible crimes probably took place almost constantly". The passage is clearly self-mocking, but I venture that this serves less to expose an unfounded class anxiety than as a *palliative for its persistence*, a means of handling the enduring sense of unease that class presents to this new domain of middle-class pleasure. In this, Calder's book is in company, for such means of naming and parking class anxiety and conflict are a persistent feature of the Brutalist revival.[7] Lynsey Hanley observes it, for example, in the recent play about Sheffield's Park Hill estate, *Standing at the Sky's Edge*, where the "tangible injuries of class are reduced to a series of jokes about Ocado deliveries, designed to get us to laugh at middle-class consumer neuroses without challenging the way in which Park Hill is now marketed directly at those consumers".[8]

The progression of Calder's narrative from this introductory framing, revealing and interpolating though it is, to the book's more focused discussions might have proven my assessment to be overhasty. But when the opportunity arises to take a stand for council estates and tenures, his cursory response to the privatization of Balfron Tower hardly displays a commitment to evaluating and challenging the classed social relations in play. As I discussed in Chapter 1, this Brutalist council estate designed by Ernő Goldfinger was gifted by Tower Hamlets council to Poplar HARCA, who refurbished it for private sale. Calder briefly laments the privatization, but then shrugs it off as some kind of natural urban ecology, wherein the parties involved – the housing association which evicts tenants to sell off the estate, the developer which profits and the artists who assist in its image-cleanse – all perform their allotted role: "It would be odd if each group did not do what it is doing."[9]

Contrary to Calder, it is a key contention of this book that Brutalist council housing ceases to be itself, I mean *architecturally*, when it is separated from engagement with social relations, losing what is radical in its aesthetic form to become a mere style, at once depoliticized and functional to middle-class and developer appropriation. It is not by cleansing Brutalism of its class qualities that its aesthetic significance is revealed, but rather by *cleaving* to them. Yet this is not to champion the second main trend in the Brutalist revival. Though erroneously dismissed by Calder for foregrounding social concerns, he accurately characterizes this trend as the calibration of Brutalist forms to a certain image of the welfare state, understood (whether as a past to mourn or a future at our backs) as an integrated whole comprising concrete modernism, mass housing and class identity, a whole positively coded as a progressive, socialist or utopian achievement.

Owen Hatherley is clearly Calder's target (all the more evidently so in being not referenced once) and though Hatherley's 2008 book *Militant Modernism* is justly feted for its political appraisal of modernist architectural form, one can indeed find therein a celebration of class and architecture as an achieved, positive identity. For example: "Modernist urban planning could be seen as one of those moments where the workers – the Labour movement – got ideas above its station, the period where, as per Bevan or Lubetkin, nothing was too good for ordinary people."[10] A clearer and more typical instance, though, is this observation from the National Trust: "[Balfron] Tower ... stands as testament to a particular historical moment; when a vision of a utopian post-war Britain, coincided with an architectural movement, Brutalism, and a material, concrete. ... Balfron Tower is the welfare state in concrete."[11]

It is true that under the welfare state, coherent self-identity was partially achieved for sectors of the working class in the global north, their interests incorporated in Keynesian social and economic planning. And council housing was a significant plank of this class identity. Yet retrospective understandings of a positive and integrated identity of class and architecture obscure the central dynamic of class, a dynamic evident then and intensified today, namely its *fraught* and *crisis-ridden* nature. They obscure also the racialized and exclusionary nature of this figure of the "ordinary people" for whom nothing was too good. This misunderstanding of class articulated in the Brutalist revival leaves us with the hitherto unexplored problem, central to this book, of how class *as crisis* figures in this architecture, as I turn to now.

Crisis and Non-Identity in Class and Class Architecture

The quality, affordability and security of working-class housing during the ascendency of the welfare state was, in the main, far better than the miserable situation today, after 40 years of privatization, demolition, deregulation and welfare retrenchment. But the persistence during the welfare state of industrial strife, unofficial strike action and work refusal suggests that in practice a life tethered to industrial labour, and the social and cultural forms, housing included, that accompanied it, was no utopia incarnate. Moreover, to the degree that secure working-class identity was achieved, it was an identity conditional upon the stratifications and exclusions of racialization, gender and colonialism.

Working-class identity was a central component of the tripartite "national compact" between state, business and labour, as Robbie Shilliam shows in *Race and the Undeserving Poor*. In the national compact, "class" was "subordinated to national-racial affiliation", a patriarchal and industrious "white working class" that was "firmly installed within imperial coordinates and their racist determinations" vis-à-vis Black and other racially minoritized subjects at home and in the Commonwealth.[12] To be clear, this is not class but racialized identity, identity *masquerading* as class – though it was the dominant mode by which class was spoken and legislated for by state actors, and spoken and claimed by significant sections of the working class and its institutions, as Satnam Virdee tracks through some eye-opening examples.[13] We might frame this as a national-cultural dimension of the Marxist argument – contrary to received wisdom on the political left and right – that the workers' movement took shape as an internal dynamic of capitalist modernization.[14]

Today, though, with the dismantling of the welfare settlement and the neoliberal expulsion of labour from the national compact, the fraught experience of class is less confined to the stratifications and exclusions of racialization, gender and colonialism and is instead increasingly generalized.

Witness the global offshoring and secular decline of manufacturing labour, the historical bulwark of working-class power; the long-term decline in real wages; the move to the heart of the wage relation of precarity and under-employment; the extension of super-exploitation and informal work attendant on the tendential rise in populations superfluous to capital's need for labour; soaring personal debt; welfare retrenchment; and the withdrawal of capital and state from bearing the costs of working-class social reproduction.[15] Under these conditions, the working class is ever more revealed to be a condition not of identity but of *crisis* – a condition of exploitation, insecurity and dispossession, pulled out of shape by the tangle of social relations of which it is comprised.[16] Here, "what human beings are, is contingent or stochastic; there is no way in which they are as such, in themselves", as G. M. Tamás encapsulates the fraught non-identity of class.[17]

These are the bleak conditions with which class analysis must grapple if it is to have any social traction and consequence. But they also give to working-class politics a *wrenching* and *propulsive* force of radical change, a force inherent in Marx's understanding of the working class, or proletariat, as a living contradiction: "a class with *radical chains*, a class of civil society which is not a class of civil society, a class [*Stand*] which is the dissolution of all classes".[18] For, *without a place of its own*, without an achieved and satisfied identity accommodated to society, or a positive ground upon which such an identity could be established, class politics must of necessity push out *into the social realm as a whole* – a restless and wrenching engagement with the gamut of social relations that cleave and buffet each particular working-class experience. While liberal politics contents itself with fashioning and bolstering the "liberty", in Marx's cutting phrase, of the "*confined* individual, confined to himself", proletarian politics *recovers the flux of the social* – indeed, the flux of the natural, the planetary, the cosmic – as the terrain of its practice, thought and vision, even as, or because, the social is lived as crisis.[19]

By the same token, neither can working-class *architecture* achieve self-coherent identity. Architecture is so interwoven with the social relations of land, construction and speculation that it is the most capitalist of arts. In Fredric Jameson's phrase, "Of all the arts, architecture is the closest constitutively to the economic, with which, in the form of commissions and land values, it has a virtually unmediated relationship."[20] Under these conditions, as Tafuri contends, the pursuit of liberated architectural forms – self-coherent "islands of realized utopia" – is mystifying, an ersatz solution that leaves unchanged the underlying conditions of social life.[21] As he writes in *Architecture and Utopia*, "The search for an alternative within the structures that condition the very character of architectural design is indeed an obvious contradiction of terms."[22]

Such claimed architectural autonomy not only mystifies, it has *directly served* modern capitalist development. This was the function of modernism's utopia of the *plan*, which furnished the model for the Keynesian rationalization of production, distribution and consumption of the post-war industrial city – the city, "structured like a machine for the extraction of surplus value", as the realization of the architectural avant-garde.[23] Le Corbusier is the incomparable figure here, of architecture as ideology of the plan, of the total integration and active involvement of "the whole anthropo-geographic landscape".[24] Take as example this ecstatic passage from his *Radiant City*: "Give us plans; show us plans; explain those plans to us. *Unite* us. ... If you show us such plans and explain them to us, then the old dichotomy between 'haves' and despairing 'have-nots' will disappear. There will be but a single society, united in belief and action."[25]

From this appraisal of the integration of architecture in capital, Tafuri draws the logical conclusion: "just as there cannot exist a class political economy, but only a class criticism of political economy, so too there cannot be founded a class aesthetic, art, or architecture, but only a class criticism of the aesthetic, of art, of architecture, of the city itself".[26] *There can be no class architecture*. It is an exacting standard, to be sure, seemingly leaving Marxist perspectives on architecture with only the domain of critique, devoid of architectural practice.[27] Yet I want to take Tafuri's stringent disavowal of architectural autonomy to be less a refusal of the material existence of class architecture than a *wrenching* and *propulsive* insistence that it can achieve *no self-coherent identity*.

My approach can be schematized as follows. Class architecture, as we will see through the Smithsons' Brutalism and Robin Hood Gardens, is wrought out of fraught and hostile social relations, relations that course through and condition it from within. Just as the working class has no identity to realize, so class architecture does not declaim its autonomy from capitalist society, succumbing to "the 'resolve' illusion", wherein it would be lost to an accommodation with its social surround.[28] Rather, it faces up to the social relations that cleave through it, critically handling them in built form, exposing its limitations and contradictions, and therein forging new socio-architectural forms for living in, pulling against and visioning beyond capitalist society. These new forms are necessarily fragmentary. As the working class is a fraught and fractured non-identity, class architecture avers unifying wholes, revealing itself instead in parts, fragments and voids – which is not its limitation but its experimental force, its untimely opening to worlds in and against this society.

Matter and Society as Found

I turn now to consider the Smithsons' Brutalism from this perspective of class architecture. My point is not that their Brutalism is only or primarily class architecture, but that class architecture is a conceptual means to draw out and critically develop the dynamic of the social in their Brutalism, provoked to do so by the problems confronting Brutalism and housing today. I start, though, with the aesthetic, the domain of the material, before turning to the ethic, the domain of the social, exploring later in the chapter how they come together in Brutalist form.

The "rough poetry" of Brutalism designates an expressive architecture of exposed, unrefined or *raw* materials. As Brutalism has come to be known, it takes shape quintessentially in concrete, patterned by the relief impressions of the wooden form-work into which it is poured in situ, or by the gravel aggregate revealed by bush-hammer and sandblast treatment – hence the commonly stated origin of the term, in Le Corbusier's post-war style, of *béton brut* (raw concrete), as pioneered in his Unité d'habitation (1947–1952) and Maisons Jaoul (1954–1956). But a fixation on concrete has blinkered our understanding of the Brutalist approach to materials, which has numerous additional sources and features.

Writing in *Architectural Design* in January 1955, the Smithsons' derive their approach not from concrete but from Japanese traditional architecture, or its filmic and photographic representation, where they found a "reverence for the natural world and, from that, for the materials of the built world".[29] Indeed, "It is this reverence for materials – a realization of the affinity which can be established between building and man – which is at the root of the so-called New Brutalism."[30] As such, there's a Brutalist approach to *any* material, albeit that some were more favoured than others. The Smithsons were not keen on brick, preferring "wood, and concrete, glass, and steel, all the materials which you can really get hold of", materials which they took to against buildings of the 1940s which appeared, apparently, "as if they were not made of real material at all but some sort of processed material such as Kraft Cheese".[31] One can appreciate, then, how it is that they could consider their Hunstanton Secondary School in Norfolk (1950–1954) to be "the first realization of the New Brutalism in England", despite the decided absence of exposed concrete.[32]

As for the *brut* in Brutalism, this also has other sources than Le Corbusier's use of concrete. It draws, via fellow Brutalist Eduardo Paolozzi, on the visceral and expressive materiality of Jean Dubuffet's *art brut*, a vital and elemental art produced by those untrained by or untethered from the class-bound normative structures of beauty and culture.[33] Significantly for the development of Brutalist materiality, in *art brut* one can also find a turn against the *subject* of the beautiful, as constructed in the modern aesthetic paradigm founded by Kant. As David Lloyd writes, the Kantian aesthetic is "the organization of the senses toward an increasing *distance* from the object", wherein the "Subject without properties" of the bourgeois public sphere is established in contradistinction to racialized and classed others who *suffer*, in Kant's phrase, the "charms of sense".[34] For Brutalism, on the contrary, it was precisely these charms of sense, of the self-destabilizing immersion with matter, which were sought out and championed.

Materials – and now the as found enters the picture – were to be used directly as encountered, or *as they are found*. Materials were not covered over or modelled through geometric form – as per the International Style modernism of the 1920s and 1930s – but valued in themselves for their expressive qualities, particular forces, morphological capacities and contingent effects. In the Smithsons' singular turn of phrase, engaging with matter as found was "the seeing of materials for what they were: the woodness of wood; the sandiness of sand".[35] It was an attention to both qualities and capacities, such that the Brutalist question to ask of any material was also, "what can it do?"[36]

Though it is not a term the Smithsons use, we see in this approach to matter a break with the long-dominant aesthetic schema of *hylomorphism*, a schema that approaches matter as *base* and *inert*, only shaped by active imposed form. It might be a leap to say that in pitching against hylomorphism Brutalism establishes a *class* politics of matter, but it is notable that hylomorphism is intimately associated with capitalist industry and its social structure of *work*, where the division between active form and inert matter is correlated with the classed division of society into active governors and passive governed, vital intellectuals and brute manual labourers.[37] By contrast, the as found is an *immanent* engagement with matter, where materials, in Deleuze and Guattari's critique of hylomorphism, "natural or artificial, and both simultaneously", are "in movement, in flux, in variation, matter as a conveyor of singularities and traits of expression".[38] And those who would engage with matter as found – architects, but also artists, inhabitants, viewers – do not do so by "confronting it as a scene detached from [themselves], but by entering it and moving about in it".[39]

In this as-found way, materials take on an unsettling, even *agential* role – the architect decentered as an agent to become a "kind of resonator that builds in response to a poly-incidence of conditions".[40] These are John Voelcker's words, architect and fellow member of Team 10. He continues: this is "a re-orientation of spirit in which the specialist-architect who aimed at putting the built world into a pre-determined and pre-planned order has been replaced by the man-architect [sic], who is almost passively receptive to the sequence of situations in which he finds himself".[41] As the rough poetry of Brutalism is drawn out through matter, then, the architect also *yields* to it: "this matter-flow can only be *followed*".[42]

Wrought in these ways through materials, capacities and forces, Brutalist architecture is experienced also as *image* – it has "Memorability as an Image", in Reyner Banham's terms (the third of his three defining characteristics of Brutalism, accompanying materials as found and legibility of structure).[43] Banham refers to Brutalism's visually arresting scale, shape and heft, but image here is not a retreat from visceral matter to the refined aesthetic sense of the optical, for "an Image", he writes, "is what affects the emotions".[44] That is to say, Brutalism constructs a *haptic* mode of vision, where the eye is invested with the sense of touch, "press[ing] visual material toward the nervous system", as Highmore describes Paolozzi's monstrous bronzes.[45]

We can turn now from the material to the social dimension of Brutalism, adding in features of the social as we proceed. It is apparent from the Smithsons' 1957 statement that the architectural ethic, insofar as it names a critical and reflexive engagement with society, did not refer to a domain *separate* from the aesthetic. Brutalist rough poetry was achieved only insofar as *the style itself* was a direct engagement with social relations, had an "objective" relation to "mass-production society". This was engagement with society in the full breadth of that term, but pertained in particular to urbanism and mass housing – or *habitat*, as had been the quasi-ecological research problem of CIAM since 1949.

Here the social was approached no less as found than were materials, a point that is commonly missed in the literature. It is a crucial feature of being "objective about 'reality'" that architecture was not to proffer or impose a social ideal, but to be *critically immanent* to social relations as they are encountered. It is on these terms that the Smithsons' Brutalism comes closest to being a class architecture, where architecture cleaves to "the realities of the situation, with all their contradictions and confusions, and trying to do something with them".[46] This is the source of its critical orientation *and* its dynamism, where, as Highmore encapsulates, "the lack of transcendence, the permanent uncertainty of any resolution ... propels brutalism back into the world as a form of ethical realism".[47] Brutalist rough poetry was not, then, "meant to redeem society, but rather to create something of value in confrontation with it", as Alex Kitnick puts it, to which end it had a strident quality, a "brute" injunction to social relevance.[48] Indeed, Peter Smithson goes so far as to make this injunction the standard by which Brutalism *stands or falls*: "We are interested in expressing not ourselves, but what is going on and building which denies what is going on is just the opposite of brutalism – it is chi-chi, which is a sort of evasion."[49]

The Violent Consumer

Before turning to *how* Brutalism engages the social, a potential difficulty presents itself. If the Brutalist confrontation with society is class architecture, fashioning built form from the fraught confusion of social relations, is it an obstacle that the Smithsons were not Marxists? Indeed, is it an obstacle that they coined the phrase New Brutalism in direct *opposition* to a certain Marxism in architecture? For the *New* here did not refer to an earlier incarnation, but served to place the movement in critical relation to the then ascendant style of New Empiricism, a style associated with Communist

Party members and sympathizers in the London County Council's architecture department.

To the first question, the simple answer is no. Class architecture is too awkward, complex and overdetermined by social relations to be evaluated in terms of the political identifications of its architects, identifications (or lack thereof) which do not at all delimit or exhaust the political dimensions and potential of architecture. As to the second, there is a definite liberal ground to the Smithsons' political orientations, and their critique of the welfare state can have a neoliberal tone. But their primary object of critique here was New Empiricism's thinly diluted Swedish modernism, with its populism of pitched roofs, brick walls and picture windows, which they irreverently characterized as "People's Detailing", rather than the Marxism as such of the style's champions, if Stalinism is to be called that.

An apparent obstacle *is* presented, however, by the Smithsons' ideas about class, occasional though they are, for this takes us to the heart of the thesis of this book. I address their approach to class here to then put it aside.

In a strident retrospective assessment of Robin Hood Gardens, the Smithsons declare it to have been a *socialist* endeavour – a "building for the socialist dream", "it wants to be universal, greater than our little State".[50] Yet, as Dirk van den Heuvel shows, there is no indication that they were especially exercised by socialism, beyond an attraction to Swedish-style social democracy, to society as the "togetherness of one extended family".[51] Moreover, their social democracy comes with an understanding of class that is decidedly uncritical – first, in the Swedish vein, of society aggregating around the dominant "culture group" of the middle class, and then, when the fraught realities of class society inevitably unsettled this picture, an angry turn against the working class.[52]

This turn is partially evident in a 1970 BBC television documentary about Robin Hood Gardens, *The Smithsons on Housing*, directed by avant-garde novelist B. S. Johnson and filmed during the estate's construction. It opens with a startlingly downbeat presentation of working-class propensity to vandalism, Alison Smithson speculating that instead of building new homes, "It may be that [architects] should only be asked to repair the roofs and add the odd bathroom to the old industrial houses and just leave people where they are to smash it up in complete abandon and happiness."[53] But when she picks up the point again in her 1974 essay, "The Violent Consumer, or Waiting for the Goodies", the objectionable class dimensions of this appraisal are let loose. The occasion, though unstated, was vandalism of Robin Hood Gardens.[54]

The societal problem of vandalism prompts Alison Smithson here not to a critical appraisal of the social violence of class and inequality, which sunders society as a whole, but to rail against the working class, with a conceptual edifice brimming with the clichés of middle-class contempt. As against the middle-class "builders in the community", the "bill-paying other half", here is a "*class of resentment* that has largely taken the place of the *working class*", a class "belligerent with [consumerist] desire", lacking all "sacredness for the results of labour", negligent of private and public property, "the immediate beneficiaries of the welfare state [who] smash and foul those portions of cities provided specifically for them".[55] It is true that in the Marxist paradigm I set out above there's nothing *angelic* about the working class, riven as it is by constraint and contradiction, and a certain disrespect towards labour is integral to class politics.[56] But Alison Smithson's appraisal of class is clearly not headed in those directions.

The essay reads like a wounded attempt to shield Robin Hood Gardens and its architects from criticism, and from the broader turn against modernist council estates, by laying blame on the *undeserving poor*.[57] Here Smithson tapped into a discursive and policy framework that has had a leading role in the history of council housing – from the earliest council homes and the birth of the welfare state, where it served to exclude certain sectors from council housing and commandeer the *deserving* working class for the national compact, to the neoliberalism of Margaret Thatcher, Tony Blair and since, where it is deployed to stigmatize council estates, priming welfare retrenchment and estate demolition.[58]

It is dispiriting indeed to see this framework deployed by an architect of Robin Hood Gardens, not confronting but perpetuating the hostile discourses of class society. But it is a wounded outburst after the estate's completion; insofar as ideas of class featured in the Smithsons' writings around the design of Robin Hood Gardens, they were of the problematic but commonplace variety of Swedish-style social democracy. Moreover, the point, as I have been suggesting and will pursue through the book, is that the non-identity of class is figured in the Smithsons' Brutalism *not in what they write about class*, or write about class directly, but *in what they write about and construct in architecture*. Returning to this, I move now to consider how expressive materials and fraught social relations are brought together into architectural form, where form has a Brutalist specificity, to be understood in terms of *topology* and the intuition and provocation of *problems*.

Brutalist Form: Topology and Problems

Brutalist architecture is confronted by the question of how it can remain true to the expressive, processual and conflictual material and social forces that it fashions, without these being subsumed in and subordinated to architectural form. In Highmore's phrase, how are "forms" to "have the capacity to negotiate and figure contradictory and conflictive material"?[59] It is a question that informs Banham's movement-defining 1955 essay "The New Brutalism", where he identifies in the Smithsons a "topological" approach to form, or what he also calls their "aformalism".[60] Brutalist aformalism, Banham argues, turns against the formal unity of classical proportion and symmetry, governed by principles of geometry, to instead fashion architecture on the topological principle of *form in process* or *deforming form*, governed by such qualities as "penetration, circulation, inside and out".[61]

Banham refers in particular to the Smithsons' competition entries for the Golden Lane estate (1952) and Sheffield University (1953). The Sheffield entry comprised gangways and a full-width continuous deck, in an angular horseshoe shape that connected the academic faculties – poles of attraction which "continually recharged movement" – and cupped a half-open and half-closed inner green, opening up the traditional university quadrangle to site and city.[62] The structure both facilitated and was *shaped by* movement. Space and form were "generated by flows of people rather than as containers of functions", in Crinson's words.[63] For Banham, in what has become a quintessential description of Brutalism, "no attempt is made to give a geometrical form to the total scheme", where "large blocks of topologically similar spaces stand about the site with the same graceless memorability as Martello towers or pit-head gear" (Figure 2.1).[64] In the Smithsons' topological idiom, here they were developing a "non-Euclidean" architecture, an architecture "more complex, and less geometric", "more concerned with 'flow' than with 'measure'".[65] And they understood this approach to be of no small significance. As Alison Smithson prefaced the "Team 10 Primer", this

Figure 2.1 Sheffield University axonometric, 1953, revised 1978. (Alison Smithson. Smithson Family Collection)

"non-Euclidian idea" is "contemporary to all our difficulties, social and political, economic and spiritual".[66] Einstein, Schönberg, Bergson, Mondrian and Joyce, among others, "jumped out" of the deterministic "Euclidian groove", she writes. "They set the great top spinning again and expanded the universe – the outside and the inside universe." Society and architecture only tinker with these ideas, she chastises, "gnawing at the edges", when they should instead "join the riot".[67]

As is apparent in the Sheffield competition entry, this topological approach entails a loosening of parts from integration in the whole, a loosing of the different forms in process of which a building is comprised, where parts or forms become "things in themselves" with "their own internal disciplines and complexities".[68] For this, the Smithsons drew inspiration also from Jackson Pollock. In a Pollock drip painting, there *is* a whole, with "clarity of intention", but it is "more like a natural phenomenon, a manifestation rather than an artefact", "complex", "n-dimensional" and "multi-vocative".[69] Immersed in a built structure, as in a painting by Pollock, there is no fixed point or primary form around which to manoeuvre; rather, one is always "in the middle", moving through interleaved but distinct forms in process, as they are found.[70]

Loosened from overbearing formal integration, the architectural whole and its parts also remain *open to that from which they are formed* – open, in our terms, to their material and social outside – such that form is in continuous and dynamic interplay with its environment. In deforming itself, it takes its social and material surround with it. Brian Massumi, prominent in the return of topological thinking in the humanities, puts it like this: "Forms figure less as self-enclosures than as open co-dependencies of a shared deformational field. The continuity of that field of variation is inseparable from the forms populating it. Yet it exceeds any one of them, running across them all."[71] Or, to use a term I adopt from Gilbert Simondon, form is a *modulation* of that of which it is formed, where "to modulate is to mold in a continuously and perpetually variable way".[72] Here, then, we have a theory of form that is adequate to the Brutalist theory of matter, where modulation, as Simondon addresses directly, is posited against the active-form and passive-matter distinction of hylomorphism.

The emphasis Massumi places on continuity of transformation leads him to view built architectural form as secondary to the process that exceeds it, as "residue of a process of change, from which it stands out (in its stoppage)".[73] But that is not how I consider it in this book. Rather, the forms in process of Robin Hood Gardens are modulations of materials, social relations, site and environment that bear process *in their built articulation.*

Their topological qualities of inside and outside, circulation, thresholds and so forth at once shape and are *extended by* the social and sensory *experience* and *use* of the architecture. It is for this reason that Banham's presentation of the topological qualities of Golden Lane includes a favourable remark about the unusual prominence of *people* in the architectural drawings, where "the human presence almost overwhelmed the architecture".[74]

It remains to be seen how the *social* features in these deforming forms. The key operator here is the social *problem*. Forms, the Smithsons insist, are not dreamt up out of an architect's mind, or readily available to be drawn from a more or less derivative stock, where the architect "drops back into a formula" – that approach is "a sort of lie".[75] For Brutalism, rather, "form evolves *out of circumstance*", out of encounters in the social and material world, the world as found.[76] There is an "involuntarism" to architectural form here, and to the thought that accompanies its fashioning, if we draw from Deleuze. "Something in the world *forces us* to think", where this something is "an object not of recognition but of a fundamental *encounter*".[77] And encounters produce or solicit problems, the catalyst for the emergence of form. The "strangeness" of an encounter "perplexes" thought, "awaken[s] thought from its natural stupor" and forces it "to pose a problem".[78] Provoked in this way, problems emerge in "a range of affective tones: wonder, love, hatred, suffering".[79]

Form emerges, then, through sensing, teasing out, grappling with and materially fashioning problems. As a process, it is experimental and faltering. If architecture "ruptures", if it "realizes the priority and force of form", as Anna Kornbluh writes in *The Order of Forms*, it does so by cleaving to the fault lines, tensions, complexities and limits of social problems, the "encounter with limits" conditioning form from within.[80] In no way, then, are problems *resolved* in form. In modulating social problems, form is necessarily groping, incomplete and open. We can see, then, how a topological understanding of form can lend itself to class architecture, to bring that concept back in, for both are characterized by a processual grappling with social complexities and limits without resolution.[81]

If the social figures as a terrain of problems, problems that anticipate and summon the emergence of form, we must ask, what were the *specific* problems that engaged the Smithsons? What problems provoked the forms of Robin Hood Gardens? In the broadest sense, the key problem was "mass housing" – mass working-class housing, or "building for the greatest number". The Smithsons put it plainly in a 1950s text that reappears in their 1970 book *Ordinariness and Light*: "In England the key problem is that of the council house."[82] This was a problem of capacity and supply, certainly, but for the Smithsons it was also one of form, for they continue: "We are involved in mass housing not as reformers but as *form givers*."[83] They sought forms adequate for the contemporary city, the district and the street, as much as for the home, and for the dynamic interplay and codetermination of these scales of association – this is their "ecological approach to the problem of habitat", to "evolve an architecture from the fabric of life itself".[84]

As it should be for an architecture of the encounter, the social problem of mass housing was mediated and complicated through the particularities of a commission and its site – its social, topographical and environmental features. And this situated mediation is responsible for identifying and fashioning the additional and different problems that are articulated in the various deforming forms that comprise a building. As for Robin Hood Gardens, I consider it to have comprised four main problem-mediating forms, each of which can be named by one of the "affective concepts", as Christine Boyer characterizes them, through which the Smithsons grappled with each problem-form: *streets in the sky* (the problem of the street); *ordinariness and light* (home); *repetition and difference* (mass); and *charged void* (landscape). It is to these problem-forms that four of the following chapters are devoted, starting with the streets in the sky.

To conclude this chapter and to prepare for the analysis of the estate's forms, its themes can be reprised in a schematic of the Brutalism of Robin Hood Gardens. This estate is a work of architecture comprised of different deforming forms, forms which are at once material and social – and hence also spatial, environmental, sensory, affective, atmospheric, temporal and so forth. Each form interrogates and modulates a particular problem, a problem integral to working-class housing and habitat in class society. These forms are loosened from determination by formal unity, allowing each to have its own qualities, complexities and effects on the whole, where each is at once distinct, overlapping and folding in and out of the others. Each form bears and grapples with the limits of the problem it surveys, rather than settling into resolution. And each form is processual, enlivened by the material and social forces, uses and experiences that it facilitates. This latter provides an architectural rationale, alongside the political one, for the presence in this book of residents' accounts of their experience of the estate and for the inclusion of their portraits, which sometimes overwhelm the architecture with the "looked-at, lived-in life of the building".[85]

Coda on Utopia and Class Architecture

I established the concept of class architecture in contradistinction to the *utopian* in architecture, with some good cause. Whether as the modernist utopia of the plan, which furnished the model for the post-war industrial city, or as "islands of realized utopia" amid social conditions left unchanged, utopian architecture serves the world as it is while masquerading as doing the opposite. And these are not the only reasons to shy away from the concept in the context of Brutalism. A distorted figure of utopian modernism has endured as a formulation of the political right, ever since the first privatizing assaults on public housing empowered themselves by characterizing these estates and projects as deluded utopias – "utopia" was put "on trial" and found "guilty", in the words of Alice Coleman, Margaret Thatcher's favourite urbanist.[86] In a more mundane sense, the association of Brutalism with the utopian is too often today a lazy cliché, where utopianism is vaguely equated with welfare-state values, more or less hopefully or dismissively, but either way effectively ending rather than inciting architectural ideas and problems.

Yet I want to keep open a line of connection between class architecture and utopian thinking. This is not least because Jameson's appraisal, in 2005, that "Utopia seems to have recovered its vitality as a political slogan and a politically energizing perspective" is all the more evident today. Amid the runaway crises of capitalist society and the pervasive – if still nascent and faltering – sense of the imperative to reconfigure social life against and after capitalism, the *visioning* and *agential* power of utopia is a vital resource.[87] There is more to emancipatory politics than this, but Jameson encapsulates this utopian function in his claim that "one cannot imagine any fundamental change in our social existence which has not first thrown off Utopian visions like so many sparks from a comet".[88]

Jameson is of course himself a leading figure in the renewed vitality of utopian thinking, where his formulations in fact share much with the sensibility of class architecture – the dynamic of incompletion and non-identity, the wrenching of form out of social crisis, the significance of architecture to the transformation of social life. It is notable, then, that Jameson has forged his thinking about the utopian in architecture by tarrying with Tafuri. As Gail Day shows, while in the mid-1980s Jameson regarded Tafuri's refusal of the possibility of class architecture to be "paralyzing and asphyxiating", he later contends, in 2001, that Tafuri's "implacably negative judgments", as I have formulated it here too, "are not demoralizing or paralyzing but rather energizing and productive of future praxis".[89]

Where the zigzagging line of connection between class architecture and utopianism becomes more complicated is around the problematic of class. The case I made above, and will pursue through this book, is that the deforming forms of Brutalism become most wrenching, inventive and transformative – most *utopian*, in Jameson's sense – the more they grapple with the problems of class society, the more they bear the "restlessness within its very self" of the working class, as condition and standpoint, into architecture.[90] Jameson's writing about architecture, on the other hand, is less engaged with the problem of class, and in this I suggest it loses some of its capacity for a utopian architectural thought adequate to the social conditions of today. I would not make too much of it, but it is not insignificant that Jameson's most renowned essay on the utopian in architecture, for all its insight, concerns a well-to-do private residence – Frank Gehry's home in Santa Monica.[91]

Against lazy characterizations of the Smithsons as utopian architects, Crinson has identified an "*anti*-utopian" bent to their architecture.[92] This is an architecture of "disabused realism", without illusions as to what architecture alone can achieve – though for Crinson this is no *retreat*.[93] Their disabused realism *all the more* compels architecture's experimental, critical and ongoing grappling with the rough and conflictual realities of the social world. And this, I want to suggest, is what the Smithsons bring to architectural *utopianism*, if that term is to be used (sparingly) in connection to their Brutalism. It is how we can understand the self-description of their work, deployed only once or twice, as a "fragmentary utopia".[94] Class architecture is a disabused realism and a fragmentary utopia in one.

Notes

1 Alison and Peter Smithson, "House in Soho, London", *Architectural Design* 23 no. 12 (December 1953): 342. The site was actually in London's Fitzrovia, at 24 Colville Place, adjacent to but not in Soho. It transpires that this foundational text was written by Alison only, as the Smithsons

later report in their review of Rayner Banham's book on Brutalism, which includes also a rare note of the sexism of their world: "The piece was initialled A.M.S. in typescript, but this was mistranscribed, an error or as an anti-feminist editorial gesture, as P.D.S. This is how one comes to found a movement!" Alison and Peter Smithson, "Banham's Bumper Book on Brutalism", *The Architect's Journal* 144 no. 26 (1966): 1590–1591, 1590. The same review credits Alison also with coining the movement's name. "New Brutalism", they write, "was a spontaneous invention by A.M.S. as a word play counter-ploy to *The Architectural Review*'s 'New Empiricism'", with the "brutal" part sourced to an unnamed English newspaper article, which Laurent Stalder has identified from a cutting in the Smithsons' archive to a piece in *The Times* titled "'Radiant City' Lawsuit: Complaint of Brutal Realism", 3 December 1952. As Stalder fills in the rather comic details, *The Times* article "reported that the French Society for Aesthetic Sensibilities had taken the Unité to court for being 'brutal,' symbolising the decline of moral order, and affronting French style and aesthetics in general". Laurent Stalder, "'New Brutalism,' 'Topology' and 'Image': Some Remarks on the Architectural Debates in England around 1950", *The Journal of Architecture* 13 no. 3 (2008): 263–281. For discussion of the different sources and shifting meanings of the term Brutalism in its early usage, see Dirk van den Heuvel, "Between Brutalists: The Banham Hypothesis and the Smithson Way of Life", *The Journal of Architecture* 20 no. 2 (2015): 293–308 and Anthony Vidler, "Another Brick in the Wall", *October* 136 (2011): 105–132.

2 Alison and Peter Smithson, "The New Brutalism: Alison and Peter Smithson Answer the Criticisms on the Opposite Page", *Architectural Design*, April 1957, 113.

3 Ben Highmore, *The Art of Brutalism: Rescuing Hope from Catastrophe in 1950s Britain* (New Haven, CT and London: Yale University Press, 2017), 15, 271; Mark Crinson, "Neo Brutalism", *London Art History Society Review* (2021): 6–7; Mark Crinson, "Brutalism: From New to Neo", talk given at Birkbeck, University of London, 19 May 2016, https://backdoorbroadcasting.net/2016/05/mark-crinson-brutalism-from-new-to-neo/.

4 Barnabas Calder, *Raw Concrete: The Beauty of Brutalism* (London: William Heinemann, 2016), 82.

5 *Ibid.*, 18.

6 *Ibid.*, 4. Calder's separation of the aesthetic from the social is fittingly carried by a robust and self-identical autobiographical voice, the book's unity of class, voice and architecture consummated in the reveal that his love of Brutalism's most establishment scheme led his friends to refer to it after him, as "the Barnican". For critique of the autobiographical voice in contemporary writing, attentive to its class dimensions, see Gary Hall, *A Stubborn Fury: How Writing Works in Elitist Britain* (London: Open Humanities Press, 2021).

7 Considered as part of the broader social process of middle-class appropriation of working-class cultural forms, the palliative quality of beautiful Brutalism can be read alongside Skeggs' argument that such appropriations are *fragile*. They are liable to be ridiculed or to fail in achieving adequate class distinction, and hence must "be continually authorized and asserted", especially so when the two classes live in close proximity, as they do in gentrifying council estates. Skeggs, *Class, Self, Culture*, 154.

8 Lynsey Hanley, "Britain Needs Decent New Council Houses – Not Just Musicals about Them", *The Guardian*, 3 April 2019, www.theguardian.com/commentisfree/2019/apr/03/britain-needs-new-council-houses-sheffield.

9 Calder, *Raw Concrete*, 83.

10 Owen Hatherley, *Militant Modernism* (London: Zero Books, 2009), 10.

11 Joseph Watson, "Towering Ambitions: Balfron Tower and the National Trust", 2014, www.balfrontower.org/document/93/flat-130-balfron-tower. Though it is not the point I am making here, this passage, taken as it is from the accompanying booklet to the Hemingway-designed apartment at Balfron Tower (see Chapter 1), illustrates how the social-democratic version of the Brutalist revival can cross over into beautiful Brutalism, becoming an alienable quality for the extractive aesthetics of the latter, a wholesome historical image of organic community with which to market these estates for middle-class consumption.

12 Robbie Shilliam, *Race and the Undeserving Poor* (Newcastle: Agenda Publishing, 2018), 75, 80.

13 Satnam Virdee, *Racism, Class, and the Racialized Outsider* (London: Red Globe Press, 2014). This is not at all to cast white members of the working class as *emblematically* racist, as today's stigmatizing discourses of class tend to have it. Of course, *anti*-racism had a profound and powerful place in the historical workers' movement, articulated with its foundational principles of solidarity and internationalism. But I will illustrate the point I make here with an example from East London that concerns a figure dear to the social-democratic left, George Lansbury. It illustrates too the counter-trend in working-class anti-racism.

As the first Labour Party mayor of Poplar, Lansbury is renowned for leading the Poplar Rates Rebellion of 1921. Seeking, and soon achieving, rates equalization across London, so as to share the burden of poor relief, 30 Poplar councillors were jailed for diverting payments that were due to the London County Council and the Metropolitan Police to local poor relief. *Poplarism*, as this became known, is a far cry from the activity of London Labour councils today, caught up as they are in the finance–housebuilding complex. But there is another side to Lansbury.

In 1920, when he was editor of the *Daily Herald*, the leading newspaper of organized labour, Lansbury presided over a series of articles that deployed sickening anti-Black racial fantasies to stoke working-class support for Germany against France in dispute over the Ruhr. Under the headlines "Black Scourge in Europe" and "Sexual Horror Let Loose by France", Edmund Dene Morel wrote of France "thrusting her black savages ... into the heart of Germany", of the "barely restrainable beastiality of the black troops" unleashed in the rape and murder of white women, and warned that, "If the manhood of these races, not so advanced in the forms of civilization as ourselves, are to be used against the Germans, *why not against the workers here or elsewhere?*" In a preface and editorial, Lansbury endorsed Morel's article, inviting female readers to ponder over these "sexual outrages", while refuting the charge of racism in a manner that further entrenched it: "we champion the rights of the African native in his own home", "nature has given us all qualities of temperament suitable to the conditions and climate in which we are born" and so forth. When Claude McKay, Jamaican-born poet, novelist and communist, wrote to the paper to object, Lansbury refused to publish his letter. McKay's letter was published instead in Sylvia Pankhurst's Bow-based communist weekly the *Workers' Dreadnought*, starting his period of journalism for the paper – just one illuminating episode in his extraordinary peripatetic biography. Robert C. Reinders, "Racialism on the Left: E. D. Morel and the 'Black Horror in the Rhine'", *International Review of Social History* 13 no. 1 (1968): 1–28, 1–2 and Claude McKay, *A Long Way from Home: An Autobiography* (London: Pluto Press, 1985).

14 This point is made by a number of communists and Marxists, most notably Jacques Camatte, Mario Tronti, Moishe Postone, the journals *Théorie Communiste* and *Endnotes* and G. M. Tamás, who puts it succinctly: "Socialism as a political movement was a tool of

capitalist modernization not only in the East, but also in Central and Western Europe." G. M. Tamás, "Telling the Truth about Class", *Socialist Register* 42 (2006): 1–41, 11. See Nicholas Thoburn, "Do Not Be Afraid, Join Us, Come Back? On the 'Idea of Communism' in Our Time", *Cultural Critique* 84 (2013), 1–34.

15 "Afterword", *Endnotes* 1 (2008): 208–216; Aaron Benanav, *Automation and the Future of Work* (London: Verso, 2020).

16 Beverley Skeggs, "Introduction: Stratification or Exploitation, Domination, Dispossession and Devaluation?" *The Sociological Review* 63 no. 2 (2015): 205–222; Nicholas Thoburn, "The People Are Missing: Cramped Space, Social Relations, and the Mediators of Politics", *International Journal of Politics, Culture and Society* 29 no. 4 (2016): 367–381.

17 Tamás, "Telling the Truth About Class", 3.

18 Karl Marx, "A Contribution to Hegel's Philosophy of Right", in *Early Writings*, trans. Rodney Livingstone and Gregor Benton (Harmondsworth: Penguin, 1975), 256.

19 Karl Marx, "On the Jewish Question", in *Early Writings*, trans. Rodney Livingstone and Gregor Benton (Harmondsworth: Penguin, 1975), 230, translation modified. For a more fully developed account of the non-identity of the proletariat, see Thoburn, "The People Are Missing".

20 Fredric Jameson, *Postmodernism: Or, the Cultural Logic of Late Capitalism* (London: Verso, 1991), 5.

21 Manfredo Tafuri, cited in Gail Day, "Manfredo Tafuri, Fredric Jameson and the Contestations of Political Memory", *Historical Materialism* 20 no. 1 (2012): 31–77, 56.

22 Manfredo Tafuri, *Architecture and Utopia: Design and Capitalist Development*, trans. Barbara Luigia La Penta (Cambridge, MA and London: MIT Press, 1976), 181.

23 *Ibid.*, 81.

24 *Ibid.*, 126.

25 *Ibid.*, 131.

26 *Ibid.*, 179.

27 For Tafuri, this is a critique that unearths and demystifies the "contingent and historical" capitalist conditions of the seemingly objective and universal discipline of architecture, just as Marx did with the putatively objective discipline of political economy. *Ibid.*

28 Tafuri, cited in Day, "Manfredo Tafuri, Fredric Jameson and the Contestations of Political Memory", 62.

29 Theo Crosby, Alison Smithson and Peter Smithson, "The New Brutalism", *Architectural Design* 25 no. 1 (January 1955): 1 . *Gate of Hell* (1953), a Japanese period drama which won the grand prize at Cannes in 1954, was their primary source – they did not visit the country until 1960. There are signs of orientalism here, but the Smithsons' approach to matter and form does not at all follow the prominent strain in the Modern Movement, Louis Sullivan and Frank Lloyd Wright in particular, where references to national architectural styles, including especially those of Japan, were components of a *racializing* and *white supremacist* architectural organicism. Charles L. Davis II, *Building Character: The Racial Politics of Modern Architectural Style* (Pittsburgh, PA: The University of Pittsburgh Press, 2019).

30 Crosby, Smithson and Smithson, "The New Brutalism", 1. These passages appear again, slightly altered, in the Smithsons' *Without Rhetoric*, on pages 4 to 6. It is a characteristic practice for them to repeat, incorporate and re-write earlier texts in later books. Henceforth I will refrain from noting these repetitions except for when it has pertinence for the discussion.

31 Alison Smithson, in Smithson et al., "Conversation on Brutalism", 40. In an amusing discussion of brick in the same 1959 interview, Peter Smithson remarks: "I am obsessionally against the brick, you know, we think brick the antithesis of machine building and yet for practical reasons we never have built in anything else. It is a tragedy." Nonetheless, "If common sense tells you that you have got to make some poetic thing with brick, you make it with brick." Alison picks up the thread: "But a time is coming now for a further stand against being pushed towards building in bricks, even if it means refusing a job that needs bricks." *Ibid.*, 46.

32 Crosby et al., "The New Brutalism", 1. As to the first Brutalist building *anywhere*, the Smithsons credit this to the Baker House dormitory (1947–1949) at MIT, designed by the Finish architect Alvar Aalto. They describe it as "the most revolutionary post-war building, which no one understood at all and said so, talking endlessly about it. ... [I]t was the first building to consciously use its access systems as places, and as the means to allow the building to explain itself. It occupies the position in architecture that Pollock does in painting, and is probably the first true Brutalist building." Smithson and Smithson, "Banham's Bumper Book on Brutalism", 1591. A common story about the etymology of New Brutalism identifies a different first example as the Villa Göth (1949) housing complex in Uppsala, Sweden, designed by Bengt Edman and Lennart Holm, which the architect Hans Asplund referred to in jest as *nybrutalism*.

33 Jean Dubuffet, "Art Brut in Preference to the Cultural Arts", orig. 1949, https://cornpone.tumblr.com/post/8698135872/art-brut-in-preference-to-the-cultural-arts-jean.

34 David Lloyd, *Under Representation: The Racial Regime of Aesthetics* (New York: Fordham University Press, 2018), 73, emphasis added, 74.

35 Alison and Peter Smithson, "The 'As Found' and the 'Found'", in *The Independent Group: Postwar Britain and the Aesthetics of Plenty*, ed. David Robbins (Cambridge, MA: MIT Press, 1990), 201.

36 Peter Smithson, in Peter Smithson and Hans Ulrich Obrist, *Smithson Time: A Dialogue* (Köln: Walter König, 2004), 18.

37 As Deleuze and Guattari put it, after Gilbert Simondon, "the hylomorphic schema owes its power not to the technological operation but to the social model of *work* subsuming that operation". Gilles Deleuze and Félix Guattari, *A Thousand Plateaus: Capitalism and Schizophrenia Volume 2*, trans. Brian Massumi (Minneapolis: University of Minnesota Press, 1987), 562.

38 *Ibid.*, 409.

39 David Sylvester, describing Paolozzi's painting and sculpture, cited in Alex Kitnick, "The Brutalism of Life and Art", *October* 136 (2011): 63–86, 66.

40 John Voelcker cited in Highmore, *The Art of Brutalism*, 15.

41 *Ibid.*

42 Deleuze and Guattari, *A Thousand Plateaus*, 409.

43 Banham, "The New Brutalism", 28.

44 To underscore the aesthetic significance of the Brutalist difference, here is Schiller on the refined sense of sight: "The object of touch is a force to which we are subjected; the object of eye and ear a form that we engender. As long as man is still a savage he enjoys by means of these tactile senses alone." Cited in Lloyd, *Under Representation*, 74.

45 Highmore, *The Art of Brutalism*, 179. Banham's haptic visuality is in tension with his more conventionally modernist opinion that the Brutalist image requires and conveys the integration

of form and function, "that the building should be an immediately apprehensible visual entity, and that the form grasped by the eye should be confirmed by the experience of the building in use". Banham, "The New Brutalism", 25.

46 Alison and Peter Smithson, "Cluster City: A New Shape for the Community", *Architectural Review* 122 (1957): 332–336, 332.

47 Highmore, *The Art of Brutalism*, 99–100.

48 Alex Kitnick, "Introduction", *October* 136 (2011): 3–6, 6. The Smithsons wrote in 1966: "Brutalist to us meant 'Direct': to others it came to be a synonym for rough, crude oversized and using beams three times thicker than necessary. Brutalism was opposite, necessary to suit the new situation, like Kahn's work at Yale. That wasn't rough or crude or oversized." Cited in van den Heuvel, "Between Brutalists", 298. Fellow Brutalist Georges Candilis put it like this: "Brutalism, yes of course. It was our slogan. The term has to be taken in the sense of directness, truthfulness, no concessions. I remember writing: 'You have to be direct and brute.'" Cited in Vidler, "Another Brick in the Wall", 108.

49 Peter Smithson, in Smithson et al., "Conversation on Brutalism", 42–43.

50 Alison and Peter Smithson, "Robin Hood Gardens, London", *The Charged Void: Architecture* (New York: The Monacelli Press, 2001), 296.

51 Dirk van den Heuvel, *Alison and Peter Smithson: A Brutalist Story Involving the House, the City and the Everyday*, unpublished PhD thesis (Delft University of Technology, 2003), 243.

52 *Ibid.*

53 *The Smithsons on Housing*, dir. B. S. Johnson (BBC, 1970), available on YouTube.

54 Vandalism of the estate in its earlier years is not something to be dismissed lightly, but it was a common social phenomenon of the time and was not remembered as a significant issue by the three early residents we spoke with.

55 Alison Smithson, "The Violent Consumer, or Waiting for the Goodies", *Architectural Design* 5 (1974): 274–279, 274, 277.

56 Tamás makes an analytic distinction between an "angelic" view of the exploited (found in Rousseau, Karl Polányi, E. P. Thompson) and a properly Marxist "demonic" view, where class has no positive identity – no culture, nature, values – outside of or prior to its fraught composition in capitalism. Tamás, "Telling the Truth about Class".

57 It is no justification for this response, but criticism of the estate and the vandalism appears to have taken a significant emotional toll on the Smithsons – understandably so. The couple's son, Simon Smithson, recalled in 2008 that "Robin Hood Gardens is a difficult issue for me because it affected my parents' careers in a very unfortunate manner, and it's been painful for us as a family. They became convinced that the commission [to build Robin Hood Gardens] was going to destroy their careers. ... [W]hen we talked to the warden and he showed us the old peoples' centre that had been smashed up and had to be locked, it shook my father to the core." To be clear, should this comment suggest otherwise, it is not an appraisal of the estate itself, which, as he states, the Smithsons believed to be their most important building. "Interview: Simon Smithson", *Building Design*, 21 February 2008, www.bdonline.co.uk/opinion/interview-simon-smithson/3107017.article. Simon Smithson, "We Called it 'Robin Hood Lane'", in *Robin Hood Gardens: Re-Visions*, ed. Alan Powers (London: Twentieth Century Society, 2010).

58 Shilliam, *The Undeserving Poor*.

59 Ben Highmore, "Rough Poetry: *Patio and Pavilion* Revisited", *Oxford Art Journal* 29 no. 2 (2006): 269–290, 284.

60 Banham, "The New Brutalism".

61 Banham, "The New Brutalism", 27. The terms *form in process* and *deforming form* are used interchangeably in this book – terms I borrow, respectively, from Michel Tapié's *Un Art autre*, which is one of Banham's references, and Gilles Deleuze, *Cinema 1: The Movement-Image*, trans. Hugh Tomlinson and Barbara Habberjam (London: Athlone, 1986), 178.

62 Alison and Peter Smithson, "Sheffield University", in Smithson and Smithson, *The Charged Void: Architecture*, 108.

63 Mark Crinson, *Alison and Peter Smithson* (Swindon: Historic England, 2018), 18.

64 Banham, "The New Brutalism", 27.

65 Smithson and Smithson, *Ordinariness and Light*, 130.

66 Alison Smithson (ed.) for Team 10, "Team 10 Primer", *Architectural Design* 32 (December 1962): 559–563, 559.

67 *Ibid.*

68 Smithson and Smithson, *Ordinariness and Light*, 84.

69 *Ibid.*, 84, 86.

70 *In the middle* is Deleuze and Guattari's term for the *plateau* condition of being flush with and flooded by a particular environment: "It's not easy to see things in the middle, rather than looking down on them from above or up at them from below, or from left to right or right to left: try it, you'll see that everything changes." Deleuze and Guattari, *A Thousand Plateaus*, 23.

71 Brian Massumi, "Sensing the Virtual, Building the Insensible", *Couplets: Travels in Speculative Pragmatism* (Durham, NC and London: Duke University Press, 2021), 135.

72 Gilbert Simondon, *Individuation in Light of Notions of Form and Information*, trans. Taylor Adkins (Minneapolis and London: University of Minnesota Press, 2020), 31.

73 Massumi, "Sensing the Virtual", 135.

74 Banham, "The New Brutalism", 27.

75 Peter Smithson, in Smithson et al., "Conversation on Brutalism", 42–43.

76 Peter Smithson, "Think of it as a Farm! Exhibitions, Books, Buildings. An Interview with Peter Smithson", in *This Is Not Architecture*, ed. Kester Rattenbury (London: Routledge, 2002), 94.

77 Gilles Deleuze, *Difference and Repetition*, trans. Paul Patton (New York: Columbia University Press, 1994), 139, first emphasis added.

78 *Ibid.*, 139, 140. Deleuze underscores that the point is not to solve ready-made problems ("as if they were drawn out of 'the city's administrative filing cabinets,' ... forc[ing] us to 'solve' them, leaving us only a thin margin of freedom"), but to *pose* problems, where "stating the problem is not simply uncovering, *it is inventing*". Gilles Deleuze, *Bergsonism*, trans. Hugh Tomlinson and Barbara Habberjam (New York: Zone Books, 1988), 15. *Ibid.*, quoting Henri Bergson, *The Creative Mind: An Introduction to Metaphysics*, trans. Mabelle L. Andison (New York, Philosophical Library, 1946).

79 Deleuze, *Difference and Repetition*, 139.

80 Anna Kornbluh, *The Order of Forms: Realism, Formalism, and Social Space* (Chicago, IL: Chicago University Press), 42.

81 If Marxism and topology seem strange bedfellows, it is worth noting that the critical appropriation of topology was a significant interest of the Situationist International and its Scandinavian offshoots, for whom topology offered a theory of space and form adequate to the non-identity of the proletariat. See Ellef Prestsæter's wonderful volume on this topic, focused on Jacqueline de Jong's topological magazine *The Situationist Times*. Ellef

Prestsæter (ed.), *These Are Situationist Times! An Inventory of Reproductions, Deformations, Modifications, Derivations, and Transformations* (Oslo: Torpedo Press, 2019).

82 Smithson and Smithson, *Ordinariness and Light*, 108.

83 *Ibid.*, 108, emphasis added.

84 *Ibid.*, 108, 22. Making it plain that this was a social problem that required new forms, Alison Smithson wrote: "The problem of reidentifying man with his environment cannot be achieved by using historical forms of house-groupings, streets, squares, greens, etc., as the social reality they presented no longer exists." Cited in Hadas Steiner, "Life at the Threshold", *October* 136 (2011): 133–155, 144.

85 Massumi, "Sensing the Virtual", 145.

86 Alice Coleman, *Utopia on Trial: Vision and Reality in Planned Housing* (London: Hilary Shipman, 1985). For Thatcher's interest in Coleman and an enthusiastic appraisal of Coleman's ideas by one of the leading ideological institutions of estate demolition today, see Create Streets, "Alice in Wonderland", 2014, www.createstreets.com/wp-content/uploads/2017/12/Interview-with-Alice-Coleman.pdf.

87 Fredric Jameson, *Archaeologies of the Future: The Desire Called Utopia and Other Science Fictions* (London and New York: Verso, 2005), xii. I am grateful to Judy Thorne and Martin Greenwood for discussion of the features and significance of utopian thought, whose own writings on the matter are acute and inventive examples of its critical value today.

88 *Ibid.*

89 Fredric Jameson, "Architecture and the Critique of Ideology", *The Ideologies of Theory* (London and New York: Verso, 2008), 349; Fredric Jameson, "From Metaphor to Allegory", in *Anything*, ed. Cynthia Davidson (New York: Anyone Corporation, 2001), 30. Day's account of Jameson's divergent returns to Tafuri contains a great deal more insight about their relation and differences. Day, "Manfredo Tafuri, Fredric Jameson", 71.

90 Marx and Engels, "The Holy Family", 36.

91 Jameson, *Postmodernism*, 108–129.

92 Mark Crinson, talk given at "Forgotten Estates", Royal Academy of Arts, 3 October 2016, www.youtube.com/watch?v=K-xktCBOd70.

93 *Ibid.*

94 Alison and Peter Smithson, "Contributions to a Fragmentary Utopia", *Urban Structuring: Studies of Alison and Peter Smithson* (London: Studio Vista, 1967), 75.

3

Streets in the Sky: Fragmented Territory and the Brutalist Street

The idea *of "street" has been forgotten.*

Alison and Peter Smithson, *Ordinariness and Light*

Life in action cannot be forced behind the netting of imposed pattern.

Alison and Peter Smithson, *Ordinariness and Light*

If Brutalist problems and forms are wrought from the fraught conditions of class society, this is no more so than with Robin Hood Gardens' streets in the sky – the problem-form with which the Smithsons confronted the crisis of the street and the limits of modernism's functionalist urbanism. This is the architectural form for which the Smithsons and Robin Hood Gardens are most known, and hence a suitable choice for the first of this book's four chapters to centre a particular form of the estate. As with all these forms, features of the streets in the sky route in and out of other chapters of the book, notably Chapter 5, where they are an object of the Smithsons' graphic design. Here I cast the problem-form of the streets in the sky widely, incorporating also the problem of territory, in the Smithsons' approach to the estate's fragmented site.[1] Taken together, street and territory are also an opportunity to consider issues of community coherence and to posit the estate's postcolonial scene against the forces of ethno-national identity that course through the present and past of council housing.

To first sketch the form and origins of the streets in the sky, recall that Robin Hood Gardens comprised two housing blocks, of seven and ten storeys, which nurtured between them a garden and artificial mound, overlooked by the kitchens, bedrooms and escape balconies. On the other

Figure 3.1 Street in the sky, west block, looking north. (Nicholas Thoburn, October 2014)

façades, with views facing *out* of the estate, were the streets in the sky. They ran the full length of both blocks at every third floor, providing deck access to the homes, semi-public sites of encounter and contemplation, bracing open-air space raised up in the sky and glorious unobstructed vistas across London, achieved through ingenious use of a counter-lever (Figures 3.1 and 3.2).

The Smithsons first proposed their formal typology of the street deck in their Golden Lane competition entry in 1953, where it was named "streets-in-the-air".[2] Whether directly or via Le Corbusier's Unité d'habitation, it was influenced by the access decks in Moscow's Narkomfin Communal House (1928–1930), the extraordinary Constructivist scheme designed by Moisei Ginzburg and Ignati Milinis, with its "daylight service corridor", as Ginzburg had it, serving as a "forum for collective social exchanges" (Figure 3.3).[3] Le Corbusier even used the phrase *rue en l'air* in this context, but where he took the Narkomfin's decks into his scheme's interior, the Smithsons returned them to the exterior façade, removed the glazing (only the lowest deck of the Narkomfin was unglazed) and increased the depth of the opening

Figure 3.2 Street in the sky, east block, looking north. (Nicholas Thoburn, February 2015)

Figure 3.3 Narkomfin Communal House, 1928–1930. (Moisei Ginzburg and Ignati Milinis. Creative Commons)

Figure 3.4 Exterior façade and southern "head" of the east block, showing the impressed bands of the three street decks and the southern lift lobbies. (Nicholas Thoburn, August 2017)

to the sky (Figure 3.4).[4] Another influence is more surprising, but grounds the Smithsons' claim that Brutalism was a response to *peasant* dwelling forms (forms "which have style and are stylish but were never modish: a poetry without rhetoric").[5] For amid the series of visual representations of Golden Lane included in *Ordinariness and Light* is a photograph of a Dayak long house in Borneo, its form and point-of-view remarkably similar to the Smithsons' diagram of the Golden Lane street deck.[6]

The deforming form of streets in the sky had renowned precursors, then, but it was not derivative. Alison Smithson imagined such transmissions and connections, as the "reuse" of "inspirational forms", "idea-energy" shared in a "fellowship [that] spans history".[7] Moreover, this transmission of form was inseparable from grappling with the particular social and architectural problems of the Smithsons' own moment.

Urban Re-Identification and the Sensibility of Play

Though widely misunderstood, if not wilfully misrepresented, as a hubristic modernist move against the terraced working-class street, the streets in the sky were a response to the latter's *crisis*. This crisis, as the Smithsons saw it, was consequent on a number of urban and architectural developments: the verticality of post-war high-rise development, a form which dominated council building in the 1960s, where streets were swapped out for internal access corridors and nondescript plots of open space; the urban dominance of the car, which degraded and substituted for safe and social street life; and the anti-urban suburbanization of the New Towns movement. A response to the crisis of the street, the street decks were also a break with modernism's governing urban model, the *functional city*, as set out in CIAM's Athens Charter of 1933, where the city was divided into four functions: dwelling, work and recreation, linked together by transportation. I turn to this break now.

Just how different was the Smithsons' approach can be seen in the content and form of their *Urban Re-Identification* grid, the display panel they took to CIAM's ninth congress in Aix-en-Provence in 1953 (Figure 3.5). Rather than comprising the four distinct functions, here the social life of the city is conceived of as four nested "scales of association", named across the top of the grid as house, street, district and city. In these scales, urban association is understood to be processual, patterned and improvised, with each scale interrelated in a "modulated continuum", thus registering the "true complexity of human associations", as the Smithsons described it.[8] It is important to appreciate that these scales did not provide a new model in place of the Athens Charter, for they were themselves becoming outmoded, a starting point from which to develop a *new* "ecological approach to the problem of habitat", to "evolve an architecture from the fabric of life itself" (hence at CIAM 10 in Dubrovnik in 1956, the Smithsons substituted the term "cluster" for the four scales, geared to specific and situated patterns of association that traverse and draw from each scale).[9]

This approach, and its break with CIAM's functionalism, is dramatized in the very structure of the grid. Measuring 83 x 275 cm, *Urban Re-Identification* has 24 panels comprising visual and textual material associated with the Smithsons' competition entry for the Golden Lane estate, ostensibly the architectural object of the presentation. The grid form was instituted under Le Corbusier's direction at CIAM 7 in 1949, as a tool of inception, analysis, synthesis, presentation and comparison that sought to foreground the four functions through a set of diagrammatic protocols.[10] In

Figure 3.5 *Urban Re-Identification* grid, displayed at CIAM 9 in Aix-en-Provence. (Alison and Peter Smithson, 1953. Smithson Family Collection)

Urban Re-Identification, however, the grid becomes party to the *undoing* of functionalism.[11] Though in its shape and visual structure it broadly accords with CIAM's protocols, the geometric order of the CIAM grid and its linear readability is visibly overwhelmed, as "life falls through the net" of the four functions.[12] More specifically, it is overwhelmed by *play*.

Play provides both the social quality and the dynamism of *Urban Re-Identification*'s scales of association. It features in photographs of working-class children playing hopscotch, skipping, bicycling, in assorted impromptu patterns of activity and rest. The photographs are by the Smithsons' friend and collaborator Nigel Henderson, taken in 1951 outside his house in Chisenhale Road, Bow, a heavily bombed part of East London. They constitute a full 10 of the 24 panels, of which all but one are untethered from explanatory text. This foregrounding of children's play is significant in its own terms – it would become a key focus of Team 10, the successor group to CIAM, pursued most concertedly by Aldo Van Eyck.[13] But the Smithsons' intent here is also for play

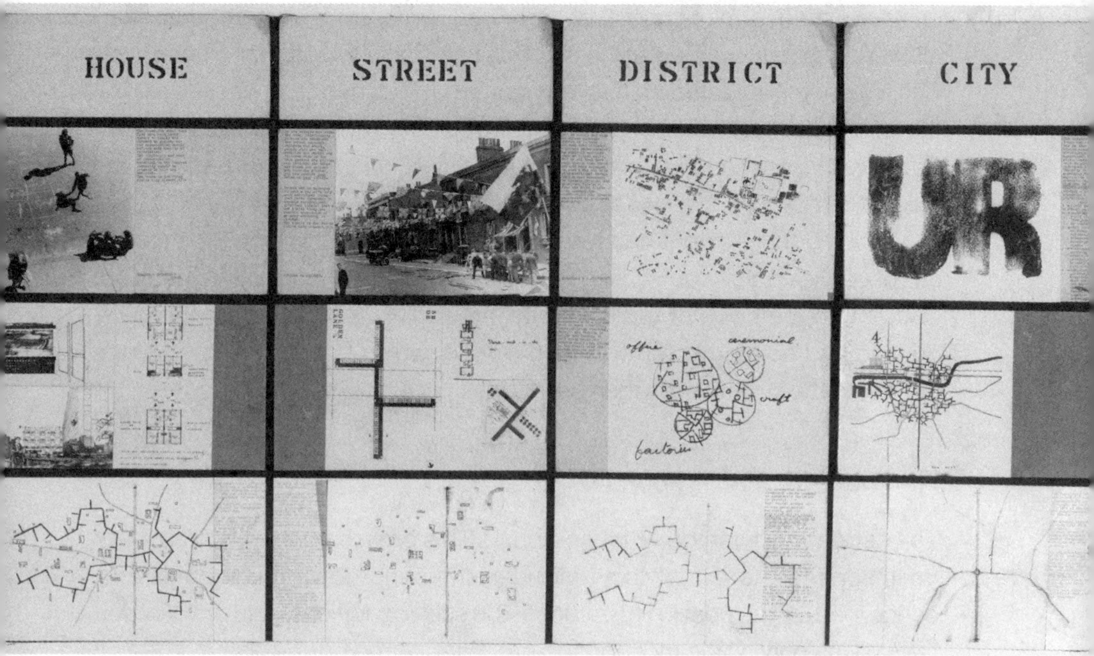

to serve as a figure for the *sensibility of the street*, a sensibility of "improvisation, invention, an urban choreography, a territorial flexibility, an impromptu sociability".[14] Playful, this street sensibility was framed also in spatial terms, as an "horizontal" mode of association against the "vertical living" that hitherto came with building high.[15] Verticality had deprived families of outdoor life and rendered sociability difficult, "by the complete absence of horizontal communication at the same level, and the ineffectiveness of vertical communication". Here the "*idea* of 'street' has been forgotten".[16]

As is usual with cultural representations of children, the Smithsons' figure of the playful, impromptu street bears a significant dose of optimism and hope for the future (a figurative use of the child we have rightly become wary of, after Lee Edelman's critique of "redemptive futurism", the child as occlusion and redemption of the social violence of modernity).[17] But the content and affective mood of Henderson's photographs bring also a more ambivalent quality. The Smithsons' grid posits a problem and a sensibility that sought to identify, tease out and overcome the crisis of functional urbanism, seeking new forms through the complex sociality of the street, but without an established form to carry over or revive. Henderson's photographs, after all, were of a post-war street life that was being finished off. Hence, as Peter Smithson later reflected on this moment, what was needed "was the invention of another kind of street". It "wasn't ... a question of saying the street must be revived. It is a matter of thinking what the street did, and what is the equivalent of it if it is no longer necessary, if the street is dead."[18]

Holding this thought and turning to Robin Hood Gardens, the estate's street decks could scarcely suggest an achieved solution, fully formed and buoyant, to the crisis of the inner-city street. This is patent from the geographic and economic territory of the build, which I consider now before moving to the street decks themselves.

Fragments of Site as Found

The estate was infamously traffic-bound. This pressed on the minds of the Smithsons to the extent they considered turning down the commission, concerned for the possibility of success in such conditions. And the broader terrain was only a little more hospitable. Sited at the north-eastern edge of London's shipping docks, in the 1970s this was a geography of industrial decline, the docks finished off by containerization and the new deep-water dock downriver at Tilbury. Inhospitable setting, industrial decline – these name the *class* conditions of the territory, where class is not identity but crisis. There was no bind here between geography, people and labour – no working-class identity – and the scheme's move to re-establish one carried a strong counter-tendency, as is apparent in B. S. Johnson's BBC television film *The Smithsons on Housing*, which, broadcast in 1970, served as a public introduction to the scheme. Understood by Johnson and the BBC to have been a less-than-successfully-achieved film – "boring to anyone without a special interest in architecture", wrote Johnson, who, a friend of the Smithsons, struggled with them over style and direction – it is today a strange and awkward document, though no less enticing and insightful for it.[19]

The film portrays East London in interregnum between industrial and post-industrial terrain. The site scenes are shot at an industrial scale, without a coherent image of human form or community to ground it. They include long panning shots of Robin Hood Gardens half-formed, with distant views of the estate, vast and hulking, at once comparable in scale to the shots of the Thames, ships, cranes, roads and power station, and yet strange, like nothing around. In part, these images suggest the "Roman" endeavour, as the Smithsons later described the estate, of sufficient scale and monumentality to have a catalytic force of urban renewal.[20] One might hence have expected Alison Smithson's accompanying voiceover to present a unifying plan upon tabula rasa, that conceptualization of territory, cleansed and dehistoricized, that is integral to industrial modernism. It is something of a surprise, then, that her narrative has a rather different content and sensibility, presenting the relation between territory, people and architecture not as an integrating whole but, as van den Heuvel describes it, an "as found" arrangement of existent, broken and incomplete social patterns, connecting routes and structures, a narrative of "picking up, turning over and putting with".[21] This approach informed the couple's exhaustive research on the social and economic history of the territory, developed through various means and mediums, including site walking, brass rubbings, diagrams and photomontage. Here a different quality of the as found comes into view than I discussed in Chapter 2. It is still a method of immersion in matter and society, but now the as found is attentive to the existence and handling of the world *in fragments*.

The Smithsons' approach to fragments is considered in a career-reflective essay from the late 1980s, "The 'As Found' and the 'Found'".[22] Fittingly for the topic, the essay is brief and fragmentary, far from a systematic or comprehensive account, but it indicates that the as found was derived originally from Henderson's street-life photographs of East London. In these they encountered vernacular practices and expressive forms, playful reappropriation of space, a liveliness of ordinary artefacts and a brute poetry of fragments – "children's pavement play-graphics", "items in the detritus on bombed sites, such as the old boot, heaps of nails, fragments of sack or mesh and so on".[23] Here, "the 'as found' was a new seeing of the ordinary, an openness as to how prosaic 'things' could re-energize our inventive activity" in a "society that had nothing".[24]

As this remark suggests, amid the essay's constellation of concerns is an underlying cause and ambition. The as found is an *enchantment* of objects, rooted not so much in the unconscious – as in the Surrealist "found object", with its delimiting chains of psycho-sexual meaning – but in the conditions and inflections of the *ordinary*, of everyday life. It is not the ordinary one might expect, however, for it is wrenched out of shape by crisis, in two senses. First, quite simply, the ordinary here is a *classed* condition, a condition of working-class East London, of poverty and limited means, of those who "had nothing". Second, it was infused by the social and psychic devastation wrought by World War II, still very much present in the minds of Henderson and the Smithsons at this time. Henderson's compulsive walks and photographic practice, the origin of the as found, were means of self-therapy following a severe nervous breakdown caused by his experience as a war-time pilot, and war continued to register too in the topography of East London, still scarred by bombsites well into the 1960s.[25] The integral experience of war to the emergence of the as found also gives it another distinction from the Surrealist found object, the latter's sensory *shock* considerably diminished by contrast, leaving the field open for a post-Surrealist theory of the object. As Henderson put it, "Houses chopped by bombs while ladies were still sitting on the lavatory, the rest of the house gone but the wallpaper and the fires still burning in the grate. Who can hold a candle to that kind of real life Surrealism?"[26] Sensory shock is not entirely evacuated from the object as found, but its place in Henderson's self-therapy indicates that it combines with a quality of *care*, a tentative and exploratory means of living amid fragments, amid crisis.[27]

As the Smithsons pick up the as found from Henderson, its domain expands from urban drifting and street photography to architectural practice. The context of war ebbs away and crisis and convulsion are transposed into a sensitivity to contingency, irresolution and the social and economic life of a territory.[28] In particular, the as found becomes a method of site preparation. It conveys immersion in the social and material environment of a site, engagement with the "situation of flux and change", with a site's different temporalities and trajectories, with parts that structure a site and parts for which the use has drained away – all drawn into a contingent relation where "anything and everything can be raised by association to become the poetry of the ordinary".[29] This returns us to *The Smithsons on Housing*.

In Alison Smithson's voice-over, the site's fragments are of considerable scale: the 1806 East India Dock; the Brunswick Wharf Power Station; the 1844 railway; the river Thames. They are also mobile: the ships as "decoration" for the site, as "connectors of people to their district, and to the world around", approaching the estate from the east before the Thames loops south and around the Isle of Dogs – for Adrienne Sargeant, an early resident, the latter was a favourite childhood view from her living-room window.[30] Such fragments provided the means of knitting together the scheme and its territory, the "fix" as Alison calls it – but in a mutable way. The East India Dock, intended as a key visual fix for the taller east block, was filled in during the build. Yet in the film's narrative it becomes a means to illustrate the contingency of the estate's fragmentary conditions, wherein the scale of relations now shifts from large to small. Walking the site prior to the build, Alison and the couple's son, Simon, collected china shards – ships' ballast or cargo fallout, their prior functionality uncertain – which were assembled and set in 54 tiles of shutter-formed concrete to fashion a mural for the estate's old people's club. *Art of the "As Found"*, the mural was titled (Figure 3.6). A photograph of it is the only image included in "The 'As Found' and the 'Found'", but though there are existent photographs of the completed work in situ, the image we see there, aptly so, is of the work incomplete, half the tiles arranged in pattern but as yet un-set as a whole, still in fragments.

As Mark Crinson advises, it would be a mistake to dismiss this as-found approach to the site as "a fetishising of things peripheral to the job of designing the estate".[31] Indeed, we might think of the mural as bearing a *truth* of the scheme. As a "Roman" endeavour, Robin Hood Gardens was of course a structure of great disruption and site clearance. But this is held in tension with a different tendency. What the Smithsons' mural crystalizes is an architectural method that seeks also to knit the structure with the site as found – not erasing but working flush with the fragmented territory as it is, attentive to multiple histories and temporalities, to use and disuse, to situated lives and cultures and to the expressive qualities of ordinary matter.[32]

Streets of Representation and Lived Reality

Turning from the site to the streets in the sky, critics have been all too ready to see here a fragmentation of sorts. Not content with merely describing their putative failings, Charles Jencks took the extraordinary step of mocking up and photographing a street deck scene of impending violent attack. The photograph illustrates his case against Robin Hood Gardens in *The Language of Post-Modern Architecture*, his influential critique of modernism. Featuring a man with hands raised over his head, clasping an object with which to

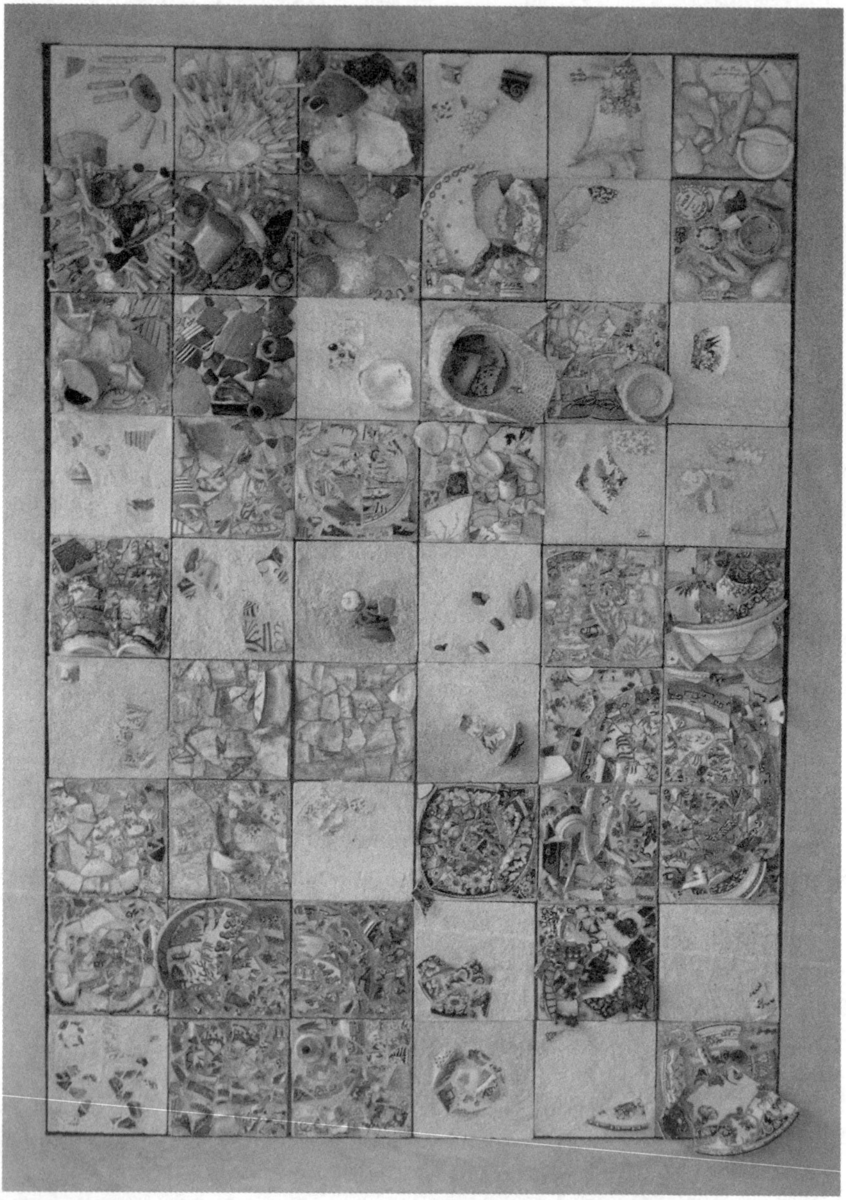

Figure 3.6 *Art of the "As Found"*. Tile mural in the estate's old people's club. (Alison and Peter Smithson, 1968–1970. Smithson Family Collection)

strike, the caption describes how the "architectural critic Paul Goldberger mimes a mugger's threatening gesture – commonplace in these corridors".[33] Goldberger is smiling, conveying that this is some kind of joke, but in no sense does that diminish the entitled and symbolically violent act that is this ersatz representation.

Jencks had a keen eye for symbolic and imagistic means to make his broader thesis, the prime subject of which is the first-stage demolition of the Pruitt-Igoe public-housing scheme in St Louis, Missouri. Represented in Jencks' book in photograph and text, it provides him with the preeminent myth of the failure of modernism.

> Modern Architecture died in St Louis, Missouri on July 15, 1972 at 3.32 p.m. (or thereabouts) when the infamous Pruitt-Igoe scheme, or rather several of its slab blocks, were given the final *coup de grâce* by dynamite. Previously it had been vandalised, mutilated and defaced by its black inhabitants, and although millions of dollars were pumped back, trying to keep it alive (fixing the broken elevators, repairing smashed windows, repainting), it was finally put out of its misery. Boom, boom, boom.[34]

Robin Hood Gardens does not fit neatly with this thesis, however, for it was *completed* the year Jencks deemed modernism to have died. For a volitional image of its supposed failure, Jencks hence had to resort to his fabrication. There is continuity in the two images nonetheless, for both the Pruitt-Igoe text and the Goldberger photograph identify a leading cause of deprivation with architecture itself, and both racialize the amalgam of poverty, public housing and violence – the vandalizing "black inhabitants" of Pruitt-Igoe and the "mugger" in Poplar, that 1970s moral-panic trope of Black criminality which Stuart Hall et al. took apart in *Policing the Crisis*.[35]

It is not that there were no drawbacks to the street decks at Robin Hood Gardens. They did not meet the ground but required lifts at either end, unlike at Sheffield's Park Hill (designed by Jack Lynn and Ivor Smith, who had been taught by the Smithsons, and commonly regarded as the first and fuller achievement of the streets in the sky).[36] The decks could be littered. Their stairwells were sometimes taken for drug use. They did not, in other words, resolve the constraints and crises of class society. But that was not their aim. Only the utopian idea of architecture, in Tafuri's sense, with its resolve illusion, would claim for built form that possibility. As the street decks fashioned a new socio-architectural form from class society, confronting its crises and limitations, the constraints of class, of limited means, of deprivation, remain.

Neither did the street decks facilitate a neat and self-identical *community*. Community is a useful word to name the social and emotional bonds and support networks that were clearly central to life at Robin Hood Gardens, frequently remarked upon by residents, and to name the designed-in sociality of the estate's decks and other forms. It is a useful word too to hold against the image of social and psychic alienation that is imputed to council housing by the dominant stigmatizations. But the word community can also obscure the complexities of urban social life with a fuzzy image of togetherness, life's complexities lopped off. Fitzgerald lived in the west block from 1982 until its demolition, and much enjoyed the estate. I asked him whether it felt connected to its urban environment and if it had a strong community. He was not convinced by the question. "I think that sociologists try to make too many connections where perhaps none exist, or they exist in forms which aren't as tangible as those words seem to mean to me. ... The idea of community comes from villages where people grew up together, went to school together, worked at trades locally ... I don't think you can say community when you have millions of people!" The notion of community "is pretentious, because most people don't even know their neighbours". As he playfully narrated his pseudonym for my sound recording, I wondered if his skepticism at my sociological terminology might have extended also to naïve ideas of *class*: "Fitzgerald speaking, horny hands of the soil and of the sea."[37]

This discussion of community is an opportune moment to comment on the place of drugs on the estate. For a period of time in the mid- to late-1990s, heroin misuse was a significant problem at Robin Hood Gardens. As Dheraj Shamoo recalled, it achieved national news coverage when a woman (who was not a resident) was filmed on the adjacent Poplar High Street using heroin in a car, a child in the back seat, having apparently purchased the drugs on the estate.[38] Residents spoke with us about the problem in nuanced ways. Motiur Rahman, a resident for 23 years, recalled that heroin arrived almost overnight, evident in a sudden difference visible in some of his neighbours: "their faces changed, their bodies changed, you could see the difference, their interests changed". Asked why, he said that hard drugs "hit estates at different points". "Somebody moves in with an interest in drugs and that spreads, it just so happened that lots of the boys saw this as a way out, saw it as cool. Whatever it was, it just hooked them, and they were not necessarily poor boys or boys with difficult backgrounds, some of them were well to do from good families – religious families – so they had all the right upbringing – the right talk. ... It was just too easy – the estate was left all to itself you know, no support from outside."[39] For Darren Pauling, who lived at Robin Hood Gardens for 16 years from the mid-1990s, "Yes there were drugs on there at one time but it sort of took care of itself. You didn't really hear of burglaries and that – there were, and I didn't know everyone on the estate, but over the course of the time I had been there I think I have known only two or three burglaries, one of those just recently."[40] Musa said something similar about the drug users keeping largely to themselves, as did Rani Begum: "I know there are people living here that do take drugs. But it has never bothered me and it's never affected me. I do feel safe and I do love the flat I am living in and even the area I am living in. I'm quite happy because I know every place you go there is bad and good anyway."[41]

Of course, users could also be intimidating and disruptive of social life, as Del Schwenninger-Walter found, remarking on how the council's continual failure to maintain the security doors into the buildings exacerbated the problem.[42] And Musa remembers how, around the turn of the millennium, the green "became an intoxicated park, as opposed to the park that we recalled, so we wouldn't take our children".[43] He views the causes of the problem as both a lack of local-authority investment in the estate and cuts to community support, especially the closure of youth clubs, which left bored youth susceptible. "They were the best of people. Many of those I know have sincere intentions, but they can't help themselves due to addiction. Drugs ruined them, their family, their marriages."[44] After a time, he said, the problem diminished considerably, certain individuals and families left, some were imprisoned, there was not any longer a drug community as such.

The street decks did not resolve the crises of class society, then, yet almost all the residents we interviewed talked enthusiastically about their social and architectural qualities, describing a complex of uses, emotions, sensory associations and pleasures that do indeed suggest that here were fragments of a "street form for the present day".[45] Khaled Elgahari, a resident since childhood, compared the open-air quality of the decks favourably to the new apartment blocks rising around the scheme, with the latter's internal corridors and "rows of doors crammed together like a prison".[46] When we asked William and Laetitia Fakamus if they would not prefer a private balcony, the couple responded that balconies in the new developments might look attractive, but they consolidate an insular approach to life, the correlate of a housing industry that "cares more about money" than the "meaning of life". "Here we all know each other", William said, "but if you go into a private balcony you will know nothing or nobody" (Figures 3.7 and 3.8).[47] For Laetitia, walking along the decks could recall the catwalks of her youth as a fashion model, while as a Christian she imagined the wonder of God's global embrace in their expansive visual connectivity to aeroplanes, cars, pedestrians and river boats.[48]

Musa spoke with me after his family had moved into the first phase of Blackwall Reach, where he found the loss of the street decks to be one with a loss of community.

> Why? Because you don't see each other. There isn't a community. You go into the lift, you come back to your apartment, you live with your family, you go back out – it is a life very much based on living with you and your family, without a communal feel. The children don't get to see what we saw as children. There's no street in the sky, there isn't any intermingling, [the building] doesn't allow friendships to bond. ... That warmth in that sun that you would feel every evening [on the decks] is something that you can't get here. Although we have a [private] balcony, you don't get that warmth. Why is that? Because you shared it with the community. You shared it as a young boy with an aunt, who's not your mother but a mother of your friend or an uncle who is a father of a friend or simply a neighbour. You're just having a conversation, she or he gets to know who her son's friends are, you get to know their mother or father. You build a closer bond, often you would feel as if you were all a family, which came with respecting and maintaining that respect by supporting and finding solutions for one another ... Although Robin Hood Gardens had its communal problems related to drugs, I would call it the golden age – a memory of joy and laughter. If there is a golden age or a golden community, for me and my family it would be living our lives in Robin Hood Gardens.[49]

On our visits to the estate we sometimes saw young children playing on the decks, kicking balls, scootering, riding small bicycles. One boy we met, as his mother explained, liked to walk visitors to and from the lift at one end of the street deck outside his home, which he did with us until something in the view caught his attention (Figure 1.7). Play was a feature too of Motiur Rahman's

Figure 3.7 William and Laetitia Fakamus and family. (Kois Miah, November 2016)

Figure 3.8 William and Laetitia Fakamus and family by the green. (Kois Miah, November 2016)

sense that the value of the decks lay in facilitating an open-air sociality: "We always talked about the walkways being like Bangladesh. People did unbelievable things on them, like riding bikes – I don't mean one bike but four bikes going past each other. They played Carrom Board, it was so wide. In Eid, the doors would be open in every house and you would have all these people, swaths of people going up and down the corridors in their glitzy outfits, going to people's houses, eating samosas. It gave you the opportunity to live an outdoor life."[50] Abul Hasnath also recalls how the larger deck areas at the "heads" of the buildings were regularly used for Carrom Board matches – a chair would be flipped over another, a Carrom Board placed on top, friends and neighbours would gather, and games would go on into the night (Figure 3.9).[51] He talks especially evocatively of the "buzzing" street sociability during Ramadan. Rather than retire to bed between night prayer and pre-sunrise meal, groups of friends, sometimes non-Muslims included, would often stay up through the night chatting on the street decks.

On a more everyday level, Abul recounted that you could peek through the maisonettes' deck-facing windows to see if anyone was about and go and have a chat. Or he would take time to himself with a cigarette, watching the construction at Canary Wharf, getting "that moment of serenity, that moment of peace you wanted, just by standing on that landing".[52] Abul now keenly feels the loss of this socio-spatial form in the Blackwall Reach building his family moved to, with its hotel-like quality of front doors opening from narrow, windowless, internal corridors (Figure 3.10). "By God, do I miss our balconies", Abul reflected, "It was a huge, huge thing that we lost".[53] In different ways, it is a loss to himself, his parents and his children. Now, living in the same Blackwall Reach building as four of his close friends from the estate, Abul has even attempted to recreate the street decks' impromptu sociability by erecting a gazebo-cum-gathering space in his ground-floor garden, but in a private space he knows this is battling against the odds.

Picking up the remarks by Motiur and Abul about reminders of Bangladesh and social life during Ramadan, one sees here the postcolonial threads of the global in the local, the local *as* the global, "an inventory of the elsewhere on every street", as Les Back and Michael Keith put it.[54] A quality of the estate's social and cultural life, this postcolonial scene also prompts consideration of the racialized symbolism and structures of council housing, necessary for critically understanding the latter's present and past.

Figure 3.9 A west-block head maisonette and triple-height street deck, with lift-lobby to the left. (Kois Miah, April 2015)

Figure 3.10 Five friends on the estate's green. (Kois Miah, November 2020)

Council Housing and Racialization

In right-wing narratives about council housing today the fraught social relations of class are refashioned into an identity, the *white working class*, via the racist canard that the scarcity of council homes is due to preferential allocation to immigrants and their descendants. It is the leading way that class has been framed in the UK in recent years, pre- and post-Brexit, an artefact of racist, ethno-nationalist discourse. During the welfare settlement, the white working class was a condition of *integration* in racialized nationalism, but today its traction and volatility are because this pseudo-class formation is itself in crisis, as Robbie Shilliam has argued. With the ejection of labour from the national compact, attendant on the collapse of the welfare settlement and the decline of British capitalism, the benefits of whiteness that accrue to the so-called white working class are in significant retreat. It is a situation to be grasped through anti-racist and internationalist class solidarity – or through a wounded and melancholic revival of racial nationalism, doomed to fail even in its own terms, and all the more dangerous for that.

The white working class is not in any sense, then, a constituency outside of its role as a "tool of domination", even as it is "partially self-authored" by significant numbers of working-class whites.[55] It is not *class*. This ill-fitting identity and its constitutive exclusions take hold *against* rather than *as* class.[56] In the realm of housing, it disguises the *true* class dynamics of the shortage of affordable, secure and safe homes, namely Right to Buy sales, estate demolition, deregulation, welfare retrenchment and housing finance and investment – the combined assault from government and the finance–housebuilding complex on working-class housing and social reproduction.

This is not to let the political left off the hook, however, for there are significant racist dimensions to the claim on *our* council housing in socialist understandings of the post-war class settlement. It is an uncomfortable truth, but the welfare state was achieved on the backs of expropriation from the colonies, actively pursued by Clement Attlee's now lionized 1945–1951 Labour government, to the tune of £750 million in "loans" (some 8% of UK GDP) that were enforced through the financial mechanism of the Sterling Area.[57] And Attlee's welfare state was also a "warfare state" – "clearly the Labour government's primary concern", in John Newsinger's assessment.[58] During Atlee's premiership, Britain conducted brutal and bloody imperial adventures in Vietnam, Indonesia, Greece, Malaya, Kenya, India, Palestine, Iran and Korea. It also began development of British nuclear weapons, having endorsed the US nuclear bombing of Hiroshima and Nagasaki in 1945, allowed the USA to establish bases in Britain for its B-29 bombers and commenced a massive rearmaments programme.[59]

But to stay centred on the welfare state, its central material plank of council housing bore racial nationalism at its core. Council housing was "the prime element through which the provision of social assistance was politicized and racialized", argues Shilliam, a key benefit of (white) labour's inclusion in the national compact.[60] Or, as Miles Glendinning puts it in his global study of mass housing, though extolled through lofty rhetoric of the kind "decent homes for all", the "underlying agenda was to use housing to define membership of the 'imagined community' of national society", housing "bound up with authoritative, patriarchal social structures and strategies of forcible intervention or segregation". "One of the very foremost weapons in the armoury of the disciplined, 'strong state' and 'strong city' of the twentieth century was housing."[61] And mass public housing was also integral to the economy – "municipal capitalism", Sidney Jacobs wryly calls it. "Primarily attempting to deflect class struggle and maintain the profitability of both finance capital and the construction industry, council housing constitutes a very capitalistic solution to problems encountered at a particular conjuncture of Western Capitalism."[62]

Integral to this was the paradigm of the deserving (of social security and welfare) and undeserving poor, a distinction with roots in chattel slavery.[63] While all UK governments since Thatcher's premiership have stigmatized council estates as concentrations of the undeserving and feckless, during the welfare state, council housing was allocated to, and hence a means of fashioning, the deserving working class against the undeserving poor. This manifest in the exclusion of Black and Asian citizens from council tenancies and their confinement in poor-quality and overcrowded private-rental and owner-occupation sectors well into the 1970s. As Jacobs puts it, "until inhibited by the 1968 Race Relations Act, councils persistently evading their responsibilities to house black applicants made no bones of their intentions to give priority to the white population".[64] It was not until the 1977 Housing (Homeless Persons) Act, with its shift to a needs-based system, that real change occurred. And when councils finally took responsibility for housing Black and other racially minoritized groups (reluctantly so, forced upon them by rising Black homelessness) they were first concentrated in "difficult to let" estates, and then subject to dispersal policies driven by racist fears of "black ghettos" in the heartland of British cities.[65] In 1988, for example, Tower Hamlets council was found by the Commission for Racial Equality (CRE) to have discriminated against Bangladeshi and other racially minoritized residents over a ten-year period, under both Labour and Liberal administrations, by allocating them to poorer-quality estates.[66]

As much, then, as the postcolonial streets of Robin Hood Gardens tell a vital story of the global flows and cultural complexity that comprises London's post-war working class, they also stand against the ethno-nationalism of right-wing narratives about council housing today and the structural history of this tenure that is obscured by the social-democratic image of past class identity. The streets in the sky impress upon us that council housing, even or especially at its height, was shot through with the contradictions, dispossessions and racializing violence of an imperial power. Hence, today, council housing should be understood, experienced and fought for not as a utopian achievement under assault, where once nothing was too good for the working class, but through and against the fraught social relations that have always conditioned it from within.

Notes

1 Though the distinction is not hard and fast, I reserve the word *territory* for the socio-economic terrain of the site and locale, discussed in this chapter, and *ground* and *landscape* for the constructed spatial form of the estate's green and mound, in Chapter 7.

2 Since streets are traditionally in the *air*, to my mind the mutation through use of the Smithsons' phrase into streets in the *sky* is more evocative of their elevated quality, up in the sky. Hence it is the mutation that I use in this book, though it was not to my knowledge used by the Smithsons themselves. The Smithsons also claim coinage of the term *deck* in this context. Alison and Peter Smithson, "Banham's Bumper Book on Brutalism", *The Architect's Journal* 144 no. 26 (1966): 1590–1591.

3 Moisei Ginzburg, cited in Jane Rendell, *The Architecture of Psychoanalysis: Spaces of Transition* (London and New York: I.B. Tauris, 2017), 44. Rendell discusses the mutual influence of Le Corbusier and Ginzberg. As for the Smithsons, their only reference to the Narkomfin that I know of is in their 1981 image-based scrapbook on the Modern Movement, which includes one small photograph of the building without comment. Alison and Peter Smithson, *The Heroic Period of Modern Architecture* (London: Thames and Hudson, 1981), 59.

4 Though the Smithsons were greatly indebted to the Unité, what they praise as "the most significant building of our time, existing in space but outside time, like the Temple of Poseidon

at Paestum", they describe its lifts, interior streets and apartments in less-than-favourable terms: "Man scurries along from Victorian lifts down gloomy corridors to the solitary confinement of his private drawer." Alison and Peter Smithson, *Ordinariness and Light: Urban Theories 1952–1960 and their Application in a Building Project 1963–1970* (London: Faber and Faber, 1970), 87.

5 Alison and Peter Smithson, *Without Rhetoric: An Architectural Aesthetic 1955–1972* (London: Latimer, 1973), 6.

6 The only comment is the caption: "Sea dayaks' long house. Some houses are a quarter of a mile long and hold ninety families." Smithson and Smithson, *Ordinariness and Light*, 59.

7 Alison Smithson, "Transmissions and Connections", in Alison and Peter Smithson, *The Charged Void: Architecture* (New York: The Monacelli Press, 2001), 37.

8 Alison and Peter Smithson, *Urban Structuring: Studies of Alison and Peter Smithson* (London: Studio Vista, 1967), 26.

9 Smithson and Smithson, *Ordinariness and Light*, 108. The term "cluster", meaning "a specific pattern of association", was itself temporary, "a clearing-house term during the period of creation of new types". Smithson and Smithson, *Urban Structuring*, 33.

10 Annie Pedret, *Team 10: An Archival History* (London and New York: Routledge, 2013), 58–69. Pedret includes an image of the model grid wherein the protocols were first specified, which shows that the Smithsons' grid shares much of the basic visual form.

11 Annie Pedret, "Dismantling the CIAM Grid: New Values for Modern Architecture", in *Team 10 1953–81: In Search of a Utopia of the Present*, ed. Max Risselada and Dirk van den Heuvel (Rotterdam: NAi Publishers, 2005).

12 This was as much true for the small scale as it was for the large: "Behind the geometric façades our washing, our china dogs and aspidistras look out of place. Life in action cannot be forced behind the netting of imposed pattern." Smithson and Smithson, *Ordinariness and Light*, 21.

13 Rob Withagen and Simone R. Caljouw, "Aldo van Eyck's Playgrounds: Aesthetics, Affordances, and Creativity", *Frontiers in Psychology* 8 Article 1130 (4 July 2017): 1–9.

14 Peter Smithson, cited in Ben Highmore, *The Art of Brutalism: Rescuing Hope from Catastrophe in 1950s Britain* (New Haven, CT and London: Yale University Press, 2017), 272.

15 Smithson and Smithson, *Ordinariness and Light*, 50–51.

16 *Ibid.*, 51–52.

17 Lee Edelman, *No Future: Queer Theory and the Death Drive* (Durham, NC and London: Duke University Press, 2004).

18 Peter Smithson, in Beatriz Colomina and Peter Smithson, "Friends of the Future: A Conversation with Peter Smithson", *October* 94 (Autumn 2000): 3–30, 9.

19 B. S. Johnson, letter to John Drummond, 26 July 1970, in Jonathan Coe, *Like a Fiery Elephant: The Story of B. S. Johnson* (London: Piacador, 2004), 286.

20 Alison and Peter Smithson, "Robin Hood Gardens, London", *The Charged Void: Architecture* (New York: The Monacelli Press, 2001), 296.

21 Dirk van den Heuvel, *Alison and Peter Smithson: A Brutalist Story Involving the House, the City and the Everyday*, unpublished PhD thesis (Delft University of Technology, 2003), 228–229. The quotation is from Alison and Peter Smithson, "The 'As Found' and the 'Found'", in *The Independent Group: Postwar Britain and the Aesthetics of Plenty*, ed. David Robbins (Cambridge, MA: MIT Press, 1990), 201.

22 *Ibid.*

23 *Ibid.*
24 *Ibid.*
25 Highmore, *The Art of Brutalism*.
26 Nigel Henderson, cited in *ibid.*, 72.
27 There is an intriguing associated quality to this care, a certain *animism* to Henderson's object as found, the quality, he writes, of a "talisman": "It feels as if he [the object as found] has dropped from outer space at *that* precise spot to intercept *your* passage and wink 'its' message specifically *at* and *for* you." It also bears for him a sense of deep time, cosmological time and inorganic time, as Highmore puts it. Henderson, cited in Highmore, *The Art of Brutalism*, 168–170.
28 Crinson formulates the significant impact of the war on New Brutalism thus: "In their self-mythology, the caesura of totalitarianism and war had separated this New Brutalist generation from the 'heroic' modernists of the 1920s. The separation brought with it productive anachronisms, temporal foldings that could both estrange modernism and make it truer to itself." Mark Crinson, "Eye Wandering the Ceiling: Ornament and New Brutalism", *Art History* 41 no. 2 (April 2018): 318–343, 322.
29 Smithson and Smithson, "The 'As Found' and the 'Found'", 201.
30 Adrienne Sargeant, interview, 15 August 2016.
31 Mark Crinson, *Alison and Peter Smithson* (Swindon: Historic England, 2018), 70.
32 In contrast, the site preparation for Blackwall Reach was very much in the framework of tabula rasa, its social- and site-cleansing aim encapsulated by a text adorning the construction hoarding: "1,575 homes. 20 Acres. One brand new community." The site's history did play a role here of sorts, but it was flattened and corralled according to the vapid messaging of regeneration. The marketing brochure commandeered local maritime history and even a photograph of the hitherto maligned Robin Hood Gardens, now described as the Smithsons' "pioneering housing estate". "Blackwall has always been associated with visionaries and pioneers", it flattered the potential buyer, "an area steeped in history with an exciting future", "the next big thing in East London urban living". *Blackwall Reach, London E14*, marketing brochure, no date.
33 This is the caption in the later editions of the book, renamed in 2002 as Charles Jencks, *The New Paradigm in Architecture* (New Haven, CT and London: Yale University Press, 2002), 19. Peter Smithson himself objected to the representation in a 1977 letter to *Architectural Design* (issue 7–8). In reply, Jencks claimed in the following issue that Goldberger is miming not an attack on the person but vandalism, referring readers to the book's caption, which in earlier editions is more ambiguous: "Goldberger mimes an act that often occurs."
34 Charles Jencks, *The Language of Post-Modern Architecture*, 2nd edn (London: Academy Editions, 1978), 9. The word "black" is removed in later editions. The place of anti-Black racism and Black American experience in the architecture, demolition and myth of Pruitt-Igoe, and Jencks' place therein, is explored in Elizabeth Birmingham, "Refraining the Ruins: Pruitt-Igoe, Structural Racism, and African American Rhetoric as a Space for Cultural Critique", *Western Journal of Communication* 63 no. 3 (1999): 291–309.
35 Stuart Hall, Chas Critcher, Tony Jefferson, John Clarke and Brian Roberts, *Policing the Crisis: Mugging, the State and Law and Order* (London: Macmillan, 1978).
36 The street decks were reached through two lifts and a stairwell at both ends of each block. (Earlier in the estate's life there were also stairwells at each crank of the two buildings – two in the west block, one in the east block – which opened directly to the garden. These were

closed for reasons I am unsure of.) In the southern heads, the lift shafts were folded into the main structure by the larger maisonettes, and the lift lobbies led into an open area, at a height of two and three storeys, at the start of the decks. At the northern tails, the decks tapered off as they reached each lobby, and the lift shafts stood apart.

37 Fitzgerald, interview, 3 March 2015.

38 Dheraj Shamoo, interview, 7 September 2014.

39 Motiur Rahman, interview, 4 December 2015.

40 Darren Pauling, interview, 5 September 2015.

41 Musa, interview, 28 October 2020. Rani Begum, interview, 10 September 2014.

42 Del Schwenninger-Walter, interview, 27 August 2014.

43 Musa, interview, 28 October 2020.

44 *Ibid.*

45 Smithson and Smithson, *Urban Structuring*, 10.

46 Khaled Elgahari, interview, 1 February 2015.

47 William Fakamus, interview, 11 July 2017.

48 Laetitia Fakamus, interview, 11 July 2017.

49 Musa, interview, 28 October 2020.

50 Motiur Rahman, interview, 4 December 2015.

51 Abul Hasnath, interview, 29 October 2020.

52 *Ibid.*

53 *Ibid.*

54 Les Back and Michael Keith, "Reflections: Writing Cities", in *Stories of Cosmopolitan Belonging: Emotion and Location*, ed. Hannah Jones and Emma Jackson (London and New York: Routledge, 2014), 20.

55 Robbie Shilliam, *Race and the Undeserving Poor* (Newcastle: Agenda Publishing, 2018), 108.

56 Put otherwise, the degree to which working-class whites *challenge* the identity of the white working class is the degree to which they manifest class politics.

57 Tony Norfield, "Origins of the UK Welfare State", *Economics of Imperialism* blog, 8 October 2015, https://economicsofimperialism.blogspot.com/2015/10/origins-of-uk-welfare-state.html.

58 John Newsinger, "War, Empire and the Attlee Government 1945–1951", *Race and Class* 60 no. 1: 67–76, 72.

59 *Ibid.*

60 Shilliam, *The Undeserving Poor*, 92.

61 Miles Glendinning, *Mass Housing: Modern Architecture and State Power – A Global History* (London: Bloomsbury, 2021), 3, 6.

62 Sidney Jacobs, "Race, Empire and the Welfare State: Council Housing and Racism", *Critical Social Policy* 5 no. 13 (1985): 6–28, 18.

63 Shilliam, *The Undeserving Poor*.

64 Jacobs, "Race, Empire and the Welfare State", 20. This racialized non-allocation was achieved through numerous housing polices and informal practices, wherein the paradigm of the undeserving poor is prominent. Three instances can suffice as examples. At the centre of the deserving working class is the nuclear family – disciplinary mechanism, of women especially, and means of discouraging supposedly irresponsible working-class procreation. It was hence for this family form that council housing was built and allocated to, in neglect of other types of households – larger, multi-generational and single-parent

families – where Black and Asian populations have been over-represented. Second, through the 1950s to the early 1970s, demolition and slum clearance was the main route to council housing, but local authorities – whose decisions in these matters were opaque – deliberately avoided clearing areas known to have high proportions of Black and other racially minoritized residents. Third, dispersal policies meant that racially minoritized families had to wait longer for accommodation. For example, in Birmingham between 1969 and 1975, "the five properties on either side of one allocated to a Black tenant were to be reserved automatically for whites". *Ibid.* Norman Ginsburg, "Institutional Racism and Local Authority Housing", *Critical Social Policy* 8 no. 24 (1988): 4–19, 10.

65 Jacobs, "Race, Empire and the Welfare State", 22.

66 Commission for Racial Equality, *Homelessness and Discrimination: Report of a Formal Investigation into the London Borough of Tower Hamlets* (London: Commission for Racial Inequality, 1988). The case is discussed in depth in Jennifer Maureen Lowe, *Social Justice and Localities: The Allocation of Council Housing in Tower Hamlets*, unpublished PhD thesis (Queen Mary, University of London, 2004), a reference I take from John Boughton, *Municipal Dreams: The Rise and Fall of Council Housing* (London: Verso, 2018).

4

Ordinariness and Light: The Unhomely at Home

Art begins not with flesh but with the house. This is why architecture is the first of the arts.
Gilles Deleuze and Félix Guattari, *What Is Philosophy?*

In a real building the light and the space and the air are one.
Alison and Peter Smithson, *Without Rhetoric*

I turn now from the streets in the sky to the homes of Robin Hood Gardens, to develop an understanding of the co-constitution of the ordinary and domestic, the *homely*, with the rush of the outside world, the Brutalist *unhomely*.

The emphasis on mass provision of good-quality, working-class housing was central to the Smithsons' Brutalism. Viewed from the framework of class architecture, it had a practical goal – the opening of a little livable territory, a home, from hostile social conditions. But it was also *expressive*, rendering home open to those social conditions, modulating them in the architecture, as the homely comes to bear the outside, the unhomely, in its form. This is the problem that the Smithsons name *ordinariness and light*, a beguiling phrase that titles the book they published during the build of Robin Hood Gardens. In this chapter I reconstruct this problem through the formulation of the homely and unhomely in Deleuze and Guattari's reading of *art brut*, before tracing its articulation in the architectural thresholds of Robin Hood Gardens, in residents' lived experience of home, and in the place therein of racism and its resistance.

House and Universe

In our conversations with residents it was common to hear enthusiastic accounts of the streets in the sky, with their commanding views across

London and their opening to the vertiginous expanse of sky. But one conversation was especially instructive for the problem at hand, in that it foregrounded not the views as such but the formal arrangements by which they were enabled. Responding to a question about the estate's Brutalist style – the unpainted concrete, the chunky, hulking look – Wayne Alison, a long-time caretaker of the estate, surprised me by describing apparently opposite features: "People would say, yes, it's all concrete – but, no, it's not ... It's completely open, you can walk [on the street decks] from one side of the building to the other side and it's just air coming in, you can breathe."[1]

Wayne had no objection to concrete, that is not the point here. What his remark makes apparent is that the concrete form of the estate constructed an openness from which, in a certain sense, the concrete *falls away*. A feature of the street decks, it characterized the estate's homes too. Robin Hood Gardens provided well-proportioned domestic space, comprising flats and maisonettes of one to four bedrooms, all with dual aspect – each apartment extending the full width of the building – and opening out through walls of windows to the expansive views, to the light (Figure 4.1). "You know, the whole wall in the living room is glass", as Motiur Rahman put it, "could you say that

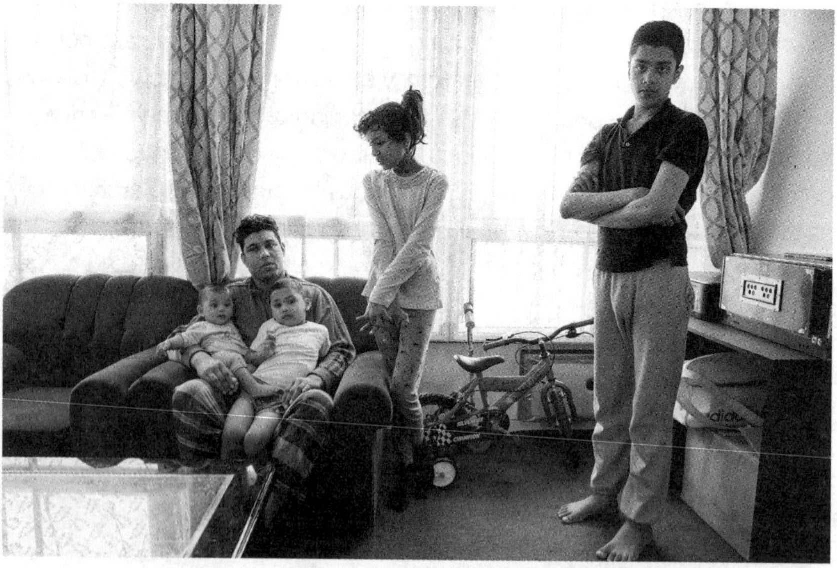

Figure 4.1 Samir Uddin and his children, in front of their garden-facing living-room window. (Kois Miah, September 2015)

about any other block of flats? You get the light from both sides." It is a quality that can be teased out with the help of Dubuffet's *art brut*, a key source of the *brut* of New Brutalism.

In discussion of Dubuffet, Deleuze and Guattari argue that the foundational condition of *art brut* is *home*, the expressive production of lived territory: "Art begins not with flesh but with the house. This is why architecture is the first of the arts."[2] But liveable and expressive home is constituted not, as one might expect, in enclosure. In Deleuze and Guattari's typology, only the *major* subject (bourgeois, white, male) achieves separation of home from its outside, the social serving to fashion, facilitate and bolster the subject's autonomy to the extent that, paradoxically, the social becomes mere background, the private and domestic largely untroubled by the world outside.[3] By contrast, the "cramped space" of *minor* experience (working-class, racially minoritized, gendered) leaves the home pulled out of shape by the conflictual social relations that cleave through it, as "the family triangle connects to other triangles – commercial, economic, bureaucratic, juridical – that determine its values".[4] *This* is the home to which *art brut* corresponds, as it modulates in aesthetic form the minor or working-class condition of being riven by social relations. The home is not closed in upon itself but constituted in a series of differently oriented, interlocking "frames" – wall, window, floor – which serve as interfaces between inside and outside, the finite and the infinite. They are "faces of a dice of sensation", where liveable territory is at once formed and nurtured, and opened to that which *unforms* it – home is *created* through this relation with the impersonal and vertiginous outside.[5] It is a dynamic that Stephen Zepke has argued to be key to Brutalism, an architecture with two mutually constituting tendencies: "House and Universe, *Heimlich* and *Unheimlich*, territory and deterritorialization".[6]

In challenging the stigmatizing representations of Robin Hood Gardens, it is right to foreground the ordinary, homely qualities of the estate. They were indeed significant achievements, central to the Smithsons' design and to residents' experiences. But advocates for Brutalist public housing should not *retreat* to the domestic, disavowing the unhomely and thus surrendering the unsettling expressive qualities of this architecture to middle-class consumption of Brutalism, as if these were not of concern to working-class residents. *Art brut* teaches us that, in Brutalism, home is coupled – tentatively, experimentally – with the unhomely, with that which disturbs it from outside, lifting home into other socio-material planes, planes elemental, impersonal, cosmic, with which it is co-determined. As I introduced this argument, it was *light* that was the primary quality of the unhomely outside. These apartments were built with relatively modest resources. It is true they were well proportioned and roomier than one finds in today's private-sector equivalents, but they were hardly large living spaces. Their difference lay, rather, in being not the crammed in rows of Victorian tenements that they replaced, nor sentimental re-imaginings of traditional workers' homes, but homes built up in the expanse of sky – not locked away from the light but modulated by it, formed at the threshold between closed and open, inside and outside (Figure 4.2).[7]

While light is a *particular* quality of the estate, I want to suggest that in the Smithsons' formulation it is also a *figure* for the unhomely outside *in all its material variety*, where each of the deforming forms of Robin Hood Gardens bears an unhomely coupling, more or less pronounced, with the homely.[8] As such, ordinariness and light, homely and unhomely, house and universe is something of a formula for the scheme as a whole. With regard to the estate's homes, the focus of this chapter, there are particular architectural features

Figure 4.2 Father and children at the entrance to their maisonette, illuminated by the estate's deck-facing triangular windows. (Kois Miah, September 2015)

that facilitate this coupling of the homely and the unhomely, features that are best understood in the topological framework of the *threshold*.

Expand the Threshold

In the Smithsons' topological understanding of deforming form, the different scales of urban association are in a modulated continuum, where "forms, from the smallest of scales up, were part of a dynamic continuum of cultural life", as Hadas Steiner puts it in a text I rely on here.[9] Recalling the minor mode of home discussed above, "the structural relationships of habitat, literally and figuratively, forced habitation out of seclusion".[10] The various scales do so by meeting, or being modulated by each other, at their thresholds.

The primary threshold for the Smithsons was between home and street, for this is where children first meet the outside world. It is a threshold that looked "inward to family and outward to society". "On the one hand, the lessons of the house infused the city by way of the threshold. On the other", as Steiner quotes from *Ordinariness and Light*, the "looseness of organization and ease of communication essential to the largest communication should be present in this, the smallest", the home.[11] Both sides of the threshold are, then, in a relation of projection and introjection with the other, the outside and the inside reverberating together. But further, the threshold has a particular quality of its own, a socio-spatial quality, whereby experience is *intensified* as the subject passes through. The threshold, as Steiner draws from Jakob von Uexküll's anthropology, is "the crucial point at which organisms become aware of the subtle differences in qualities that differentiate the states around them".[12]

At Robin Hood Gardens, the threshold between home and street informs the architecture in a number of ways, to the aim of reinvigorating built form "by fostering meaningful encounters at the threshold of intimacy".[13] The street decks – semi-public spaces, open to residents, their visitors and the curious, but not to the city as a whole – blended with the estate's homes at the threshold of the doorways, which turned off in pairs at right-angles to the decks, creating threshold "eddy spaces", as the Smithsons called them. Here the homes claimed a little of the deck for their own, and vice versa. For Adrienne Sargeant's family, it was a feature that facilitated the joyful occasions on warm summer evenings when they would pull chairs

Figure 4.3 Moyna Miah and his grandchildren outside the eddy space between their home and the street deck. (Kois Miah, April 2015)

out onto the deck and eat their dinner raised up in the open air.[14] The eddy-space threshold was prominent too in Moyna Miah's experience of the estate, his pleasure in sitting out on the street deck with his semi-permanent arrangement of a chair and stools (Figure 4.3). On the other façade, though the fire-escapes-cum-balconies were not deep enough for chairs, they were accessed by "huge doors", as Motiur Rahman put it, so "you could sit inside the room and open up the doors – it felt like you were outside".[15] And for ten of the largest maisonettes at the buildings' southern ends, the Smithsons brought from their Golden Lane design the threshold space of the "yard garden", an expanded balcony the size of a small room located between the street deck and the front door, open to the elements and the views over the green (Figure 4.4).

The Smithsons understood the threshold between home and outside to feed also into the activity of *play*, to pick up again this theme, where the street decks provided threshold play spaces for children not yet old enough to progress onto the green. And the view of the green afforded by the kitchen windows and escape balconies enabled parents and carers to keep an eye on older children down below, a *visual* threshold filled with the

Figure 4.4 Mrs Hoque, with Runa Khalique and Aklima Begum, in her maisonette's "yard garden". (Kois Miah, September 2015)

complex emotional texture of parent–child relations as reins are loosened and autonomy gained (Figures 4.5 and 4.6). This is dramatized in Kim's recollection of her father's evening return from work, soon to call her to return from the green, though here the intensive threshold between home and outside was carried in the apartment's electric lights: "We had already been in and had our dinner, then we would go out to play, and we knew the minute that balcony light came on, we would run! We would go down the hill the other side and into the basements and wouldn't come back out!"[16]

In these examples, one sees actualized the Smithsons' aim to *multiply* the threshold as a vitalizing feature of socio-architectural form, to "restore authentic experience", as Steiner has it, "by expanding the perceptual qualities of the threshold to the entirety of the urban encounter".[17] As I have presented it, the intensity of the threshold has a *joyous* quality, a quality that comes from a calibrated dialing into the unhomely outside, and also a quality of homely *care*.[18] These are the leading affects of the estate's thresholds. But there is also some ambivalence here, the outside handled too as *threat*. Robin Hood Gardens was at once a structure of light, of the embrace of thresholds with the outside, and a weighty, almost fortified, structure of defence. An

Figure 4.5 Del and Gaby Schwenninger-Walter, on their maisonette's escape balcony in the west block. (Kois Miah, September 2014)

Figure 4.6 Azezzun Zahraah, on her maisonette's escape balcony in the east block. (Kois Miah, September 2014)

excursus through two of the Smithsons' other homes can aid in explaining this, following Jonathan Hill's observations about how light is designed differently into Upper Lawn Pavilion (1959–1982), the Smithsons' retreat in the Wiltshire countryside, also known as Solar Pavilion Folly, and House of the Future, their contribution to the 1956 *Daily Mail* Ideal Home Exhibition.

On one hand, when approached in terms of site, materials and purpose, Upper Lawn Pavilion could not be more different to Robin Hood Gardens. A small country retreat, the two-storey structure is a timber box with floor-to-ceiling windows on three sides and clad with aluminum sheets and teak (Figure 4.7). In the as-found way, it is built on the ruin of a workers' cottage (condemned prior to purchase and demolished for the build), whose chimney stack and an exterior wall contribute structural support for the first floor on the northern side. It gives the pavilion a perched and impermanent quality, and allows for the ground-floor doors to fold back, opening the interior to the courtyard. The plan of the cottage is partially retained, though the pavilion is shifted to one side, such that the cobbled floor of the old kitchen and one of the cottage windows are now outside, providing a terraced space with a view

Figure 4.7 Upper Lawn Pavilion, Wiltshire, 1959–1982. (Alison and Peter Smithson. Smithson Family Collection)

through the boundary wall. Yet, on the other hand, if we foreground the topological qualities of Upper Lawn – its deforming forms, its thresholds – it can be understood as the light of Robin Hood Gardens taken to its purest form.[19] As the name Solar Pavilion suggests, it is structured around the threshold of light and, more widely, of climate and environment. "Upper Lawn", Peter Smithson explains, "was placed in an eighteenth century English landscape with the conscious intention of enjoying its pleasure ... submitting to the seasons", in "rooms which could be open-to-nature", to the "long view".[20] Dialed to the maximum into the outside, overheating and heat loss from its single-glazed, south-facing expanse appear to have been acceptable consequences of the sought-for submission to the environment.[21] Later, though, defenceless against the loud parties and motorcycle noise of new neighbours, the pavilion lost its charm, and in 1982 the Smithsons sold it on.[22]

Light is key to the structure of the House of the Future also, but in a rather different way. This small, modular structure imagined the home of a young, childless couple in the year 1981. Built of plastic and filled with plastic furnishings and objects, the walls, floors and ceilings comprised one flowing surface. Rectangular at plan, it was designed to be slotted into gridded rows of identical homes, with the living spaces surrounding a patio open to the sky above, all the home's windows facing onto this only source of light (Figure 4.8). Though House of the Future looked playfully futuristic and tends to be understood that way, it has an ominous undertone, a bunker-like quality, as Beatriz Colomina observes, where "Almost every detail of the house can be explained as a defensive system against pollution, noise, dust, cold, views, germs, and visitors."[23] "Air, then" – or light and sky – "rather than plastic, is the real material of the house".[24] But in contrast to Upper Lawn, light is not to be submitted to, so much as to be achieved under conditions of *defence* against the outside, an outside bearing the implicit threat of nuclear devastation.

At Robin Hood Gardens, it was not nuclear threat which informed the design, but the daily reality of traffic noise and pollution, due to the inhospitable terrain of the site, bordered as it was by major roads – on the west side by Cotton Street, one of only two routes onto the Isle of Dogs, and on the other by the thunderous approach and exit to Blackwall Tunnel under the Thames. (Between the tunnel road and the estate was squeezed the low-traffic Robin Hood Lane, the source of the estate's name, a corruption of an earlier Robin Wood Lane.) It is for this reason that the guiding theme of the

Figure 4.8 House of the Future, *Daily Mail* Ideal Home Exhibition 1956, with view from the interior patio into the kitchen. (Alison and Peter Smithson. Photograph by John McCann. Smithson Family Collection)

estate was "protection".[25] It was for protection that the scheme was designed around the garden "stress-free zone", protected against the roads by the two blocks. And this informed the acoustic sensitivity to the homes' internal layout – the street decks and living rooms placed on the traffic-facing sides, internal stairs and hallways as a "buffer zone" in the middle, and the quieter living spaces of the kitchens and bedrooms facing the garden (Figure 4.9).

It was also for protection that the estate was bordered on two sides by a concrete "acoustic boundary wall" – ten-feet high, canted outwards at the top, and constructed close to the roads so as to deflect away traffic noise as near to source as possible (Figure 4.10).[26] In fact, the Smithsons were in part drawn to the private car, as is most apparent in Alison Smithson's book *AS in DS: An Eye on the Road*, her "sensibility primer" for the perceptual and emotional experience created by automotive movement through the countryside.[27] Here the car itself is a kind of threshold, a modulation of landscape. But they came to recognize the "destructive effect of cars – their obtrusiveness in

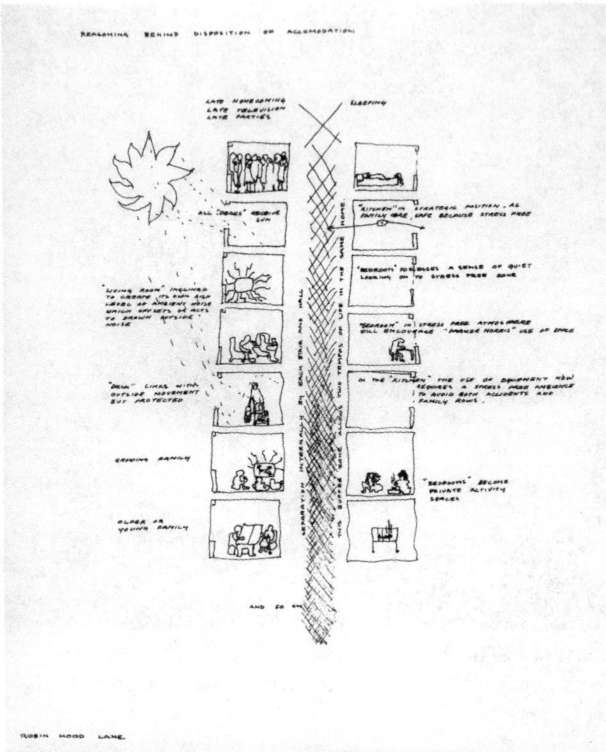

Figure 4.9 *Reasoning Behind Disposition of Accommodation, Robin Hood Lane*. (Alison and Peter Smithson, date unknown. Smithson Family Collection)

places, their ability to get everywhere, their pollution".[28] A "big road", as they express it so well, "is an overwhelming territorialising force in itself, absorbing all its margins into itself".[29] This was to be resisted, warranting at Robin Hood Gardens the decisive countermeasure of the acoustic wall. It had mixed results. As is almost universally observed, including by residents, the boundary wall had an unappealing, prison-like quality, which was hardly mitigated, as the architects had hoped, by the vertical gaps formed diagonally at every three feet (although the aesthetic would have been softened if Virginia Creepers had been cultivated here, as in one of the architectural drawings).[30] However, as a response to the problem of the road – an overwhelming territorial force, encroaching on its margins – the wall can be appraised more positively. Though seemingly opposite to the estate's calibrated openings to the outside, the acoustic wall was actually integral to this threshold dynamic.

Figure 4.10 Acoustic boundary wall along Cotton Street, at the entrance to the west block. (Kois Miah, April 2015)

One might say that it is where the different structures of House of the Future and Upper Lawn combine into one – the wall's *defensive* function facilitated the estate's *opening* to the outside, repelling that which would impair the ordinariness and light.[31]

A further feature of the defensive threshold can be added if we follow Mark Crinson and read protection from today's revanchist forces of urban development back into the design. Likely this is what most offended the estate's neoliberal opponents – its strident and starkly visible fortification against an economic order for which there is supposed to be no alternative. Robin Hood Gardens, Crinson writes, was "an aggressive form of protectiveness, a defensiveness that is both necessary and symbolic about the place of the home among the effects of car mobility, industrial-scale pollution and rampant economic violence".[32]

Stigmatizing Representations of Home

The co-construction of the homely with the unhomely was as an inventive and joyful architectural feature of the estate, but this is not at all how the estate's critics in government and media viewed it. From these quarters, the unhomely qualities of Robin Hood Gardens were spun into an image of hulking horror that overwhelmed domestic life, an image that all too often garnered authenticity by ventriloquizing the estate's putatively brutalized residents. It is worth presenting some examples.

In *The Guardian*, Simon Jenkins' colourful appraisal of this "prison without a roof endured by 600 people for half a century" was seemingly confirmed by his claim that "Not one current resident to my knowledge has stepped forward in its defence." "The tenants and Tower Hamlets council want the place down, and now."[33] For Margaret Hodge MP, who turned down the first listing application, anyone seeking to save this "concrete monstrosity" "should try living in it or raising a family there".[34] In one influential guide to London architecture, the estate's "almost manic system of walls and moats" make it a "particularly depressing place to live in".[35] Another book takes Robin Hood Gardens to be such a self-evident monstrosity that there is no need to ventriloquize its residents, taking two whole pages to describe its "inexcusably, unarguably, unmitigatingly awful", "austere", frighteningly utilitarian, "interminable concrete".[36] An editorial in *The Guardian* at the time of the 2008 listing dispute put it more politely, but with no less certainty, again apparently authenticated by the views of residents: "Sadly, its 'streets in the sky' walkways and too-narrow staircases meant it did not work for families."[37]

These stigmatizing accounts have performative effect, shaping and distributing social moods and symbolic frames that help propel agendas in social and economic policy. The same is true of filmic representations, though here the logical consequence of stigmatizing the estate's architecture is more fully realized, as residents' *homes* becomes sites of monstrosity too. Robin Hood Gardens featured in two episodes of *Luther*, the televisual police drama. In one memorable scene, the eponymous detective played by Idris Elba sought to extract information by dangling a resident loan shark over the side of a street deck.[38] The scene is architecturally framed and shot from different angles, attentive to the space and form of the deck and façade, as if such scenarios were natural to the scheme. But the most disturbing sequence is when a maisonette is discovered to be the site of a gruesome murder, the home plastered in graffiti tags which decorate a scene of torture and death by suffocation.[39]

In another example, the music video for the song "Getting Nowhere" (2010) by Magnetic Man, featuring John Legend, the architectural forms and spaces of Robin Hood Gardens are again incorporated into a narrative of urban anomie and despair. BMX-riding youth in hoodies figure social doom as they cycle about the estate's street decks and moats, while curtain-tweaking elderly people and video-gaming children are seemingly marooned in the estate's homes. The grim symbolism is crowned by the presence of a horseman of the apocalypse, no less, who the youth mirror in certain key respects. In a scene worthy of Peter Jackson's *Lord of the Rings*, the black-clad, hooded and sword-wielding horseman rears up his horse atop the estate's mound. The video gives the estate a more cinematic quality than found in *Luther*, and the accompanying scenes of distressed office workers and corporate skylines hardly present a positive counter-pole, befitting its dubstep genre. Nonetheless, there is little here to differentiate the representation of this council estate from the dominant stigmatization.

A final example works a little differently. Robin Hood Gardens had a fleeting appearance in a well-known 1980s commercial for Levi's jeans, where the east block was cast as an imposing Soviet monolith against an expanse of fake snow.[40] Shot in grainy black-and-white, the commercial's handsome protagonist smuggles his jeans through Russian border control, then traverses various urban scenes of authoritarian conformity, before trudging through the snow towards the looming Robin Hood Gardens to find sanctuary in his apartment, at last free to unwrap his prize. The estate is firmly positioned on the bad pole of the commercial's set of oppositions between consumer individuality and authoritarian conformity, yet it is the aesthetic of this pole, and hence the estate too, from which, paradoxically, the commercial's image of the jeans is fashioned. It is something like a corporate version of the post-punk visual aesthetic found in the urban photographs of Joy Division shot by Kevin Cummins in Manchester five years earlier, an early example, perhaps, of beautiful Brutalism – Brutalism at once denigrated and appropriated for middle-class self-making.

Experiences of Home

I turn now from the stigmatizing representations of Robin Hood Gardens to residents' impressions of the estate as home. It would have been no surprise to find that condemnation of Robin Hood Gardens by residents was neither as trenchant not as universal as is conveyed by Hodge, Jenkins and company. But in conversations with those for whom it was a home – rather than a scrim for fantastical projections – we found that these verdicts had little relation *at all* to residents' views.

Adrienne Sargeant moved into Robin Hood Gardens in 1974, aged nine, and lived in two apartments, a four-bed then a one-bed, until 2011 (Figure 4.11). She saw the filming of the Levi's commercial, returning home from school one day to find with amusement an unseasonal expanse of snow across the green. But she did not at all find the estate imposing or monolithic. For her, the apartments' generous proportions and variable configurations of rooms were an exciting change from the cramped and standardized pre-war tenements where she had lived previously. As a young girl, Adrienne and her friends would walk from their Preston Road home on the adjacent Isle of Dogs to sit and watch the later-stage construction of Robin Hood Gardens, recalling now that it looked "fancy" and "massive". When her family moved in, the garden was a "wonderland", "the hill was fantastic – like something you'd never seen". She remembers the strong attachment held by her father, who

Figure 4.11 Adrienne Sargeant, on an east-block street deck. (Kois Miah, August 2016)

hailed from Barbados and worked as a bus conductor: "he absolutely loved it here, absolutely loved it".[41]

Darren Pauling, a leading member of the Tenants' and Residents' Association, organized a survey where 130 families out of 140 surveyed preferred refurbishment to demolition of the estate, so countering the flawed consultation and informal polling that the council used to claim residents' preference for demolition while refusing to hold a formal ballot.[42] Unpicking the council's consultation in a 2010 letter to the local press, Darren turned the tables on the pejorative use of concrete in condemnations of the estate. Here, Robin Hood Gardens stands as a bulwark against the encroaching forces of the "concrete jungle" of hulking, unthinking and imposed urban development. "I have lived on the Robin Hood Gardens estate for over a decade and in Poplar all of my life", his letter began. "I love where I live. But I am sick of seeing overdevelopment of what was once a green and pleasant area being turned into a concrete jungle."[43]

Pat Murray and her husband John had lived in the east block since 1977, in a two-bedroom maisonette which, like any other up and down the country, the couple had made their own (Figure 4.12). The Lowry-esque picture in

Figure 4.12 Pat Murray at home. (Kois Miah, September 2015)

Pat's portrait was painted by John. "We were living in Tottenham with John's sister", Pat recalled on how she was housed by the council. "I didn't like it when we moved in but it gradually got better. I'm a Catholic and my neighbours are Muslim and they are lovely. Why can't everyone just get along? They do my shopping for me and help me. I love the space in this flat which I don't think I will get anywhere else."[44] Kois and I visited Pat and John during our first exhibition of residents' portraits, to give them the publicity poster that featured Pat's photograph. Sadly, Pat passed away shortly afterwards.

Residents' appreciation of the estate's homes was also expressed in "signs of occupancy", in the Smithsons' phrase.[45] The Smithsons intended the doorway "eddy spaces" as places for residents to furnish with pot plants, and they sometimes did. Jimmy Yorke, caretaker on the estate until his retirement and resident for ten years from the mid-1980s, used to grow tomatoes on his street deck, where it caught the sun, recalling how on summer evenings neighbours would stay out on the decks until nine or ten, drinking tea and walking about.[46] The architects may have been less pleased by the practice of some residents to paint the exterior concrete of the apartments, but these were their homes and the council's neglect allowed the concrete structures to gain some rather appealing and playful decoration. The deck-side exterior of Moyna Miah's maisonette was decorated with three large purple circles running diagonally up the divider between the triangular windows which separated the homes (Figure 1.6). This addition or another had set off a process – the exterior façade of a stretch of six or seven maisonettes here was painted in light tones of blue, green, grey and lilac, with one covered completely in vibrant purple. In the east block, at the point the deck tripled its height, one of the large head maisonettes was painted white, accompanied by a potted Bay Tree. A west-block equivalent, where Abdul Kalam grew up, greeted walkers along the deck with an expanse of two corner walls painted sky-blue (Figure 3.9). An image of this and other photographs by Abdul feature in Jessie Brenan's book about the estate, *Regeneration!*, where he describes a more impermanent effect of light and colour created during Ramadan: "everyone's up at the break of dawn to eat just before they fast", so the "whole estate lights up. Everywhere else is dark, and at five in the morning the whole estate's alight. ... Little things like that, it's quite beautiful."[47]

These and other laudatory comments about the estate's qualities of home, and other aspects of its lived experience, should not be taken to mean that there were not considerable problems (Figure 4.13). If Robin Hood Gardens modulated class society in its built forms, fashioning liveable home out of the hostile social relations that pull working-class and racially minoritized lives out of shape, it was not, for this reason, ever distinct from the damaging effects of capitalist society. Residents referred to water leaks and local-authority neglect, disinvestment and disrepair with depressing regularity. "Lots of other council estates were getting new kitchens fitted or new bathrooms and none of that was done at Robin Hood Gardens", remarked Dheraj Shamoo. "You complained to the council [about mould on the walls] but no one came to do anything about it." "If you sign a contract, you stick to your side of the bargain by paying the rent and all the service charges and everything else, you should expect them to provide a good service as well."[48] Shofiqul Hoque, chairman of the local mosque and resident for 20 years, was keen to leave, reporting that "the flat has been leaking, and dirty water from next door enters my flat. It's torture here because of this. It is comfortable as we have space outside but everything inside is damaged."[49] Darren Pauling's letter to the press itemized the issues: "residents were faced at that time with huge disrepair and electrical problems, leaks, poor heating and

Figure 4.13 Father and daughter frying chapatis. (Kois Miah, May 2015)

hot water maintenance, no internal decorations for 20 years, double glazing only on one side of the blocks, broken down lifts, etc.".[50] And yet, even when residents presented shocking accounts of disrepair or were suffering severe overcrowding, it was not uncommon for their remarks to be accompanied by enthusiastic accounts of the estate's forms, spaces and social life. In such conversations, residents would often shuttle between condemnation and celebration, their experiences not blended but held together and variously felt and expressed.

Home against Racism

Of all the social ills that can disrupt and degrade the experience of place and home, racism can be the keenest. Until the 1970s, council housing was internally regulated by the racializing distinction between the deserving and undeserving poor, a distinction which served to exclude Black, Asian, and other racially minoritized populations from council tenancies.[51] But Robin Hood Gardens opened as this racializing bar on housing allocation began to loosen, and so its story is threaded with the experience, including racism, of racially minoritized groups.

Black and Asian children can be seen on the street decks and playing in the green in Sandra Lousada's very early photographs of the estate. Adrienne Sargeant remembers her family being one of a few Black families living there in its early years. They experienced racial aggression. An unpublished PhD thesis about Robin Hood Gardens from 1982, by John Furse, comments on the presence of vile racist graffiti on site.[52] Furse also encountered racism in interviews with white residents. A woman in her thirties complains to him, for example: "It's not like it was when we first came – it's the blacks and the Chinese here now."[53] For Adrienne, though, this racism was not particular to the estate, but a feature of wider society. And one of Furse's interviewees, a man in his early twenties of Caribbean heritage, provides a disturbing spatial mapping of local racism which suggests it may have featured *less* in Robin Hood Gardens and its Poplar locale than in neighbouring wards of East London.

> I don't get no trouble [at Robin Hood Gardens] – they don't bother me much. They think I'm a "Paki" – Trinidad – it's the hair and the "tash." No – I feel O.K. here – with my sister. No-one tries it with me – I carry this blade ... strapped to my arm ... no it's

O.K. – they don't bother me. ... The National Front is more towards Whitechapel – we don't go down Brick Lane – we keep this way ... this side of The Londoner – that's where Poplar starts – other side is Limehouse – Chinese there – we stay this side. You get the Front in Stepney – I don't bother ... Skins ...[54]

I have not been able to ascertain whether Robin Hood Gardens became an estate to which the local authority allocated proportionately more Black, Bengali and other racially minoritized families, though Furse suggests this was the case, relative to the nearby Lansbury estate. What is clear is that through the early 1990s the estate became majority-non-white, with British Bangladeshis the largest minority and then the majority.[55] How did racism condition the experience of the estate during this later period? For Motiur Rahman, "the only case of racism or anything close to it" that he experienced over 23 years at Robin Hood Gardens was with a particular family in Anderson House (administratively part of the estate) "who were quite open" about their racism. "I got the sense that they didn't like this huge influx of Asian people. ... They had their good days, when you could actually say hello and walk past them and you felt like you were a normal person, and there were other days they would call you a Paki or you would have your scarf taken off you."[56]

For Abul Hasnath, racism was sometimes a feature of interaction on the estate's football pitch in the early 1990s, noting that this was the period when Derek Beackon, in nearby Millwall ward, became the first elected councillor of the avowedly racist British National Party. He recounted a racist attack when he was 12 years old, curling up in a cocoon while being kicked by a group of boys, one of them saying: "You Pakis are like wolves. Together you think you're special but on your own you're nothing." Abul insists, though, that the racism came in from outside, that these were not residents, and by the mid-1990s it was largely gone. "The white residents that were there were very well integrated with Bengalis. We really got on" (Figure 4.14).[57]

From the perspective of a white resident, Darren Pauling had a similar view, and indicated an important class dimension to anti-racism. "You'd talk to everyone", he said about his early memories of the estate. "I was brought up in East London so we've always had a big mix of ethnic minorities around. It was a docking community, basically – always blacks, Asians, Chinese, all welcome about the area. We had Chinatown just down in Limehouse. You've always had an influx of people. Who usually take that influx? Mainly poor,

Figure 4.14 The estate's football pitch. (Kois Miah, April 2015)

impoverished, working-class families, because straight away, it's better in numbers, so let's make friends, you know?"[58]

Musa, who lived with his family in a three-bedroom maisonette in the west block from 1987 until demolition, having moved in aged four, encountered racism from white residents. He recounted a violent attack on his father. And there were undercurrents of racial hostility from some residents – "you could *feel it* in certain families and occasions, feel their heat, their aggressive talk".[59] But as the Bangladeshi community grew from minority to majority on the estate, his overriding sense is that Robin Hood Gardens served as *protection* from racism – protection from everyday racist aggression and also from its more structural forms and effects. The estate's theme of protection here takes a *social* dimension, where home served to fashion a pocket of defence and security against the hostile, racializing relations of its social world, home not confined to the domestic unit, important though that is, but extending through the estate as a whole. As Musa put it, "our recollection of the estate as we were growing up is as a safety net, a home. For my father it was the same. ... When they [the National Front] were marching in Brick Lane and he was in his home here, that was a safety net. So, yes, the estate in itself became a protection, a home." Regarding the more everyday effects of racism, he remarked on how the estate and local youth clubs, with their residentials and camping trips, helped build resilience and commonality across different cultures: "Because we are from a particular minority, everything can feel like a struggle. I'm taking about the 1990s. When you're going for a job opportunity, you almost feel insecure conversing with someone of different ethnicity. You may feel as though you're not able to eloquently express yourself. Or you're not able to see commonality between different cultures."[60]

I do not mean to say that there was *uniformity* to this protection, or autonomy from hostile social relations. It was a checkered experience, where racializing relations and racist encounters at once intruded upon Robin Hood Gardens and were variously held back, dissipated, fought off and ejected by the estate-as-home.

Coda on Peter Eisenman at Robin Hood Gardens

To my knowledge, there is only one other text that engages seriously with how Robin Hood Gardens handles class in its built form, and that is architect Peter Eisenman's essay "From Golden Lane to Robin Hood Gardens: Or If You Follow the Yellow Brick Road, It May not Lead to Golders Green". Included in the same 1972 issue of *Architectural Design* as the Smithsons' publication of Robin Hood Gardens, it is perhaps the most significant architectural criticism of the estate. Moreover, Eisenman approaches the problem of class architecture in terms resonant with this chapter's typology of home and its outside. For these reasons, and that Eisenman judges the estate a *failure* in these terms, his essay warrants some extended consideration.

Eisenman's contention is essentially that Robin Hood Gardens is a paradoxical attempt, and a failure as such, to fit the revolutionary structure and vision of the Smithsons' Golden Lane design into a *middle-class* housing form. Robin Hood Gardens, he claims, does not challenge but accepts the world as it is, satisfying "the welfare state and its agency in the Greater London Council (GLC), which seems content in offering the working class ... a bourgeois existence".[61] By contrast, as the pedestrian street decks of Golden Lane branch out over the city – in their open-ended connectivity, fragmenting rather than deflecting the spatial surround, negating automotive transport – they articulate the condition and promise of working-class architecture in their immediate opening to the outside. This undoes the bourgeois division and hierarchy between private and public, for "the private cell is now in direct contact with most scales of urban structure".[62] One might say that for Eisenman, Golden Lane is all light and no ordinariness.

The street decks carry over into Robin Hood Gardens, but paradoxically so, for Eisenman argues that the scheme *succumbs to the private*. It runs to ground on the slab-blocks' delineation of what he sees as the semi-private space of the green, a vision of "English urban order", which sets off a series of mediations and hierarchies between outside and inside.[63] From the roads, through the green and its slab-block boundary, to the street decks, the apartments' interior staircasing and the inner sanctum of home, the division and hierarchy of the private and the public is reasserted, working-class inhabitants content and contained with their domestic amenities and motor cars, "dead[ened to] any expectation of future change".[64]

Leaving aside Eisenman's somewhat Puritan notion, which one can also find in Tafuri, that domestic amenities spell disaster for the prospects of revolutionary change, he is right to observe and affirm a more forceful "confrontation with the motor car" in Golden Lane than in Robin Hood Gardens. And the later scheme, as we have seen, was indeed contained by the city's roads; it did not remove or transcend them. I think he makes an error, though, in reading the street decks in a positive relation to the car, asserting that "the primary pedestrian connection is now thought of as being vertical, to the motor car; horizontal connection is by car alone".[65] For connectivity is not the best way to interpret the street decks' manifold social and sensory affordances, and the car was not at all the scheme's pre-eminent means of connectivity. I have discussed the estate's measures *against* the car, though it is true that the relation was not only hostile. It suggests of the Smithsons more than a grudging acceptance of residents' need for cars that one diagram of the estate's moats includes a Citroën DS, the beloved vehicular means of Alison Smithson's *AS in DS: An Eye on the Road* (the diaries for which were mostly written around the time Robin Hood Gardens opened).[66] And a diagram of the scheme's visual and pedestrian connections includes also the estate's traffic routes, as does a similar diagram which gives the same weight to the estate's traffic patterns as it does to pedestrian desire paths.[67] However, the connectivity of Robin Hood Gardens was not primarily to the car and roads but to the green and the Poplar locale. In interviewing residents, we did not inquire if they owned cars (the estate provided garage units for 70% of the apartments), but in answer to a question about connectivity, they referred in every instance to the ease of *pedestrian* circulation in and out of the estate to the nearby shops on Poplar High Street, to Chrisp Street Market, to Woolmore School. And when transport was mentioned, it was invariably in reference to the estate's location near multiple bus routes, not to cars.

The criticism of Eisenman that I would most emphasize, though, concerns his contention that the estate loses the classed opening of the private to the public, the homely to the unhomely. Eisenman's mistake here is threefold. First, his focus on connection blinkers him to the significance and class dimensions of *protection* to the scheme, as this chapter has shown. Second, he misses the specific quality and importance of the estate's *thresholds*. As we saw, it is through the spatial form of the threshold that the outside, the unhomely, is both experienced *and constructed*. The "dice of sensation" is *made* through particular architectural configurations of the threshold, in their multiform variety. Eisenman celebrates that Golden Lane reduces the "transitions" (thresholds, in our terms) between outside and inside, but Robin Hood Gardens shows that, on the contrary, it is not in reducing but in *multiplying* thresholds that the architectural articulation of the outside on the inside is more fully achieved. Third, and related, it is in multiplying thresholds that the private and the public, the homely and the unhomely, are constructed *in parity*. The estate was not at all a surrender to self-satisfied petit-bourgeois identity at home, but a series of thresholds that *forced home out of seclusion*, a modulated continuum of thresholds between ordinariness and light.

Notes

1 Wayne Alison, interview, 18 January 2016.
2 Gilles Deleuze and Félix Guattari, *What Is Philosophy?*, trans. Hugh Tomlinson and Graham Burchell (London: Verso, 1994), 186.
3 Gilles Deleuze and Félix Guattari, *Kafka: Toward a Minor Literature*, trans. Dana Polan (Minneapolis: University of Minnesota Press, 1986). Nicholas Thoburn, "The People Are Missing: Cramped Space, Social Relations, and the Mediators of Politics", *International Journal of Politics, Culture and Society* 29 no. 4 (2016): 367–381.
4 Deleuze and Guattari, *Kafka*, 17.
5 Deleuze and Guattari, *What Is Philosophy?*, 187.
6 *Ibid.*, 186. Stephen Zepke, "Modernism Forever: Towards a New 'New Brutalism'", unpublished conference talk, no date.

7 There is a notable consonance here with Ginzburg and Milinis' Narkomfin Communal House, wherein the *class* qualities of the modulation of light come forward. In this *social condenser* (an architectural form designed to inculcate new collective-social mentalities and routines for socialist society) Ginzburg too sought a calibrated opening of the inside to the outside, the home to the environment, and this as integral to constructing a *proletarian* sensorium. In the Narkomfin, as he put it, "The windows open accordion like and transform the living cell into an open terrace, surrounded by greenery. The sense of a room is lost: it becomes a platform integrated within nature." Moisei Ginzburg, cited in Victor Buchli, "Moisei Ginzburg's Narkomfin Communal House in Moscow: Contesting the Social and Material World", *Journal of the Society of Architectural Historians* 57 no. 2 (1998): 160–181, 169. As to its class dimensions, Ginzburg's response to Le Corbusier is revealing: "You write that the peasant does not appreciate flowers and does not listen to the songs of larks. Well of course, he does not have the spirit for such when he is overburdened by work. We want our peasant to enjoy the songs of larks. And we know that for this we must ease the burden of his work and introduce culture into his life." Culture edging out work, home loosened into landscape – here, Victor Buchli suggests, the Narkomfin was moving towards Marx's vision of the emancipated many-sided individuality of communism. *Ibid.*

8 Following Massumi, we could make this point philosophically with Bergson and Deleuze, for whom the outside is, ultimately, light: "the 'abstract surface' is light itself". Brian Massumi, "Sensing the Virtual, Building the Insensible", *Couplets: Travels in Speculative Pragmatism* (Durham, NC and London: Duke University Press, 2021), 149. As Deleuze writes, "If different examples of architecture ... are visibilities, places of visibilities, this is because they are not just figures of stone, assemblages of things and combinations of qualities, but first and foremost forms of light that distribute light and dark, opaque and transparent, seen and non-seen, etc." Gilles Deleuze, *Foucault*, trans. Seán Hand (Minneapolis: University of Minnesota Press, 1986), 57.

9 Hadas Steiner, "Life at the Threshold", *October* 136 (2011): 133–155, 153.

10 *Ibid.*

11 *Ibid.*, 141.

12 *Ibid.*, 145.

13 *Ibid.*, 141.

14 Adrienne Sargeant, interview, 15 August 2017.

15 Motiur Rahman, interview, 4 December 2015.

16 Kim, interview 28 August, 2015.

17 Steiner, "Life at the Threshold", 145.

18 One might conceptualize the joyous quality of the outside here with Spinoza, for whom joy is an increase in the capacity to affect and be affected outside of the self, where the outside is not only social but also material, atmospheric etc.

19 That the Smithsons understood Upper Lawn and Robin Hood Gardens to share the same problem-form is hinted at by two of Peter Smithson's photographs of the different schemes. One of his photographs of Upper Lawn, taken in 1978, is a close-up of a window from the outside. It looks through the interior and out through the far window onto verdant countryside, revealing the space inside only to the extent that the glass pane reflects the shape of a building behind the photographer, and incorporates a partial outline of the photographer himself, with the far window in place of his face. Six years earlier, he took a near-identically framed photograph of Robin Hood Gardens, positioned on a street deck, looking through a

maisonette and out onto the estate's garden, the photographer again reflected in this photograph of the threshold of ordinariness and light. The photographs are included, respectively, in Alison and Peter Smithson, *Upper Lawn: Solar Pavilion Folly* (Barcelona: Edicions de la Universitat Politècnica Catalunya, 1986), no page numbers and Alison and Peter Smithson, *The Shift* (London: Academy Editions, 1982), 35.

20 *Ibid.*, cited in Jonathan Hill, *Weather Architecture* (London and New York: Routledge, 2012), 246. In these ways, Upper Lawn also displays the Smithsons' prescient interest in a more *ecological* approach to architecture, where "a society becoming more climate, nature, energy-resource responsive ... will allow us to begin to think of a new form of restorative habitat for a future light touch inhabitation of the earth". Alison Smithson, "Saint Jerome: The Desert ... The Study", in *Alison and Peter Smithson: From the House of the Future to a House of Today*, ed. Max Risselada and Dirk van den Heuvel (Rotterdam: 010 Publishers, 2004).

21 As Hill puts it, "these 'failings' were important to the experience offered by Upper Lawn, questioning familiar notions of domestic shelter and privacy. 'Camping out' at a 'primitive' 'Solar Pavilion Folly' the Smithsons tested the assumption that some loss in environmental comfort is amply compensated by, and even necessary to, a more complete experience of nature and weather." Hill, *Weather Architecture*, 246, quotations from the Smithsons.

22 A playful sign of the processual qualities of Upper Lawn, the Smithsons list its dates as 1959–1982, extending beyond its structural completion in 1962 to the duration of their inhabitation.

23 Beatriz Colomina, "Unbreathed Air 1956", *Grey Room* 15 (2004): 28–59, 49.

24 *Ibid.*, 54.

25 Alison and Peter Smithson, "Robin Hood Gardens, London", *The Charged Void: Architecture* (New York: The Monacelli Press, 2001), 296.

26 The acoustic wall ran along Cotton Street and Poplar High Street. A shorter and lower stretch of the wall was sited next to the tunnel road, though in its separation from the estate by Robin Hood Lane it felt less a part of it.

27 Alison Smithson, *AS in DS: An Eye on the Road* (Delft: Lars Müller Publishers, 2001 [orig. 1983]).

28 Alison and Peter Smithson, *Italian Thoughts* (privately published, 1993), 41. To say a little more about the Smithsons' changing views about the private car, in the 1950s and early 1960s it signified for them personal and social mobility, "a certain sort of freedom" to be made key to town planning, where (the great mistake of the times) even urban motorways might be introduced to impart a comprehensibility and identity to large cities. Alison and Peter Smithson, *Ordinariness and Light: Urban Theories 1952–1960 and their Application in a Building Project 1963–1970* (London: Faber and Faber, 1970), 144. Even then, though, Golden Lane was designed as if its urban inhabitants were to have no need of cars, and while *AS in DS* has an affirmative quality, the book's preface bears an ominous verdict: "The car has rolled into the city like an assassin." Otto Das, in Smithson, *AS in DS*, 55. Perhaps the Smithsons' overarching view, albeit an impossible one, was that the car should be kept at a distance, in the manner as they saw it of Le Corbusier's Plan Voisin: "The automobile used at the scale at which it is a moving poetic thing and not a stinking object." Peter Smithson, "On Le Corbusier", in Alison and Peter Smithson, *The Heroic Period of Modern Architecture* (London: Thames and Hudson, 1981), 26.

29 Smithson and Smithson, *Italian Thoughts*, 37.

30 Alison and Peter Smithson, "Sketch: Acoustic Boundary Wall", in *Robin Hood Gardens: Re-Visions*, ed. Alan Powers (London: Twentieth Century Society, 2010), 62.

31 Kate Macintosh, architect of the stunning Dawson's Heights estate (1964–1972) in Southwark, South London, has said that the acoustic wall may actually have had little noise-reducing effect, which if true is significant, but I am suggesting that it was a measure against the encroachment of the road in a wider sense. Certainly, it was hard not to feel thankful for it when one was inside the estate. "Finding Brutalism with Kate Macintosh: Interview by Stephen Parnell, Winchester, 20 April 2017", in Simon Phipps, *Finding Brutalism: A Photographic Survey of Post-War British Architecture*, ed. Hilar Stadler and Andreas Hertach (Zurich: Park Books, 2017), 247.

32 Crinson, *Alison and Peter Smithson*, 73.

33 Simon Jenkins, "This Icon of 60s New Brutalism has Its Champions. So Let them Restore It", *The Guardian*, 20 June 2008, www.theguardian.com/commentisfree/2008/jun/20/architecture.

34 Margaret Hodge, cited in Hugh Muir, "Diary", *The Guardian*, 19 February 2008, www.theguardian.com/politics/2008/feb/19/1; Margaret Hodge, cited in David Rogers, "Hodge Scoffs at Latest Attempt to List Robin Hood Gardens", *Building Design*, 18 March 2015, www.bdonline.co.uk/hodge-scoffs-at-latest-attempt-to-list-robin-hood-gardens/5074417.

35 Edward Jones and Christopher Woodward, *Guide to the Architecture of London* (London: Phoenix, 2013). This remark is notable because Woodward was an architectural assistant to the Smithsons (along with Kenny Baker) on the design of Robin Hood Gardens.

36 Ed Glinert, *East End Chronicles: Three Hundred Years of Mystery and Mayhem* (London: Penguin Books, 2006), 251–252.

37 Editorial, "Building Blocks", *The Guardian*, 16 June 2008, www.theguardian.com/commentisfree/2008/jun/16/architecture.art.

38 *Luther*, Season 3, Episode 1, BBC Television, first broadcast 2013.

39 Robin Hood Gardens features in similarly stigmatizing and clichéd ways in an episode of the criminal-forensics television drama *Silent Witness* and in the feature film *U Want Me 2 Kill Him?*, dir. Andrew Douglas (2013).

40 Titled *Airport Russia* and first broadcast in 1985, now available on YouTube, it was the first of the famed series of UK Levi's commercials produced by Nigel Bogle and John Hegarty.

41 Adrienne Sargeant, interview, 15 August 2016.

42 Darren Pauling, interview, 5 September 2015.

43 Darren Pauling, "I'm Sick of Concrete Jungle Creeping Up on Robin Hood Gardens", *The Docklands and East London Advertiser*, 6 December 2010, www.eastlondonadvertiser.co.uk/news/i-m-sick-of-concrete-jungle-creeping-up-on-robin-3415390.

44 Pat Murray, interview, 14 September 2015.

45 Alison and Peter Smithson, "Signs of Occupancy", *Architectural Design* 42 no. 2 (1972): 91–97.

46 Jimmy Yorke, interview, 23 July 2014.

47 Abdul Kalam in *Regeneration! Conversations, Drawings, Archives and Photographs from Robin Hood Gardens*, ed. Jessie Brennan (London: Silent Grid, 2015), 65.

48 Dheraj Shamoo, interview, 7 September 2014.

49 Shofiqul Hoque, interview, 13 September 2015.

50 Pauling, "I'm Sick of Concrete Jungle Creeping Up on Robin Hood Gardens".

51 Shilliam, *The Undeserving Poor*.

52 John Furse, *The Smithsons at Robin Hood Gardens*, unpublished PhD thesis (University of Sussex, 1982), 154, 188.

53 *Ibid.*, 141. In another example, a white man in his forties remarks to Furse: "It's Blacks ... they don't know different – as soon as they move in the trouble starts. They don't know no better. Before they came there was no bother – it's them that causes all the damage – you can see it ... they don't live like us do they? Don't know how to behave. There's so many of them now ... more than there used to be – that's the trouble. Now it's the Chinese – all the same." *Ibid.*, 147.

54 *Ibid.*, 155. The pub mentioned here, The Londoner (now demolished), sat at the junction of East India Dock Road and West India Dock Road, one mile due west of Robin Hood Gardens.

55 At the time of the council's Compulsory Purchase Order in 2013, approximately two-thirds of the tenancies and leaseholds were held by people with recognizably Bengali names. *The London Borough of Tower Hamlets (Blackwall Reach) Compulsory Purchase Order 2013: Statement of Reasons* (London: London Borough of Tower Hamlets, 2013).

56 Motiur Rahman, interview, 4 December 2015.

57 Abul Hasnath, interview, 29 October 2020.

58 Darren Pauling, interview, 10 September 2015.

59 Musa, interview, 28 October 2020.

60 *Ibid.*

61 Peter Eisenman, "From Golden Lane to Robin Hood Gardens: Or If You Follow the Yellow Brick Road, It May not Lead to Golders Green", in *Alison and Peter Smithson: A Critical Anthology*, ed. Max Risselada (Barcelona: Ediciones Polígrafa, 2011), 206–223, 221.

62 *Ibid.*, 221.

63 *Ibid.*, 213.

64 *Ibid.*, 222.

65 *Ibid.*, 211.

66 Alison and Peter Smithson, *The Charged Void: Architecture* (New York: The Monacelli Press, 2001), 302.

67 *Ibid.*, 298. See Chapter 5 for discussion of the visual-connectivity diagram.

5

An Active Line on a Walk: Figuring Form with Brutalist Diagrams

The personal graphs of Klee taught our generation to sense the self-ordaining power that resides within ideas at the moment of their inception, when they are returned from the as-yet-invented into the fabric of the new vision.

Alison Smithson, "Louis Kahn: Invitation to Otterlo, Graphics of Movement"

For those capable of attention, [diagrams] are the moments where being is glimpsed smiling.

Gilles Châtelet, *Figuring Space*

The Smithsons' Brutalism emerges through grappling with problems in the social world, problems which intrude on thinking and have volitional force. I suggested earlier that *concepts* are an integral tool for working with problems and channelling them into form. Concepts do not work alone, however. The Smithsons' deployed an array of textual, graphic, exhibitionary and publishing means, each intersecting and pulling apart, to discern, tease out, grapple with and be propelled by problems. The method was "nonsystematic, synesthetic, collagistic", in Christine Boyer's characterization.[1] And a crucial role was played by *images*. Rayner Banham famously gave one of his three defining characteristics of New Brutalism as "memorability as an Image", but that is a feature of the haptic visuality of the completed buildings.[2] My interest in this chapter is with the place of images in the problem-grappling *construction* of architecture, and with one kind of image in particular: the *diagram*.

Diagrams are schematic orderings of graphic and textual material – lines, images, words, arranged in space. They are less representational than *generative*. As I show here, diagrams are a graphic modelling that seeks to intuit, shape and provoke form, a modelling that is immersed in problems, courting contingency, open to the outside. As well as being *particular kinds* of images, then, diagrams are also a *mode* of image-making, a mode that can incorporate and mobilize other graphic and visual practices. It is a mode, I want to suggest, that suffuses the Smithsons' graphic practice and architectural sensibility, as they intuit and grapple problems into form. We can call it their *diagrammatic* Brutalism.

There is a recognizable aesthetic to much of the Smithsons' graphic work, especially their "wobbly-edged" diagrams, as Peter Cook puts it, with the accompanying loose, hand-written titling (Figure 6.9).[3] But the sketches, plans, montages and diagrams that they produced of their projects in formation comprise an array of graphic features, varying considerably in style, materials and execution, including when pertaining to the same project or problem. Fashioned from within any particular project or problem, each graphic work warrants consideration in its specificity. But it is the diagrammatic method that touches them all that I want to attend to and develop here, before turning to specific examples in the diagrams and montages of the problem of streets in the sky, as it moved towards built fruition in Robin Hood Gardens. This chapter interrupts the book's movement through the scheme's architectural forms (which I return to in the following chapter on the problem of *mass*) but not as much as one might think, because graphic visualization is immanent to the estate, preceding, running through and enduring after it.

The Self-Ordaining Power of Diagrams

Brutalism has been "almost entirely defined by the photographic image", as Alpa Depani remarks, whether in the service of its detractors like Charles Jencks or "fetishized in high contrast monochrome by its champions".[4] This is as true of the representation of the Smithsons' buildings as of any other, but it is not so for the Smithsons' *practice*, whose diagrammatic visualization can be first distinguished in *contradistinction* to the photographic image. Fredric Jameson aids us here, with what he considers to be two regimes of architectural reification: the photograph of the finished work and the architectural project drawing. The "image imperialism of photography", Jameson contends, makes of architecture a spurious unity, "the transformation of the building into the image of itself".[5] Photography in this mode blocks and excises a building's "perceptual shock", its multiple and divergent perspectives and the specific problems with which it grapples.[6] This mode of reification is commercial, imbricated in the commodity aesthetics of magazine and book publishing, where "a new set of libidinal forces comes into play so that it is no longer even the building that is now consumed, having itself become a mere pretext for the intensities of the colour stock and the gloss of the stiff paper".[7]

Against this "'bad' reification", Jameson posits the "good" reification of architects' drawings, sketches, diagrams and other work on paper. They are no less distinct from physical buildings than are photographs, no less "reified", but their substance, what it is that they grapple with, is precisely the shocks, perspectives and problems that the photograph excludes. These features and qualities are, for Jameson, of no small significance – he accords them *utopian* volition, what "makes the infinite Utopian freedom possible".[8] They contribute, a little more modestly, to "the Utopia of a renewal of perception".[9]

The promise of diagrams is scarcely less for the mathematician and philosopher Gilles Châtelet. "For those capable of attention", writes Châtelet, in his 1993 book *Figuring Space*, diagrams "are the moments where being is glimpsed smiling".[10] But Châtelet provides a more fine-grained understanding of diagrams than Jameson, and hence is more useful for our purposes. With Châtelet, we can define a diagram as a schematic ordering of lines, spaces, images and words that seeks to tease out, model and provoke dynamic relationships. Diagrams are modes of inscription particularly germane to experimental projects that break with established or clichéd ideas and practices to proceed instead through "blind spots", "fogs" and "problematics". Diagrams do not *solve* problems – they *intuit* and *pose* them. They are lodged within problems and grapple with them as the condition of their development.

In so doing, the work of a diagram is as much about *holding interpretation at bay*, clearing away the clichés that flood the perceptual and intellectual field.[11] And with this is raised the relation of diagrams to *metaphors*. Both work to describe, evoke and encourage relations – they "leap out" to figure space – but metaphors risk becoming "worn out" clichés, with passifying effect, as they dissolve the "cold" technical specificity of a particular operation with the "warm confusion" of relations of resemblance.[12] Diagrams, on the other hand, with their modest plotting and sketching – as they struggle in uncertainty to grasp elusive relations and make connections across disparate realms – are extended or prolonged through contact with the world that they model. Not that metaphors are dismissed entirely – helpfully for me, because metaphoric and figurative language has a significant role in the Smithsons' diagrammatic practice. While metaphors tend towards cliché, the direction can be reversed, with metaphors working also as proto-diagrams, shifting us from clichéd representations to awakened critical modelling. In this way, "metaphor begins the process of shedding its skin that will metamorphose into [diagrammatic] operation, and hence it is that this nook swarms with clichés that strive to invite us to view a rediscovered operativity".[13] As with Jameson, diagrams still arrest movement, abstracting a form from the complexity of socio-material relations, but they do so in a manner that remains open to those relations, soliciting their "virtual" potential to take other forms.[14]

It should be clear that Châtelet's formulation of the diagram is close to the Smithsons' method of posing and grappling with problems; it is close also to their understanding and use of diagrams. We have seen their diagrammatic practice exemplified already in the 1953 *Urban Re-Identification* grid, its subversive use of CIAM's presentational visual protocols to ward off the clichés of functional urbanism and grapple with the problem of the street and its scales of association. For Alison Smithson, such graphic visual forms have a "self-ordaining power". The phrase is redolent of Châtelet, though her reference is to the artist Paul Klee. In an unpublished text cited by Boyer, she writes: "The personal graphs of Klee taught our generation to sense the self-ordaining power that resides within ideas at the moment of their inception, when they are returned from the as-yet-invented into the fabric of the new vision."[15]

As Boyer shows, Klee was indeed a significant influence on the Smithsons' graphic practice. Their diagrams sometimes pull motifs directly from Klee's remarkable primer in dynamic graphic form, *Pedagogical Sketches* (translated into English by Sibyl Moholy-Nagy in 1953), notably the black arrow used in the metre-long, diagrammatic scroll they gifted to Team 10 members at CIAM 10 in Dubrovnik 1956 (Figure 5.1). And the painted human figure at the centre of *Urban Re-Identification* is reminiscent of the partially abstract figures of Klee's late paintings (Figure 3.5). But these direct references are of less significance than how the Smithsons take features of Klee's diagrammatic *method and sensibility* into their graphic work, a point Boyer makes with the aid of David Sylvester's essays on the late Klee, published in 1948 and 1951 and influential in the Smithsons' intellectual milieu. In addition to the self-ordaining force of Klee's images, what Sylvester calls

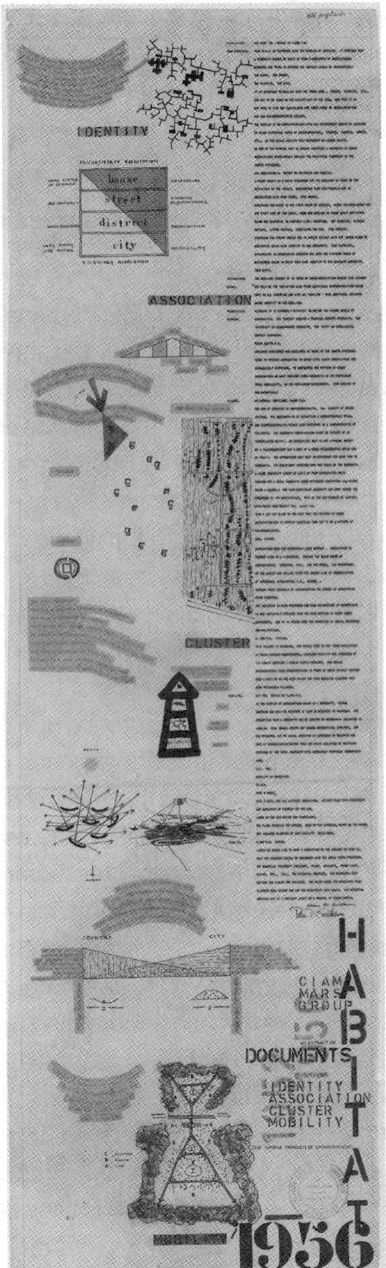

Figure 5.1 Scroll distributed at CIAM 10 in Dubrovnik. (Alison and Peter Smithson, 1956. Smithson Family Collection)

their "germinal" quality, these features include, as I consider now in turn: the dynamism of the image and its multi-focal perspectivalism; the place of the viewer in its co-production; and the generative but non-delimiting role of words and concepts.[16]

Multi-focalism, Co-production, Affective Concepts

It is *movement* that Klee's diagrams figure above all. Famously commencing *Pedagogical Sketches* with a simple curving line, an "*active* line on a walk, moving freely, without a goal", the book fashions a wonderous array of "ideograms of movement in nature", where the "movement of the motifs themselves defines fluid space".[17] These movements are dynamic and non-linear, without single points of focus, the eye instead drawn into a mutable, n-dimensional field of "lines continually changing in plane and direction", "each point of view" providing "a different view of the whole".[18]

As to how this applies to the Smithsons' graphic work, Ben Highmore has drawn attention to the multi-focal, disaggregated quality to one of the collages in their Golden Lane competition entry. Titled *Golden Lane* (1952), it comprises a line drawing of three elevations of the scheme overlaid awkwardly, without integration, on a photograph of a wrecked, perhaps bomb-damaged site, a site which in half the image presses through the shape of the proposed structure such that it is just as much a part of the image as the architectural design (Figure 5.2). The montage is made more jarring by the incongruous presence of a French film star, Gérard Philipe, collaged in the foreground, and Jawaharlal Nehru, India's first post-independence prime minister, waiving from a street deck, while a working-class man bicycles precariously across the rugged ground.[19] The diverse and conflicting parts of the image hold together, communicating something about destruction and urbanism, glamour and class, the relation of ground as found to built form – but without resolution, intelligibility held open, while the modernist constitutive condition of territory as tabula rasa is repelled. To appropriate Sylvester on Klee, every component of this image "is as crucial as every other, and there is never a point on which the spectator's eye is allowed to come to rest".[20] The viewer's imagination is in this way drawn into the image and comes to co-produce its meaning. As the eye darts about from film star to bomb-site, to Nehru, to building, to cyclist, it "return[s] to a sign already visited to find that

Figure 5.2 *Golden Lane.* (Alison and Peter Smithson, 1952. Smithson Family Collection)

it now means something other than what it meant when approached previously from a different direction". An effect on each *part* of the image, this movement effects also the *whole*, where "the perception of the picture in time produces changes in its structure".[21]

For all this polysemy and incompletion, the Smithsons' diagrams are not without meaning. The point is that meaning has an *emergent* quality, emergent for the architects as much as the viewer. Recall that for Alison Smithson, Klee's diagrams were a means of drawing forth ideas, groping towards the "as-yet-invented", ideas which pertain to problems in the world. And in that groping invention arises a role for words and concepts, which are no less volitional.

Ben van Berkel and Caroline Bos warn of a *representational* relation between architecture and concepts, where concepts have an overbearing quality of determination, pouncing on form to fix it in meaning: "While concepts are formulated loud and clear, architecture itself waits passively, as it were, until it is pounced upon by a concept. A representational technique implies that we converge on reality from a conceptual position and in that way fix the relationship between idea and form."[22] The same risk applies to the diagram, that concepts will flood it with determining ideas. For the Smithsons, however, concepts work rather differently, not determining but evoking, calling forth, provoking imagination, bearing "idea-energies".[23] They are not representational but *figurative* or *affective*. Dirk van den Heuvel has developed the former term in discussion of the expressive methods of Team 10, quoting Johan Huizinga: "The word-bound concept is always inadequate to the torrent of life. Hence it is only the image-making or *figurative word* that can invest things with expression and at the same time bathe them in the luminosity of ideas."[24] Boyer makes a related point, now directly about the Smithsons: "Expressing, questioning, and grasping experience through images generated *affective concepts* that required verbal embodiment. The Smithsons wanted to see, feel, and sense what their images, projects, *and* words could do, how these various modes of expression created rather than represented thinking, enabled orientation toward a multi-vocal rather than linear mode of expression."[25]

This is how to understand the prodigious coinage of architectural words and phrases that accompanies the progress of the Smithsons' career as an integral component.[26] New Brutalism, streets-in-the-air, urban re-identification, cluster city, conglomerate ordering, ordinariness and light, doorstep philosophy, matt building, lattice, scatter, as found, charged void – these are figurative words, they name affective concepts. As concepts they are *fuzzy*, rarely developed in a systematic way – their groping, emergent, volitional figuring of form resides in their capacity to survey and interrogate a problem while resisting closure, conveying enough meaning, but not too much, remaining open to the imagination, to the virtual. And, so often in the Smithsons' work, these concepts accompany, brush up against, refer to, or draw from visual diagrams. In association in this way, diagrams and concepts are not in *identity* – there is always a "gap", a "space between", that prevents determination of one expressive means by the other, as they work together, in their difference, to grapple with problems and provoke form.[27]

Diagramming Streets in the Sky

I turn now to consider how the Smithsons' graphic practice takes shape through their diagramming of the affective concept of the streets in the sky, first in diagrams for the Golden Lane competition, where this concept was first articulated, and then Robin Hood Gardens, where it came to built fruition.

My first example, *Golden Lane: Street Deck* (1952–1953), is much closer to a conventional architectural diagram than the more speculative *Urban Re-Identification* grid or the Golden Lane collage with Gérard Philipe, containing less of their multi-focal graphic quality (Figure 5.3). Yet it has germinal, diagrammatic features all the same. Like *Urban Re-Identification*, *Golden Lane: Street Deck* is concerned with the impromptu sociality of the street, but less in its abstract social and sensory qualities than as a refined focus on the street deck. The aerial street fills the metre-wide collage, the viewer positioned at pedestrian level looking along its length to a distant vanishing point. Movement is key to the image – the topological qualities Banham identifies of "visible circulation, identifiable units of habitation", "inside and out".[28] And this movement is *playful*, but where the agents of the joyful and spontaneous sociality of play are now primarily adults, not children. Among a number of collaged figures, including a man on all-fours playing with a toddler, are the somewhat surprising figures of Marilyn Monroe and the baseball player Joe DiMaggio (or a couple chosen for their likeness), infusing the scene with their Hollywood glamour and joyous demeanour.

For Banham, these figures, which almost overwhelm the architecture, are a "part of the total image", a part of the processual and deforming form,

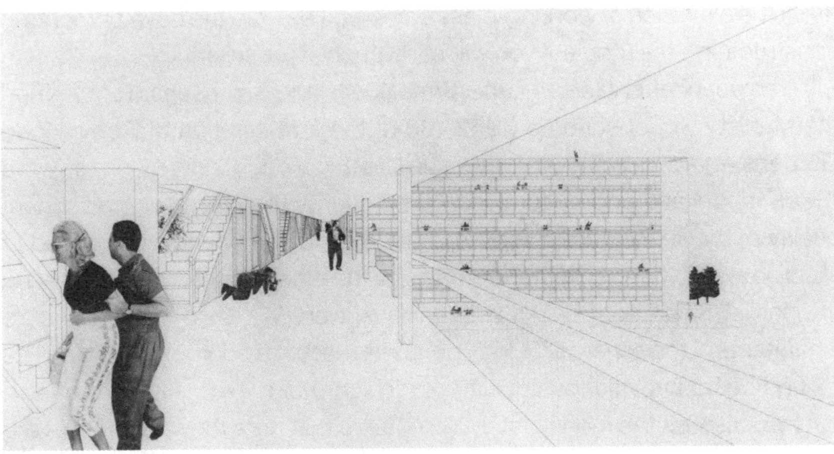

Figure 5.3 *Golden Lane: Street Deck*. (Alison and Peter Smithson, 1952–1953. Smithson Family Collection)

the "aformalism", being evoked.[29] And their specific content, a Hollywood couple, brings a sense of "dissonance" to the image, Highmore suggests, a diagrammatic breach with the given, wherein the street deck's sociality takes a fantastic or utopian quality. For here, in impoverished post-war London, "the daily grind of working-class life is miraculously swapped for glamour, youth, health, and play".[30] But can *work* become *play*? The Smithsons certainly did not take up the Marxist refrain of the abolition of work, as found around this time in the Situationist International, for example, but play here was intended to leak into and trouble CIAM's four functions, and the Smithsons adopted the prevalent Keynesian idea that automation would diminish work and release leisure time.[31] Indeed, they imagined the abandoned docks around Robin Hood Gardens becoming a water-based "leisure-pleasure zone", "a new Venice in London" (they were not to know of the nascent plans for the very different finance, property and retail redevelopment of London Docklands). For estate kids in the 1980s, in a way it was already – as Jimmy Yorke and Kim reported, it was common for groups of children, taking advantage of the docks' closure, to go swimming in nearby Poplar Docks.[32]

Granted, glamourous individuals and couples are not in short supply in *today's* graphic rendering of new housing developments, including on the hoardings surrounding the emerging Blackwall Reach, but these images serve a quite different role. They present not a dissonant and utopian over-coming of working-class grind within a working-class estate, but index and mask the *expulsion* of working-class communities from the developments in construction – the utopia, if you will, of revanchist urbanism.

Ten years after *Golden Lane: Street Deck*, the Smithsons diagrammed the Manisty Street scheme (1962–1964), the first iteration of Robin Hood Gardens, for a smaller area of the same site (Figure 5.4). Now it is Twiggy, the 1960s model and pop-cultural icon, who figures the playful and dissonant quality of the image, though she is diminished in prominence, compared to Monroe and Di Maggio, to the same size as the other figures, who are walking the garden and street decks with a more everyday air to them, plausible inhabitants of the scheme. Twiggy perches, reading a book, on a mound. The mound bears a mysterious quality, reminiscent of a flying saucer perhaps, but I will discuss the mound later. It is notable that here the street decks are not on the exterior elevation, as at Robin Hood Gardens, but face the garden. Crucially, what is also being figured here is *openness* – the *air* or *sky* of the

Figure 5.4 Collage of Manisty Street. (Peter Smithson, 1963. Smithson Family Collection)

streets in the sky. Looking back at *Golden Lane: Street Deck*, this figuration is apparent there too, the street deck's ceiling and ground rendered as empty expanses of paper, "light and airy, an almost nothing", and taking over much of the collage.[33] It is evident also in the expanse of sky in the Gérard Philipe collage, and signalled in the caption when it is included in *Ordinariness and Light*: "Golden Lane, vignette patterns of life and sky".[34]

When it comes to diagramming the streets at Robin Hood Gardens proper, the Smithsons drew out another quality through a set of four collages of street decks in the west and east blocks (Figures 5.5 and 5.6). On one side of each collage is a sectional drawing of a maisonette, with a portion of street deck and three figures at the centre. There are no celebrities, now that the image approximates to the built form. The apartments are emptied out to their pure lines, but on the other side of the images, the sky is not a voided expanse, as was the sky in the street decks diagrammed earlier, but a photograph of the views, the impressive visual scenes that were so characteristic of the street decks' built form. There is a greater realism,

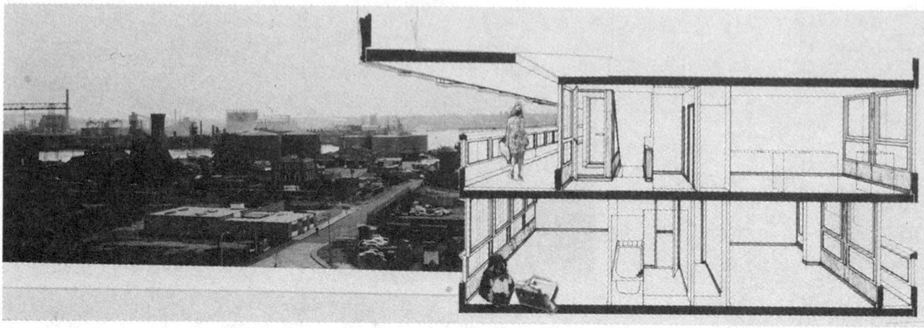

Figure 5.5 Collage of east-block street deck and maisonette no. 210, looking south towards the Thames. (Peter Smithson and Christopher Woodward, 1971–1972. Smithson Family Collection)

Figure 5.6 Collage of west-block street deck and maisonette no. 96, with Cotton Street leading south towards the Isle of Dogs. (Peter Smithson and Christopher Woodward, 1971–1972. Smithson Family Collection)

then. Indeed, the photographs were taken from the decks themselves, montaged with the earlier project diagrams. Yet the collages should not be thought of as mere representation. The diagrammatic function of figuring form is still in play, not so much in the content of the view, but in how this content evokes a *sense* of view, and a sense, which the use of photography facilitates, of elevation, of being *in* the sky.

In moving through the various diagrams of the Smithsons' streets, from *Urban Re-Identification* to these street deck collages, it is apparent that diagram and built actuality have become progressively closer together, with these last diagrams now approximating in all essential features to the street decks as built. I do not want to suggest, though, that these four *supersede* their antecedents. Rather, the most adequate diagram of the streets in the sky is the set of diagrams *as a whole*, held together in their resemblances, differences and shifting relationships to each other – much like the parts of a Klee painting. And neither do the final diagrams institute a closure or completion of the diagrammatic function. The set of diagrams *are* realized in built form, but they also accompany the scheme as *ongoing* galvanizing models, pressures on the imagination to evoke new configurations of social space. They are rivals, in this sense, to the closure that inheres in the reactionary images that cling to the estate (notably Charles Jencks' ersatz street deck "mugging", discussed in Chapter 3). Perhaps they take on especial significance today, when, having assisted in bringing the estate into form, they endure after its demolition.

To help avoid a sense of culmination in the street deck collages, my last example, one of the most curious of the Smithsons' diagrams of Robin Hood Gardens, pulls back to a more abstract figurative space. Titled *Visual Connections of the People to their District*, it is a pen-line sketch of the sightlines of the whole scheme, centred around the estate's "stress-free zone", where qualities of openness and view are figured together (Figure 5.7).[35] Stylistically influenced by Louis Kahn's 1952 diagram of Philadelphia traffic movement, the site is here demarcated by its pedestrian and automotive connectivity. Icons for eyes are distributed across the estate, with their sight lines connecting to ten or so built features of the neighbourhood, near and far, including ships routing around the Isle of Dogs, Brunswick Power Station, East India Dock and Poplar's All Saint's Church. But what is so striking is that, though the possibility of obtaining these views is created by the built forms of the estate, the buildings themselves are entirely absent. This is a diagram of the sensory qualities of openness and view that are so significant to the scheme that the architecture by which they are enabled falls away.

Diagrammatic Photography

I want to conclude the chapter by revising Jameson's division and preference for diagrams over the "bad" reification of architectural photography. Already, the street deck collages have shown us how photography can

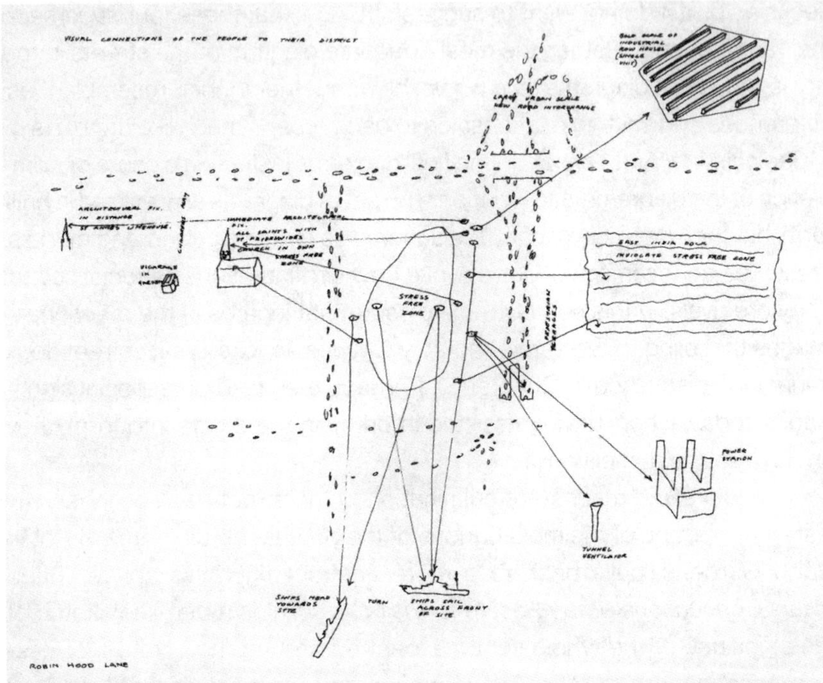

Figure 5.7 *Visual Connections of the People to their District*. (Alison Smithson, date unknown. Smithson Family Collection)

take a diagrammatic form, where it eschews formal unity to take part in the diagrams' grappling with the problem-form of the street in the sky. But photographs can also, in themselves, have a diagrammatic function.

This is evident, first of all, in the Smithsons' practice of photographing the finished estate *in fragments*. The approach is invited by the topological form of Robin Hood Gardens, this building of different parts and processes, a quality lost when attempts are made to photograph it as a coherent whole. The approach is also informed by the Smithsons' experimental use of the photographic image in *Parallel of Life and Art* (1953), their ICA exhibition with Henderson and Paolozzi, which Banham calls the "locus classicus" of New Brutalism.[36] Here a multitude of images of wildly diverse content expanded the visual field through distorting techniques of enlargement, close-up and fragmentation. Culled from newspapers, magazines and scientific and anthropological textbooks, among other sources, and derived from such means as aerial photography, X-rays and micrographs, the effect of these images was to render process and pattern against integrated form.

Photographs of fragments of Robin Hood Gardens appear in the Smithsons' 1982 book *The Shift*, including a view through a street-deck window of part of an apartment interior and out again onto the stress-free zone and mound, the opposing block just visible, as is a slight reflection of the photographer, Peter Smithson.[37] The same page carries two near-identical photographs of a three-floor section of an exterior façade of the estate, with expanse of sky above, shot from Cotton Street with a tree in the foreground – the tree bare in the winter scene and, in the second image, crowding out the building with spring-time blossom. *The Shift* includes also a low-angle, child-height photograph through long grass of play-pit climbing frames and an internal façade of the estate, and another of the mound at an angle that accentuates its contour and commanding presence. What these fragment photographs share is that they each figure a particular formal quality of Robin Hood Gardens, all the more vital for being partial, for excluding the whole. That these images are, in the main, amateur photographs gives them an additional quality of forms as found, seemingly taken while immersed in the flow of the estate.

Robin Hood Gardens was also photographed professionally for the Smithsons, by the photographer Sandra Lousada, shortly after the estate opened. Lousada, who was the unofficial photographer of Team 10 meetings, was accompanied by Peter Smithson as the two walked the grounds and the street decks, ascended nearby Balfron Tower for the long shots and visited residents' apartments.[38] Twenty or so of these images are included in the scheme's publication in *Architectural Design*.[39] They showcase the extraordinary architecture, as was their purpose, some foregrounding the sculptural and breathtakingly monumental quality of the structure. But in many of the photographs it is the estate's residents who take centre stage (in stark contrast to the publication of the Smithsons' school at Hunstanton in the 1950s, which the architects insisted, somewhat scandalously, be photographed without people and furniture). There are shots of a mother and toddler at home in their living room, adults and children about on the street decks, clothes drying on a washing line. The most striking photographs, though, are of children, visibly multi-racial, playing in the garden and play-pits, clambering over the mound, chatting, hanging out, running towards the photographer – all

Figure 5.8 Children playing on the estate's mound. (Sandra Lousada, 1971. Smithson Family Collection)

Figure 5.9 Children playing in the garden and one of the play-pits. (Sandra Lousada, 1971. Smithson Family Collection)

framed, without contradiction, by the monumental expanse of the east block (Figures 5.8 and 5.9).[40] Here the spontaneity and joy that were first expressed in Henderson's Bow photographs figure the scheme *as built* – the end of a process that was also a beginning, evoking the ever-renewed beginning that is the enlivening and extension of form through inhabitation.

We are so accustomed to the austere and unpopulated architectural photographs of Brutalist buildings that it seems positively *un*-Brutalist to photograph Robin Hood Gardens this way. Yet, along with collage and fragmentation, *this* is the more Brutalist approach to architectural photography. Against photographic reification, these images figure the extension of form into lived experience. It is not a diminishing of the architecture, or its humanization – the unhomely sculptural expanse of the estate is fully a part of these images – but the appropriation of architectural form in and as living process, open, like a diagram, to its virtuality.

Notes

1 M. Christine Boyer, *Not Quite Architecture: Writing around Alison and Peter Smithson* (Cambridge, MA and London: MIT Press, 2017), 393.
2 Rayner Banham, "The New Brutalism", *October* 136 (2011 [orig. December 1955]): 28.
3 Peter Cook, "Regarding the Smithsons", in *Alison and Peter Smithson: A Critical Anthology*, ed. Max Risselada (Barcelona: Ediciones Polígrafa, 2011), 294.
4 Alpa Depani, "Gone in Forty Seconds", *CLOG: Brutalism* (2013): 162–163, 163.
5 Fredric Jameson, *Postmodernism: Or, the Cultural Logic of Late Capitalism* (London: Verso, 1991), 124–125.
6 *Ibid.*, 122.
7 *Ibid.*, 125.
8 *Ibid.*, 124.
9 *Ibid.*, 122.
10 Gilles Châtelet, *Figuring Space: Philosophy, Mathematics, and Physics*, trans. Robert Shore and Muriel Zagha (Dordrecht: Kluwer Academic, 2000), 10.
11 This is a point made by Deleuze in description of the diagrammatic technique of the painter Francis Bacon. Bacon's random spurts of paint, his scrubbing, rubbing and wiping out of zones in the painting with a rag, stick, brush or sponge create a "graph" (Bacon) or "diagram" (Deleuze). It serves to clear the canvas of the pre-existing figurative clichés that would otherwise crowd out the painting's emerging figure, a figure that emerges from this procedure in an involuntary way. Gilles Deleuze, *Francis Bacon: The Logic of Sensation*, trans. Daniel W. Smith (London and New York: Continuum, 2003).
12 Gilles Châtelet, *Figuring Space,* 79, 10, 9.
13 *Ibid.*, 9.
14 If the diagram "immobilizes a gesture in order to set down an operation, it does so by sketching a gesture that then cuts out another. The dotted line refers neither to the point and its discrete destination, nor to the line and its continuous trace, but to the pressure of the *virtuality* ... that worries the already available image in order to create space for a new dimension: the diagram's mode of existence is such that its genesis is comprised in its being." *Ibid.*, 10, emphasis added.
15 Alison Smithson, "Louis Kahn: Invitation to Otterlo, Graphics of Movement", unpublished, cited in Boyer, *Not Quite Architecture*, 77.

16 David Sylvester, "Klee – I" [orig. "Auguries of Experience", 1948], *About Modern Art: Critical Essays 1948–97* (London: Pimlico, 1997), 35.
17 Paul Klee, *Pedagogical Sketchbook*, introduction and trans. Sibyl Moholy-Nagy (London: Faber and Faber, 1968), 16; Sylvester, "Klee – I", 35.
18 David Sylvester, "Klee – II" [orig. "Paul Klee. La Période de Berne"], *About Modern Art: Critical Essays 1948–97* (London: Pimlico, 1997), 37, 43.
19 The inspiration for Nehru's presence was perhaps his contemporaneous enthusiasm for Le Corbusier's Chandigarh, which he commissioned in 1950 as the new capital city of Punjab.
20 *Ibid.*, 39.
21 *Ibid.*, 39, 43.
22 Ben van Berkel and Caroline Bos, "Diagrams: Interactive Instruments in Operation", in *This Is Not Architecture*, ed. Kester Rattenbury (London: Routledge, 2002), 104–105.
23 Alison and Peter Smithson, *The Charged Void: Architecture* (New York: The Monacelli Press, 2001), 37.
24 Johan Huizinga, *Homo Ludens*, cited in Dirk van den Heuvel, "Team 10 Riddles: A Few Notes on Mythopoesis, Discourse, and Epistemology", in *Team 10: Keeping the Language of Modern Architecture Alive*, ed. Max Risselada, Dirk van den Heuvel and Gijs de Waal (Delft: Delft University, 2006), 97, emphasis added.
25 Boyer, *Not Quite Architecture*, 87, first emphasis added.
26 Van den Heuvel conveys the significance, style and volition of the Smithsons' figurative wordplay thus: "The concatenations of words overlap, they are sometimes interchangeable and sometimes not. ... [T]he game of words and wordplay were part and parcel of the practice of Alison and Peter Smithson and their peers: to mark their own position, to outwit their adversaries, capture the mood of the day, grasp the problems they faced, or to regenerate the tradition they sought to continue." Dirk van den Heuvel, *Alison and Peter Smithson: A Brutalist Story Involving the House, the City and the Everyday*, unpublished PhD thesis (Delft University of Technology, 2003), 25–26.
27 Huizinga again: "The eternal gulf between being and idea can only be bridged by the rainbow of imagination." Van den Heuvel, "Team 10 Riddles", 97.
28 Banham, "The New Brutalism", 27.
29 *Ibid.*
30 Ben Highmore, *The Art of Brutalism: Rescuing Hope from Catastrophe in 1950s Britain* (New Haven, CT and London: Yale University Press, 2017), 93, 90.
31 Alison and Peter Smithson, *Ordinariness and Light: Urban Theories 1952–1960 and their Application in a Building Project 1963–1970* (London: Faber and Faber, 1970), 82. For critique of the automation thesis, see Aaron Benanav, *Automation and the Future of Work* (London: Verso, 2020).
32 Alison Smithson in *The Smithsons on Housing*, dir. B. S. Johnson (BBC, 1970), available on YouTube. Jimmy York, interview, 23 July 2014 and Kim, interview, 28 August 2015.
33 Highmore, *The Art of Brutalism*, 89.
34 Smithson and Smithson, *Ordinariness and Light*, 58.
35 The date is unknown but it was certainly a working diagram, since the East India Dock, on the right, was filled in before the east-block construction reached the fifth floor, and the estate is identified here as Robin Hood Lane, as it was known during construction.
36 Banham, "The New Brutalism", 21.
37 Alison and Peter Smithson, *The Shift* (London: Academy Editions, 1982), 35.

38 Sandra Lousada, interview, 23 November 2015.

39 Alison and Peter Smithson, "Robin Hood Gardens London E14", *Architectural Design* 42 no. 9 (1972): 559–572.

40 The children take such a prominent place and dynamic role in the photographs that one might mistakenly think there was some direction involved. Lousada recounted to me a recent conversation with a student who had discussed these photographs with peers: "They said, how did you place them? I said, for goodness sake, they were playing!" I was interested if Peter Smithson had organized any aspects of the shoot. "There were certain views he wanted", but otherwise, "No, he didn't. It was: see what happened, get what you can. I just went with a camera, I didn't have tripods and lights and things like that. Of course I worked with an entourage later on, but not at that moment. When you go with an architect or sculptor or artist they start talking and it's a way of understanding what they do, and once you begin to understand what you're looking at, you photograph accordingly." Sandra Lousada, interview, 23 November 2015.

6

Beyond *Béton Brut*: Concrete, Mass and Repetition

We can use repetition as Bernini did, turn it off and on, change gear with it so to speak – it is not something to be fought against.

Peter Smithson, "Simple Thoughts on Repetition"

The exterior of a house should not reflect its interior; it should constitute a source of poetic sensation for the observer.

Asger Jorn, "Image and Form"

Materials do not immediately bespeak social relations. Yet concrete, a strange and amorphous material – actually, a composite of materials – has often been called upon to articulate, in registers both affirmative and stigmatizing, the social relations of class. In his *Concrete and Culture*, for example, Adrian Forty remarks on the close association of reinforced concrete with the politics and imaginary of twentieth-century socialism, due to its centrality to Soviet and municipal building programmes, but also to its role as metaphor of the collective bond of class. "Cement is us, comrades – the working class", writes Fyodor Gladkov in his socialist-realist novel *Cement* (1925).[1] Powerful as such metaphoric articulations of concrete and class can be, they present much scope for reductive interpretation, where the imposition of social meaning evacuates concrete of its particular materiality and delimits its meanings to a restricted set of tropes, variously emancipatory, progressive or reactionary.

This chapter seeks to avoid these pitfalls, developing a class aesthetics of concrete through its materiality, its expressive qualities and particular capacities, as found at Robin Hood Gardens. The chapter asks of this material at this site, "what can it do?"[2] Approaching the concrete of Robin Hood Gardens as an entanglement of matter and society, aesthetic and ethic, I explore here a Brutalist expressivity of concrete that is released from its tether to *béton brut*, the raw concrete from whence the movement's name. Instead, the qualities and capacities of concrete emerge through the particular problem of *mass*, a problem raised by mass housing, mass that is expressed in the *industrial scale* and the *repetition and difference* of the estate's concrete structures and surfaces.

Class Concrete

Certain class qualities of concrete are central to Charles Jencks' antipathetic verdict on Robin Hood Gardens, where the scheme's use of "homogeneous" concrete, as he puts it, signified "social deprivation" and "council housing" – a most unwholesome trinity.[3] The Smithsons also approached concrete as integral to council housing, but for them it was the means for an expressive materiality which drew from the class experience of massification and industry. In broad terms, steel-reinforced concrete provided a practicable means for mass housing. Mass housing was a driver of post-war modernism, inherited by Team 10 – building "for the anonymous collective", with "issues of habitat and *le plus grand nombre* as the key questions for architects".[4] In the Smithsons' words, "The term Mass Housing applies to all dwellings not built to the special order of an individual: houses over which the occupier has no control other than that he has chosen or has been chosen, to live there: houses for which therefore, the architect has a peculiar responsibility."[5] This was a question of capacity and supply, certainly, but for Team 10 the non-individualized, mass character of this working-class housing was also articulated *aesthetically*, in concrete.

Brutalism is iconically characterized by wood-shuttered concrete cast in situ, the timber-grain impression presenting the quintessential as-found aesthetic of raw concrete. It is one of the paradoxes of Brutalism that concrete is celebrated for such raw material qualities when in fact it has no raw state as such, just composites – cement, sand, gravel and water – and is only "'rendered plastic' through complex chains of operations prior, during and often after casting", as Katie Lloyd Thomas puts it.[6] Concrete's as-found material properties do not, then, precede its technical, chemical and aesthetic handling. This at first seems confounding, but it actually aids in appreciating the *immanence* of the Brutalist approach to materiality. In facing up to concrete's absence of a raw, pre-formed state, a truly as-found approach to concrete demands that concrete be appreciated and handled in terms of the processes, qualities, capacities, variations, limits and tipping points that arise in the numerous chemical and technical operations of its manufacture, casting, curing and ageing. Concrete helps us break, in other words, with the hylomorphic matter–form schema, which approaches matter as base and inert, shaped by active imposed form.

However, in the Brutalist aesthetic of timber-grain impression, the hylomorphic schema can creep back in. Denys Lasdun's National Theatre (1967–1976), glorious though it is, can illustrate the point. Here it took great technical effort, and associated financial cost, to produce adequate timber-grain impression across the concrete's surface, to persistently achieve this effect and not another.[7] This is not a problem in itself for the as-found aesthetic, since all working with matter will necessarily "edit and censor" its numerous capacities and contingencies, the "variegations, behaviours and historical singularities the material might otherwise exhibit".[8] But the act of editing can be hidden – and hence a sense of the potential for multiple *alternative* edits – by the generalization of one edit into a movement-defining style, especially when the style is seemingly so elemental and timeless as timber-shuttering. Moreover, insofar as here it is the timber impression *of the form-giving mould* that is made visible, at the expense of concrete's other and more contingent traits (its tendency to pit and fissure, or for its aggregate to reveal during pouring and setting), the hylomorphic schema is all too easily recharged, "concrete appear[ing] as amorphous matter that can be formed perfectly into the orthogonal shapes described by the architect's modernist concept".[9]

In any case, at Robin Hood Gardens, the Smithsons employed a different method, its structure fashioned not in timber-shuttering but in the industrial concrete of slab-block system-building (Figure 6.1).[10] Poured, in-situ concrete was the intended construction technique for the scheme, but the engineers, Ove Arup and Partners, felt the size of the structure and extent of repetition made it more suited to an industrial system of prefabricated concrete panels, choosing the Swedish SUNDH system, licensed locally to Walter Lawrence and Son Ltd., which became the lead contractor.[11] The panels were prefabricated on site, while the façade components, the mullions and balustrades which required greater precision, were cast offsite by the firm

Figure 6.1 Jo Newman-Stackable, in front of her east-block home. (Kois Miah, May 2016)

Girlings' Ferro-Concrete Ltd.[12] The scheme did actually include significant amounts of in-situ concrete: in the foundations up to ground-level; in the cranked joint sections; and in the head, neck and tail sections, where the extent of variation made prefabrication unsuitable. Indeed, a whole section of the northern end of the west block, after the second crank, was cast in situ, due to awkward access for the panel-lifting crane. Amusingly for a Brutalist scheme (the Smithsons call it a "surprise"), these in-situ components were cast using plastic-faced shuttering so as *not* to reveal the timber impression, and thus obtain the same finish as the slab-block components (Figure 6.2).[13]

None of this is to say the estate lacked attention to the expressive traits and qualities of concrete. There was a deliberate contrast of exposed aggregate on the street deck balustrades and marble-smooth finish at the doorframes, a softening at the domestic threshold. Both had an appealing texture – the balustrades in particular, with their slightly pebbled feel to the touch, though the "straw"-colour, almost "golden hue" that Fitzgerald recalled of the building in the 1980s was in later years only achieved when cast in a late-afternoon sun.[14] The concrete was originally complemented with a colour scheme applied to the lift lobbies, the apartment doors, the frames of the deck-facing triangular windows and the French doors on the

Figure 6.2 Northern "tail" of the west block, in-situ concrete in the guise of system-build. (Kois Miah, June 2015)

garden façades – grey at garage level, green at the garden and ascending with each floor through yellow, orange and blue (in the taller block), with variants of these colours picking out different flat types. The street deck soffits, which later became cluttered with pipes and wiring, were originally finished in white gloss.[15] These concrete textures and colours were part of the Smithsons' sensory approach to the scheme, which one should "smell, feel and experience" through the "full range of senses".[16] However, far more significant to the scheme's sensory form was its handling of concrete's industrial capacities, what Peter Smithson called a "machine-scale ... aesthetics of pre-cast concrete".[17]

It is a feature Peter isolates in the same 1959 interview that saw him champion architecture's confrontation with "what is going on" in society, and where he and Alison were already turning against the mere stylistic fixation on wood-shuttered concrete. The classical machine aesthetic of 1920s modernism produced buildings to look *as if* made by machines, "single object[s], turned out on a lathe, colored-up and so on".[18] Le Corbusier's Villa Savoye (1928–1931) and Villa Stein-de-Monzie (1926) are the given examples. They mimicked in the realm of architecture the industrial production of distinct and integrated objects. The Brutalist departure, Peter Smithson proposes, is a *genuine* machine aesthetic which expresses the real industrial production of a building, not as a single object but as an assemblage of complex parts at an industrial scale: "If a thing is really made of pre-cast elements, or concrete blocks, the building has to reflect the way it was built with pre-cast elements or concrete blocks, and inevitably the building will not only have a different scale from an architecture that is conceived of as being a single object made by a machine, *but it will be built at the scale of the genuine machine with which it was built*."[19] What precisely, though, is being expressed here? What is the "rough poetry" that is dragged out from pre-cast, industrial concrete? Turning now to pick out the features of this aesthetic, we find that there are pronounced class dimensions.

Mass and Scale

As much as Peter Smithson's statement above is a break with International Style modernism, it breaks also with the municipal style of New Empiricism, influential in the New Towns but feeding also into the inner city, including Poplar's Lansbury estate.[20] With its "People's Detailing", as the Brutalists disparaged it, nodding to its popularity among Communist Party members in the London City Council (LCC), this was a softened, folksy and nostalgic modernism, where an ersatz image of class identity served as cover and pseudo-rationale for the destruction of inner-city working-class social fabrics.[21] To instead take the industrial machine as the image for a mass-housing aesthetic was to *face up to* the transformations of social life intrinsic to capitalist industry, urbanism and crisis. These transformations have destroyed older forms of community; they are not chosen from within but cleave and buffet from without. Yet they were the conditions upon which something new might emerge – in contrast to the sentimentality and simulated nature of folksy imaginings of the working class, divorced from real experience.

It seemed to me that Robin Hood Gardens' resident Touris Miah articulated something of this industrial aesthetic when, taking in the view from a west-block street deck, he declared with some pride: "This building is one of a kind. Have you seen anything like it around here? There's nothing like its *scale*" (Figure 6.3).[22] The scale was an imposing *jolt* to the senses. It is another dimension of the Brutalist unhomely, though now characterized less

Figure 6.3 Touris Miah, in a lift lobby of the west block. (Kois Miah, April 2015)

by a *threshold* with the homely than by a marked *difference*: "the uncomfortable distance between an everyday world and the undeniable drama of the buildings 'themselves'", as Stephen Zepke puts it, where "the architecture establishes this distance as one of its own conditions" (Figure 6.4).[23] This unsettling scale had significant appeal to other residents of the estate. For Motiur Rahman, who remembers his first impression as a nine-year-old: "You know, it has its gritty side, but I didn't sense that when I first saw it – I was just wowed by the vastness." Asked if he found the building exciting, imposing or ugly, he replied: "It is imposing, it is also ugly, and in a weird way that is the beauty of it, the attraction of it. There are so many buildings that are not to like now. You look at the buildings springing up, they are so 'plasticky' or 'glassy' or just all the 'samey,' but Robin Hood Gardens was unique."[24] Fitzgerald, when asked his views of the designs of the first Blackwall Reach buildings, also contrasted their insubstantial qualities to Robin Hood Gardens: "Oh, frightful – so unimaginative. ... I like strong definitions, even if it's brutal! I want something you can get your teeth into or your hands on, not something you go to touch and, 'Oh, it's an apparition!' I want something you can respect and look at."[25]

Darren Pauling enjoyed the "tactile" quality of the architecture. "When you touch it, it feels strong", unlike the new buildings "that don't look as if they

Figure 6.4 Lift-tower tail of the east block. (Nicholas Thoburn, October 2014)

Figure 6.5 Garden-facing façade of the east block. (Kois Miah, May 2016)

are built to last", but "with some future destruction date" in mind. Kevin Jones, who lived in the west block for two-and-a-half years as a property guardian, had a favourite view of the estate: the sheer wall of the east-block inner façade, which greeted him as he opened his ground-floor door, "this giant block with all these windows – really beautiful" (Figure 6.5). The estate was "built on such an epic scale", he said. "I admire it because of that boldness, and that, you know, it was made for social housing. That is incredible really, the imagination and creativity that has gone into it."[26]

Repetition and Difference

The estate's mass aesthetic of industrial concrete was not only a question of scale, however, but was manifest also within the industrial process of *repetition*. It is a theme taken up in Peter Smithson's essay "Simple Thoughts on Repetition", published in *Architectural Design* as Robin Hood Gardens neared completion. That his concern is with *industrial* repetition, and with its *aesthetic* potential, is signalled in the essay's opening observation: "We seem to have lost the secret of repetition as a formal quality at a time when we use it the most."[27] Quite so. With regard to mass housing, industrial repetition is typically treated with hostility – or hostility towards mass housing is disguised and justified as hostility to repetition. Jencks' response to Robin Hood Gardens is typical in this regard, where "repetitive pattern" joins "concrete" as signifier of council housing qua social deprivation. Jencks picks up on the asymmetrical, fin-like mullions that vertically strode the façades of the estate, one of its most distinctive and unusual features, but contends that they "are not strong enough to identify each apartment" or to "override the repetitive pattern and homogeneous material".[28] Yet this misses the point. Variation in the mullions was not designed to break-up or oppose repetition, but to be an *intrinsic quality* of it.

Uniform in shape, a "T" pattern in cross-section, the mullions varied in width, depth and length (Figure 6.6). Some ran the full height of the façades, others only the height of the balustrades, with the rest at various lengths in between. Some protruded as much as a foot-and-a-half, the others held close to their supporting structure. This variation was enabled by mass production of unit parts, the industrial process whereby repetition in the hundreds is enough to write off the cost of jigs, dies and moulds. It frees up a capacity for repetition hitherto unknown, and with it *difference*. "Looked at this way", Smithson continues, "we have incredible means available to us. With these numbers we can use repetition as Bernini did, turn it off and on, change gear with it so to speak – it is not something to be fought against."[29] As such, the Smithsons saw difference or variation as the *essence* of repetition, an understanding that they shared with Deleuze, whose seminal book on the topic, *Difference and Repetition*, was published the year work commenced on Robin Hood Gardens.

Difference is not found in an array of unique identities, as is the liberal model of individuality, nor is the point that an original form is repeated, what we call standardization, the aesthetic position to which the working class is usually assigned. Instead, difference is a quality *proper to mass or serial phenomena*, where the repeated elements gain both consistency and variation *in the process* of repetition. This is "Repetition as a quality in itself", where "elements seem to gain their meaning only in repetition, i.e. were not preconceived or designed in the abstract as 'one' and then repeated".[30] A mass phenomena, this "self-differing repetition", as Zepke puts it, repetition without an original form, is also *affirmative*, a quality of life itself.[31] In the Smithsons'

Figure 6.6 Over the edge of a street deck on the west block, showing the balustrade, mullions and garage moat. (Nicholas Thoburn, September 2015)

words, "repetition is life-including, ... it can make the multiplied thing magical in its very multiplication".[32]

It is to the scale of Robin Hood Gardens as a whole that repetition pertains – "big-scaled repetition", Peter Smithson calls it.[33] The mullions pick up on and accentuate the vertical partitions of the individual apartments behind the buildings' surfaces – though not to firmly demarcate them, to reduce repetition to the identity of a domestic unit. Rather, the mullions incorporate the homes in their process of repetition and difference, where the mass character of the apartments, themselves various in type and displayed as such by the placement of the mullions, is connected to rhythmic variation across the surface of the whole. This is a type of surface the Smithsons call a "skin modulation", and, as this phrase suggests, the surfaces of these buildings are also *distinct* from the interior shape of the apartments.[34] It is a quality that can be approached in terms of class and racialization.

In the architectural organicism that Charles L. Davis has shown to be integral to International Style modernism, exterior surface was to reflect interior form, so creating an organic whole through which nativist and racializing national character was to be reflected and fashioned in architecture – an *architectural* physiognomy analogous to a racial one.[35] This, Davis argues, was a leading feature of theories and designs in US public housing in the interwar period, wherein the putatively deficient racial character of working-class whites, recent European immigrants especially, was to be checked and reshaped in the national image – morally cleansed, hard-working, monolingual and aspirationally middle-class.[36] By contrast, at Robin Hood Gardens, whose class architecture wards off such nativist formulations of working-class identity, the surface was released from the organicist requirement to consolidate an interior whole – to consolidate a *human* form at all – and instead took on distinct qualities of its own, abstract, rhythmic, sensory.[37] In a 1954 critique of functionalist modernism, the artist Asger Jorn wrote: "The exterior of a house should not reflect its interior; it should constitute a source of poetic sensation for the observer."[38] I suggest that at Robin Hood Gardens the Smithsons concurred.

The rhythmic variation of the scheme's surfaces, its skin modulation, works not through its industrial components alone, but also in connection with another mass phenomena, the estate's *environment*, where we see again the scheme's unhomely coupling with its outside. The mullions are "bridging elements", in Alison Smithson's late description of the role of architectural protrusions.[39] They work at the threshold of the building and its outside, "at play in the air, performing a role of claiming, signalling", as built form passes into its "adherent air". Indeed, it was an environmental factor that precipitated the design of the mullions in the first place, one of the numerous architectural interventions in the soundscape of the site, intended in this instance to disrupt ambient noise from sweeping across the estate's façades.[40]

It is how the mullions played with the environmental quality of *light*, however, that created their most striking surface effects. "Sun-responsive building forms", they cast extraordinary patterns across the blocks as their shapes and shadows came in and out of accentuation through the course of the sun's arc, the sun drawn in through the wide opening between the buildings at their southern end.[41] It was a quality I enjoyed on many of my visits, various over the seasons. The effect of the mid-morning sun on the west block's garden façade, best experienced while walking its cranked length, was especially impressive (Figure 6.7). Here the "combined play of light and perspective makes all parts different", as the Smithsons wrote of repetition in aqueducts, amphitheatres and viaducts, "much as a field's form can be better seen and enjoyed when the plough reveals the form of its surface through the play of light on the regular repetitive furrows".[42]

This light-enfolding surface could not be more different to the joyless cladding used at Blackwall Reach, the successor to Robin Hood Gardens, comprised of bolted-on panels of inch-thick slices of brick, known as *brick slip*. It is the surface dictated by the so-called "new London vernacular" that was dreamt up under Boris Johnson's mayoralty and has since proliferated across London's new-build skyline.[43] The purpose for Johnson was to disguise the flood of speculative property development with an aesthetic that

Figure 6.7 Mullions as sun-responsive forms, on the west-block garden façade. (Nicholas Thoburn, October 2015)

is improbably claimed to bear Georgian stylistic preferences. It is said to be tenure-blind, and thus reduce the stigmatization of social housing. In reality, though, any tenure-blindness that is achieved is the aesthetic correlate of the drive to demolish and privatize council housing, rendering social housing invisible to the eye all the better to render it absent in actuality.[44] Fake-brick cladding – there could not be a greater revenge on the expressive materiality of Robin Hood Gardens, nor a more appropriate aesthetic, dull and mendacious, for London's property industry.

Appurtenances and a Pair

Staying with the rhythmic repetition of the estate's surface, in the Smithsons' book *The Shift* they group together the mullions of Robin Hood Gardens with the oak trellis that layers their contemporaneous student dormitory at St Hilda's College, Oxford University (1970). By their skin modulation, both buildings "seemed to offer themselves in various sorts of ways for the contribution of the seasons", a point I have indicated already.[45] Unlike at Robin Hood Gardens, however, the trellis at St Hilda's sought to encourage and support the growth of plant life, conferring, along with its timber construction, a softer, more organic quality to the scheme. For Owen Hatherley, the contrast begs a class question of the Smithsons' different priorities for these two examples of domestic architecture: "Social housing was to be raw and powerful, Oxford colleges tame and retiring. There's nothing necessarily wrong with this – which should inspire more pride? – but the residents of Robin Hood Gardens were given no trellises to invite greenery across the streets in the sky."[46] The image Hatherley puts in mind here of trellises and foliage complementing the concrete façades of the Poplar scheme is appealing, as it is achieved at the Barbican for example. But as he recognizes, it would have required a degree of maintenance that one cannot picture of the local authority, and the Smithsons knew full well the limits of municipal budgets.

I would instead point to a different out-growth on the estate's façades, perverse though this may sound: the television satellite dish (Figure 6.8). The scheme's qualities of protrusion, adherent air and bridging are such that residents' satellite dishes complimented rather than embarrassed the built form, as flows of communication joined its surface modulation of light and sound. Alison Smithson made some remarks in this direction, referring

Figure 6.8 Satellite dishes on the east-block external façade. (Nicholas Thoburn, January 2022)

to the architects' unbuilt design for infill apartments at Maryhill, Glasgow (1984), which included prominent solar-capture "roses", reaching into the sky above the roofs from masts attached to the upper-floor façades. The "fibril" nature of these "appurtenances", she wrote, "make them more the building's *antennae*; like sensors, indicative of how the building's form, skin, and services, are responsive to the climate, to communications, to our *green* attitudes".[47] At Robin Hood Gardens the appurtenances in question were not designed or theorized by architects but attached ad hoc by residents, or by Sky engineers, bolted onto the mullions outside of kitchen windows or over the edge of street deck balustrades. But in this is their significance, where the little tweaks of home-making that the Smithsons hoped for the scheme exceeded their designated places and came to contribute to the architectural surface, a skin modulation as found. It is especially pleasing that it was a modernist scheme, too often now the preserve of middle-class aesthetic preference, that elevated to architecture this most class-coded of disapproved domestic protrusions.

To end the chapter with another repetition and difference takes us from the surface to the structure of the estate, the *paired* relation of the two buildings. The component architectural features of each building were repeated in each other – street decks, mullions, heads, tails and so on. And the buildings repeated each other also in their layout of social and domestic spaces, the estate "split like a kipper" in Peter Smithsons' phrase, with decks on the exterior, street-facing façades and bedrooms and kitchens placed on the quieter, inner sides, facing the garden and opposing building. This repetition generated a strong sense of relation between the two buildings, but it was a *dynamic* relation, a relation that *differed*.

Repetition between the buildings was not a closed circuit, conferring the identity of each through mirroring the other.[48] Neither were they related as model and copy. Rather, the buildings repeated each other *in their variation*, each repeating and differing a feature of the other, the dissymmetry between them opening to the indefinite play of difference. The buildings were similar in volume, but one was taller, at ten storeys, the other longer at seven, comprising 110 and 104 apartments respectively. Both were cranked at plan, but the taller, east block only once, by 10° in the middle, serving to slightly cup the green, while the longer block was cranked twice – a third of the way along, by 10° again, but this time away from the green, then by 31° back towards its partner at the tail end. The distance between the buildings differed considerably over their length, with the northern tails more than twice the distance apart than the southern heads (though the latter were still a considerable distance apart, "to get long views out and the sun in").[49] And these differences were ramified through kinetic experience of the buildings as one moved around the estate, with the variations in perspective and the changing relation of one to the other that this produced.

It is sometimes claimed that the paired blocks, disconnected from each other and formally terminated at either end, were a curtailed and truncated version of the Smithsons' vision for mass housing, as compared to the competition entry for Golden Lane, a continuous superstructure reaching out across London, or to Jack Lynn and Ivor Smith's Park Hill complex in Sheffield, where, also continuous, the topography allows the winding street decks to connect to the ground. There are clear indications that this is incorrect, however – that the paired structure was a deliberate design choice and that any extension of the scheme would have repeated it. The estate's residents' manual, republished in *Architectural Design*, contains a small stylized diagram of the scheme's structure multiplied fourfold, each pair rotated by different angles, hinting that the paired buildings might themselves be repeated into a larger agglomeration. And this image appears in a more developed variation in *Without Rhetoric* (1973), accompanying the book's discussion of repetition and serving also as the cover illustration for the UK edition.[50] Titled *Robin Hood Gardens: Extension Diagram*, and rendered in the Smithsons' distinctive "wobbly edge" graphic style, here three sets of paired buildings are grouped together and circumscribed into three individual, and one aggregate, "areas of association", with a shop placed at the centre of the three (Figure 6.9). It is unlikely that the Smithsons thought this diagrammed agglomeration might be built – there were plans for a second stage on the remainder of the LCC-owned land, up to East India Dock Road, but this was a significantly smaller plot. As an *imagined* extension to the scheme, however, this diagram can be seen as a comment on what *was* built, setting off once again the estate's ramifying quality of repetition and difference. None of the pairs of buildings bear the shape of the built scheme, and each pair is different in their cranks, angles and relative siting, such that the process of repetition and difference is now not only between each building in a pair, but also between each pair, and between each pair and the whole.

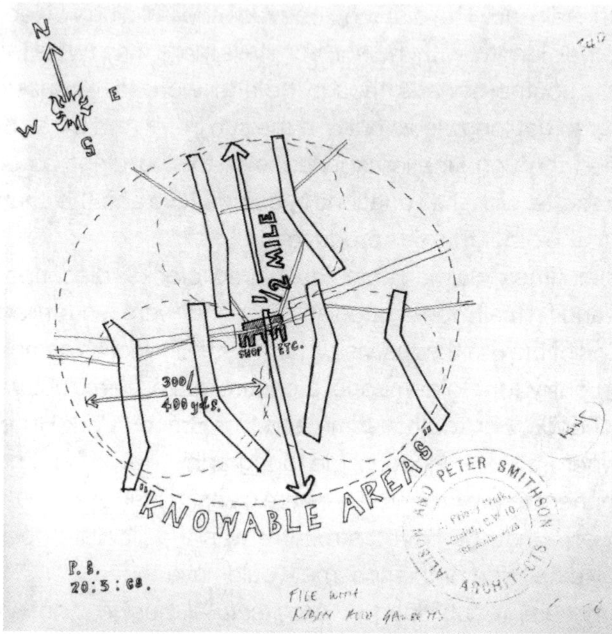

Figure 6.9 *Robin Hood Gardens: Extension Diagram*. (Peter Smithson, 1968. Smithson Family Collection)

The extension diagram is also a comment on the estate's overarching *theme*, which marks not a curtailing of, but a deliberate break with, the Smithsons' thinking from Golden Lane up to the Manisty Street stage of the Poplar scheme. In the Manisty Street design, driven by the theme of connection, the Smithsons hoped the decks "would ultimately be joined up with those of further buildings to be built when sites became available", whereas Robin Hood Gardens, as is confirmed in the extension diagram, "played down that idea of 'linkage'", establishing the scheme instead on a large and tranquil interior space of protection.[51] I turn to this interior space – the *charged void* of the green and its anomalous mound – in the next chapter.

Coda on Concrete and the Climate Crisis

Having claimed concrete for the mass aesthetics of scale and repetition, I must now stress that this association cannot hold for any *future* building. Concrete, long integral to capitalist urbanism, industry and extraction, is now known to be deeply destructive of planetary ecologies and habitable climate.[52] Concrete produces a devastating volume of greenhouse gasses – up to 2.8 billion tonnes of carbon dioxide a year, surpassed only by the total annual emissions of China and of the USA. It consumes 10% of the world's industrial water use, 75% of which is in drought and water-stressed regions. The particulate matter released in concrete manufacture and use contributes significantly to air pollution. And concrete production wrecks beaches, river courses and land masses, usually in the poorest regions, due to its consumption of colossal quantities of sand. The title of a recent article in *The Guardian* put it squarely: "Concrete: The Most Destructive Material on Earth".[53] Devastating to species life as a whole, and not only to ours, these effects are nonetheless distributed grotesquely unevenly by class, race and region.

But this is no reason to demolish the concrete structures of working-class housing estates. Quite the opposite.[54] Though the finance–housebuilding complex, including its agents in local and national government, now champions new developments on grounds of their supposed green credentials – thermal-performance cladding, green roofs, photovoltaic panels – the reality is that demolition, removal and disposal is a massive producer of carbon emissions, not least because the existent built fabrics are a major source of embodied carbon. A report commissioned by the group Architects for Social Housing in 2016 on the planned demolition of South London's Central Hill estate found that "the carbon emissions released by any deconstruction of the buildings is forty times greater than the emissions from the energy needed to carry out the demolition".[55] Then there are the huge carbon costs of manufacturing the concrete, steel and other materials for rebuild, such that 51% of the lifecycle carbon from a typical residential development is emitted before the building is even opened.[56] Yet the UK government incentivizes demolition and rebuild over refurbishment by exempting rebuild from the 20% VAT it charges on the latter.

There is an alternative, which council residents and housing movements have long demanded and Anne Lacaton and Jean-Philippe Vassal, winners of the 2021 Pritzker Architecture Prize, have shown in architectural practice. This is *renovation* instead of demolition, accompanied by a design ethics and aesthetics of sensitivity and care for the residents and concrete structures of existent working-class housing. It is not only a *social* imperative, and *cheaper*, but also the only *environmentally* acceptable engagement with these structures today.[57] In Lacaton's words, demolition "is a waste of many things – a waste of energy, a waste of material, and a waste of history. Moreover, it has a very negative social impact. For us, it is an act of violence."[58]

Notes

1 Adrian Forty, *Concrete and Culture: A Materialist History* (London: Reaktion Books, 2012), 147. The quotation is preceded: "We produce cement. Cement is a firm bond."

2 Peter Smithson, in Peter Smithson and Hans Ulrich Obrist, *Smithson Time: A Dialogue* (Köln: Walter König, 2004), 18.

3 Charles Jencks, *The New Paradigm in Architecture* (New Haven, CT and London: Yale University Press, 2002), 18.

4 Dirk van den Heuvel, *Alison and Peter Smithson: A Brutalist Story Involving the House, the City and the Everyday*, unpublished PhD thesis (Delft University of Technology, 2003), 275.

5 Alison and Peter Smithson, "Criteria for Mass Housing", in John Furse, *The Smithsons at Robin Hood Gardens*, unpublished PhD thesis (University of Sussex, 1982), 259.

6 Katie Lloyd Thomas, "Rendered Plastic by Preparation: Concrete as Constant Material", *Parallax* 21 no. 3 (2015): 277–287, 272.

7 Barnabas Calder, *Raw Concrete: The Beauty of Brutalism* (London: William Heinemann, 2016).

8 Lloyd Thomas, "Rendered Plastic by Preparation".

9 *Ibid.*, 277.

10 This mid-rise estate was built at the height of the UK's short-lived boom in system building. The boom, typically in high-rise towers, was led by Keith Joseph when both Conservative minister for housing and local government (1962–1964) and a director and major shareholder in his family's construction company. Under the corrupting influence of large construction companies, this building was characterized often by poor and inadequately tested design, over-stretched and hence shoddy labour and inadequate regulation, all of which was exposed by the Ronan Point disaster in May 1968, when a 22-storey council tower in East London progressively collapsed down one side after a gas explosion, killing four people. The collapse of Ronan Point, just as Robin Hood Gardens was about to go into construction two miles west, is the symbolic marker of the social turn against mass council housing. Stuart Hodkinson, *Safe as Houses: Private Greed, Political Negligence and Housing Policy after Grenfell* (Manchester: University of Manchester Press, 2019), 24; Miles Glendinning, *Mass Housing: Modern Architecture and State Power – A Global History* (London: Bloomsbury, 2021), 153.

11 Alison and Peter Smithson, "Robin Hood Gardens London E14", *Architectural Design* 42 no. 9 (1972): 559–572. According to Alejandra Albuerne, between 1965 and 1970 the SUNDH system was approved for 386 building projects across England and Wales before its use dropped off after 1970. Robin Hood Gardens was the third GLC-commissioned housing project to use it. Alejandra Albuerne, "Robin Hood Gardens: Reinforced Concrete Design and Construction of a Museum Artefact in Reinforced Concrete", unpublished conference paper, April 2020.

12 *Ibid.* In a late interview with Peter Smithson recorded for the British Library, he recalls some problems with the SUNDH casting, which impacted the electricity conduits and caused

subsequent trouble with cabling. He talks also about how the cranks were introduced following an initial planning rejection of the length of the west block, and notes that Alison Smithson was the lead designer of the scheme (one or the other of the couple would typically take this role). Peter Smithson, "National Life Story Collection: Architects Lives", interview by Louise Brodie, 13 of 19 (1997), https://sounds.bl.uk/Oral-history/Architects-Lives/021M-C0467X0024XX-1300V0.

13 Smithson and Smithson, "Robin Hood Gardens London E14", 560.

14 Fitzgerald, interview, 12 September 2014.

15 Alan Powers, ed., *Robin Hood Gardens: Re-Visions* (London: Twentieth Century Society, 2010), 32. Street deck views of the orange doors and the white-gloss soffit can be seen on pages 105 and 107, the former including Alison Smithson in the frame.

16 *The Smithsons on Housing*, dir. B. S. Johnson (BBC, 1970), available on YouTube.

17 Alison Smithson, Peter Smithson, Jane B. Drew and E. Maxwell Fry, "Conversation on Brutalism", *October* 136 (2011 [orig. 1959]): 45.

18 *Ibid.*, 40.

19 *Ibid.*, 39.

20 Peter Smithson remarked to Furse that Robin Hood Gardens "looks of its time" and does not have the contrived "nostalgia" of the Lansbury estate. Furse, *The Smithsons at Robin Hood*, 152.

21 This destruction was tracked at the time in Michael Young and Peter Willmott, *Family and Kinship in East London* (London: Routledge and Kegan Paul, 1957), which the Smithsons read.

22 Touris Miah, interview, 16 April 2015.

23 Stephen Zepke, *Towards a New "New Brutalism": Wandering around of Robin Hood Gardens* (Bogotá: Universidad Nacional de Colombia, forthcoming), 89.

24 Motiur Rahman, interview, 4 December 2015.

25 Fitzgerald, interview, 12 September 2014.

26 Kevin Jones, interview, 23 March 2015. Contrary to the critics of Brutalist estates like Margaret Hodge, who claim that Brutalist enthusiasts would soon lose the taste if they lived in these places, Kevin's impression of Robin Hood Gardens and its architecture moved in the opposite direction. He remarked that it is "bizarre" how his taste "totally changed" through his time living there. "I say this without any hesitation at all – by the time I left there was real sadness in me. It was definite sadness, I mean I really miss the place." This was due to his lived experience, but reading about Robin Hood Gardens and Brutalism played a role too. Other residents talked of how coming to an awareness of the estate's architectural significance impacted positively on their own views about the architecture, which were otherwise coloured by the prevalent stigmatization.

27 Peter Smithson, "Simple Thoughts on Repetition", *Architectural Design* 41 (1971): 479–481, 479.

28 Jencks, *The New Paradigm in Architecture*, 18.

29 Smithson, "Simple Thoughts on Repetition", 479.

30 *Ibid.*, 480. Deleuze makes the same point: "There is no first term which is repeated." "There is ... nothing repeated which may be isolated or abstracted from the repetition in which it was formed." Gilles Deleuze, *Difference and Repetition*, trans. Paul Patton (New York: Columbia University Press, 1994), 17.

31 Stephen Zepke, *Art as Abstract Machine: Ontology and Aesthetics in Deleuze and Guattari* (New York and London: Routledge, 2005), 35.

32 Alison and Peter Smithson, *Without Rhetoric: An Architectural Aesthetic 1955–1972* (London: Latimer, 1973), 39. They are referring here to Mies van der Rohe's housing scheme Lafayette Park (1959) in Detroit.

33 Smithson, "Simple Thoughts on Repetition", 481.

34 Alison and Peter Smithson, *The Shift* (London: Academy Editions, 1982), 66.

35 Charles L. Davis II, *Building Character: The Racial Politics of Modern Architectural Style* (Pittsburgh, PA: The University of Pittsburgh Press, 2019).

36 The crucial distinction here is with the *abject* character imputed to US Black populations, deemed *unreformable* as such. Articulated in segregationist housing policy, this had an analogue in modernist architectural theory. Davis writes: "The US housing department's official policy of racial segregation reflected the abject characteristics that modernist architects associated with black culture in modern architectural debates. European designers such as Le Corbusier simultaneously praised the primitive or instinctive genius of blacks to create the modern idiom of jazz while insisting that black Americans were too limited to engage with the rationalist principles that were required to create a modern architecture." *Ibid.*, 189.

37 This rhythmic variation was more fully achieved on the garden-facing façades, where the irregular pattern ran in all directions and incorporated the shallow depths of the horizontal escape balconies. On the road-side façades, the pattern was partially disrupted by the street decks, which took the horizontal plane for themselves and left the mullions operative more on the vertical plane. Except at the southern heads of the buildings, the mullions stopped at a level above the ground (at the first-floor escape balconies on the garden façades, and a few feet above the tarmac of the exterior moats), which served to further release the rhythmic effect of the surface.

38 Asger Jorn, "Image and Form: Against Eclectic Empiricism", in *Fraternité Avant Tout: Asger Jorn's Writing's on Art and Architecture, 1938–1958*, ed. Ruth Baumeister, trans. Paul Larkin (Rotterdam: 010 Publishers, 2011), 254–269, 259.

39 Alison Smithson, "Into the Air", in Alison and Peter Smithson, *The Space Between*, ed. Max Risselada (Köln: Walther König, 2017), 209.

40 The noise-reducing features of the estate are detailed in Smithson and Smithson, *Ordinariness and Light*, 190–191.

41 Alison and Peter Smithson, "Aspect and Prospect Responsive", in *The Charged Void: Urbanism*, ed. Chuihua Judy Chung (New York: The Monacelli Press, 2005), 244.

42 Smithson and Smithson, *Without Rhetoric*, 34.

43 Owen Hatherley, *Red Metropolis: Socialism and the Government of London* (London: Repeater Books, 2020).

44 Urban Design London, *A New London Housing Vernacular*, 2018, www.urbandesignlondon.com/documents/24/ANEWLONDONVERNACULAR_-_COMP.pdf.

45 Smithson and Smithson, *The Shift*, 66.

46 Owen Hatherley, *A New Kind of Bleak: Journeys through Urban Britain* (London: Verso, 2012), 200.

47 Smithson, "Into the Air", 209.

48 This is in contrast to a more famous two-part structure which was constructed at the same time, the Twin Towers of New York's World Trade Centre. In Jean Baudrillard's appraisal, the Trade Centre's twinned form of identical towers, each the duplicate of the other, signified the *end* of difference, the architectural expression of a monopoly capitalism that "knows how to diffract itself in equivalent variations", "to redouble itself through doubling". Jean Baudrillard,

"Symbolic Exchange and Death", in *Selected Writings*, 2nd edn, ed. Mark Poster (Stanford, CA: Stanford University Press, 2002), 143.

49 Smithson and Smithson, *Ordinariness and Light*, 189.

50 Smithson and Smithson, *Without Rhetoric*, 36.

51 Smithson and Smithson, *Ordinariness and Light*, 188, 194. The model, they note, was Gray's Inn, one of the four Inns of Court in Central London. *Ibid.*, 194.

52 As Anselm Jappe puts it in his excoriation of concrete, it "lies at the very heart of one of the core businesses of global capitalism – construction". Anselm Jappe, "Can We Cure Our Addiction to Concrete?", *Signe*, 29 May 2021, www.pavillon-arsenal.com/en/signe/11989-can-we-cure-our-addiction-to-concrete.html. See also Anselm Jappe, *Béton: Arme de construction massive du capitalisme* (Paris: L'Echappée, 2020). For all the insight of Jappe's analysis, where concrete bears the social forms and violence of capital, it has to be said that his verdict on modernist mass housing sounds alarmingly like its conservative critics. This passage gives a flavour of his view: "Then there are all the human beings who have been parked into dwellings that are devoid of meaning, perhaps indeed having a 'roof' in the physical sense, but not a place connecting them to the world anymore, no attachment point. Modernity boasts much about having developed individualism and enabled a shift beyond the rigid collective identities of yore; but what sense of personhood and one's place in the world can a child brought up behind the seventh door to the left in Building C, second staircase, 15th floor, possibly have?" *Ibid.* It is not to have a rose-tinted view of public-housing estates in capitalist society to see that Jappe here misses entirely their complex and dynamic social and cultural forms and experiences, as Caleb Femi, for example, has so powerfully articulated in his poems about life in South London's North Peckham estate, poems which include an extraordinary series on the socio-aesthetics of concrete. Caleb Femi, *Poor* (London: Penguin, 2020).

53 Jonathan Watts, "Concrete: The Most Destructive Material on Earth", *The Guardian*, 25 February 2019, www.theguardian.com/cities/2019/feb/25/concrete-the-most-destructive-material-on-earth.

54 Oliver Wainwright, "The Case for... Never Demolishing Another Building", *The Guardian*, 13 January 2020, www.theguardian.com/cities/2020/jan/13/the-case-for-never-demolishing-another-building.

55 Model Environments, in Architects for Social Housing, "Embodied Carbon Estimation for Central Hill Estate: Report by Model Environments", February 2017, https://architectsforsocialhousing.co.uk/2017/02/02/embodied-carbon-estimation-for-central-hill-estate-report-by-model-environments/.

56 Roger Harrabin, "Don't Demolish Old Buildings, Urge Architects", *BBC News*, 5 August 2020, www.bbc.co.uk/news/business-53642581.

57 Lacaton and Vassal's motto – "Never demolish, never remove or replace, always add, transform, and reuse!" – could be described as an ecological upgrade of the Smithsons' method of the as found; they have themselves noted an interest in the Smithsons. Carson Chan, "Lacaton and Vassal: Game Changer", *032c*, 4 March 2013, https://032c.com/o-architects-where-art-thou-game-changer-lacaton-vassal.

58 Oliver Wainwright, "'Sometimes the Answer Is to Do Nothing': Unflashy French duo take Architecture's Top Prize", *The Guardian*, 16 March 2021, www.theguardian.com/artanddesign/2021/mar/16/lacaton-vassal-unflashy-french-architectures-pritzker-prize.

7

The Charged Void: Intensive Landscape and the Brutalist Mound

The most mysterious, the most charged of architectural forms are those which capture the empty air.

Alison and Peter Smithson, "The Space Between"

Hills are a great formal idea, ever various, expressive of mood, expectant of weather.

Alison and Peter Smithson, "Robin Hood Gardens London E14"

In contrast to the architectural form of the tower block – too often sited with little sense of front, back and counterpart space – Robin Hood Gardens appeared to *undulate* through its ground. One of the estate's residents imagined the longer, west block as a "Cunard liner". If "you let your imagination drift", Fitzgerald reflected, "you could say it functions as a ship to carry people through time, house people through time".[1] For Manfredo Tafuri, architectural allusions to the ship are revealing of modernism's "resolve illusion", a merely "theatrical" production of emancipated community, achieved in separation from a world essentially unchanged: "The ship, the monastery, and the phalanstery are thus equivalent; in striving to reach a perfectly integrated community, they isolate themselves from the world."[2] It is a valuable insight, but not applicable to Robin Hood Gardens. If the estate's paired blocks were ships of a sort, they were fashioned through a particular and considered *engagement* with their ground, and not – as Tafuri makes his point with Sterling and Gowan's Leicester University Engineering Building (1960–1963) – as "a virtual iceberg that navigates in the sea of the park in which it is casually placed, according to a mysterious course".[3]

These qualities of the estate's engagement with its ground are the subject of this chapter, what can be called the *Brutalist landscape* of the scheme.

I explore this through two intersecting forms – the interior green as *charged void* and the estate's anomalous mound. Together, the green (or garden or park) and its mound give us a *class* landscape – a pocket of protection and set of intensive qualities, carved out from the fraught conditions of post-industrial society (Figure 7.1).

Garden as Charged Void

The undulating effect of Robin Hood Gardens was achieved not only through the choice of length over height, but through the cranks of the buildings at plan (Figure 7.2). This repeats an "old trick" that the Smithsons found in the Bernini colonnade in Rome's St Peter's Square, the Royal Crescent in Bath and the Pont-Aqueduc de Calèche near Aix-en-Provence, where the structure *harnessed* the ground in a dynamic "lock between built-form and counterpart space".[4] This lock was nuanced, with very different effects on the street and garden sides of the scheme. On the street sides (Cotton Street and the Blackwall Tunnel approach road), the lock was one of defence and inversion, part of the estate's measures against automotive traffic. The cranked contours of the buildings followed the roads, separated by the perimeter "acoustic barrier wall" (Figure 4.10). At ten feet high and canted outwards at the top, the wall deflected traffic noise as close to source as possible, while the street decks were elevated away and, inversely, residents' cars were channelled below the car-free central site into two open-air moats of garages running the length of each building. In contrast, on the garden-facing sides, the lock between building and ground served the scheme's primary aim of "protection" (Figure 7.3).[5] "Split like a kipper", as Peter Smithson describes the relation between the two buildings, they nurtured between them the green "stress-free zone" amid the urban tumult.[6]

Overlooked by all the apartments though sufficiently expansive not to feel surveilled, residents described many uses of the green, including cricket, sunbathing, barbeques, gardening, cycling, winter sledging, giant tag games that extended out and along the street decks and flirtatious self-display, teenagers conscious of eyes from the homes above (Figure 7.4). Dheraj Shamoo, who moved into the estate as part of a family of three teenaged brothers, recalled impromptu Guy Fawkes' firework displays from the mound's summit – they "looked amazing"; "everyone would go to their

Figure 7.1 The estate's green, viewed from the top of the east block. (Nicholas Thoburn, November 2015)

Figure 7.2 Nicholas Ruddock, with view of the cranked shape of the estate's west block. (Kois Miah, September 2015)

Figure 7.3 Jimmy Yorke, caretaker and former resident, in the "stress-free zone" of the green. (Kois Miah, July 2014)

Figure 7.4 Tug of war in the garden, summer Fun Day organized by SPLASH. (Kois Miah, August 2014)

balconies to watch".[7] Motiur Rahman talks of spending whole summers on the green as a child, coming in briefly for lunch, then "out again, and the next time you came in was 8pm when the sun went down. You were absolutely blissful and sort of lost in those moments." Parents would keep an eye on the children from the escape balconies and kitchens, but there was "safety in numbers"; "you could hear the kids playing"; "it felt like a little cocoon where you were just completely safe".[8]

Abul Hasnath remembers large groups of friends playing Kabaddi, Diaguti and Gula, Bangladeshi games that found their way to this Poplar green, to the amusement of his Bangladesh-born wife.[9] Wayne Alison spoke of how he always looked to the garden as he walked out of the caretakers' office: "on a summer's day, or even a summer's morning, it's beautiful, it's absolutely beautiful". Bird-watching, he spotted a redstart and its nest, a rare enough sighting, and once saw "a sparrowhawk come down and take a bird in front of my eyes. When you're in the middle of the roads and building works, you name it – nature is a wonderful thing."[10] Some resident gardeners commandeered the areas outside of their ground-floor flats, or small allotment-like plots in areas normally reserved for shrubs,

Figure 7.5 Abdul Rahim with his garden plot. (Kois Miah, May 2016)

growing vegetables, predominantly, and sometimes flowers. On our many visits to the estate we observed one garden plot in particular, at various stages of preparation and growth, but it was a long time before Kois met the gardener himself, Abdul Rahim, seen in his portrait holding a planting stick and seedling (Figure 7.5).

In their different ways these garden activities are all a kind of *play*, recalling my discussion of the estate's break with CIAM's functionalism. But to develop a theory of Brutalist landscape, we need to consider more how play here is co-constituted with the specificities of *place*. The Smithsons call it the "pleasures of territory" and "rituals of territory" – mundane and non-instrumental activity attuned to, emergent from and creating the particularities of place. "Places draw us to them for reasons beyond the feelings derived from the five senses", they wrote of the deep, complex and intuitive relation people can form with place. "Some deeper recognition is at work, felt through an unextinguishable animal sensibility."[11]

My own experience of the pleasures of territory in the green were deeply affective and multi-sensory, where *sound* played a significant role.[12] On summer weekdays, when I found myself most drawn to pass time in the green, the soundscape was an enveloping mix of birdsong, traffic (considerably muted, as the design intended), aircraft routed through nearby City Airport and human voices, all parts various over the topography and through the course of the day. It had a singular consistency. In a smaller scheme, the sheer walls of the semi-bounded site might have created a claustrophobic echo effect, but here they served to blend and soften the constituent elements of sound, partially abstracting them from source into a distinct soundscape with interlaced streams. Its impact on one's mood – calming, contemplative and a touch dissociating – is hard to imagine in a new development, with the obligatory construction of public space through points of commercial consumption. As Khaled Elgohari, a resident since his youth, remarked to me as we walked through the garden, "from a developer's point of view the green would be seen as wasted space" – where are the cafes and shops? – but these areas of undetermined use "are what makes a community".[13] It is an astute observation, that the source of residential community, or its spatial counterpart, lies not in regulated use, where space, function and economic value come to bind social life, but in a certain *indetermination*.

The Smithsons make a similar point, with their concept of the space between or charged void. I discussed in the previous chapter how the relation between the scheme's two buildings served not to confirm the identity of one in the other, but to set off a process of repetition and difference in their built features. That is only a part of it, however, for they relate also in their *interval*, the space between. The space between is an inchoate spatial and affective state produced of the relation between architecture and its surround, where a building "is only interesting ... if it charges the space around it with connective possibilities".[14] It is "a capacity we can feel and act upon but cannot necessarily describe or record", though the Smithsons tease out its qualities in some of their most evocative texts.[15]

In contrast to the gridded space of the modernist plan, the space between is a *void*. But it is a void that is *charged*, through its relation to the built surround – a space "between ... relaxedness and intensity, separateness and connection", in Max Risselada's words.[16] As a void, the space between allows for impromptu and multiple uses, a "space that is left open for interpretation", as I have indicated.[17] But here space can "evolve from a place of use into a work of art" – in the living, sensual sense of that word – where, "as with rock-pools" when the tide recedes, "what is within that space between seems extraordinarily vivid".[18] The space between has an affective quality, then, an atmosphere, a "magical emptiness" which can take over the architecture as primary spatializing force.

In a short, aphoristic text of the early 1970s, titled "The Space Between", the Smithsons put it as follows.

> The most mysterious, the most charged of architectural forms are those which capture the empty air. The faery ring, Stonehenge, the standing columns of the temple whose cella walls have gone, the empty barn, the Kahn house of the square brick columns, the chimneys of the English Renaissance ... such forms are double-acting, concentrating inwards, radiating buoyancy outwards. The drama is set up by the chairs at the round table before the knights arrive.
>
> The chimneys of the English Renaissance can also be read as architecture's own break with Rome; the center simply gone, and in place of the all summating dome the play of almost equals making magical emptiness in between and creating imaginary answering turrets beyond.[19]

I quote this passage at length because it also hints at an egalitarian politics to the charged void, "the play of almost equals". And this continues when the text returns to Louis Kahn's De Vore House (1955, unbuilt), which is described as "a brutalist place for the intellect ... not barn ... not temple ... free of the wheel of seasonal labor ... free of gods or ritual".[20]

These affective qualities of the charged void encapsulate so well the calming, contemplative and dissociating mood that I experienced in the garden, the paired buildings concentrating inwards and radiating out, a vivid atmosphere evacuated of determined function and economy, open to the unforeseen. To fully grasp the concept, though, an additional feature needs adding in. As much as the space between is "empty air", it is also *ground*. I indicated above that the Smithsons developed the concept explicitly against the geometric, gridded spatiality of functionalist urbanism. In other words, the charged void is an *intensive* rather than extensive theory of space. For this they drew on ancient Greek spatiality. Breaking with Le Corbusier's view of Greek spatial precision, purity and regularity, the Smithsons concluded from their visits to Greece that "*there was no* Greek space".[21] Places of assembly, temples, stoas "were simply put down into the charged void", "put where they had a certain convenience, meaning, and indication; it is a controlled arrangement, but not controlled through space technique as we know it".[22]

Such placement is not the *negation* of a site. That is the consequence of extensive space, where a site is emptied of qualities through its subjection to the homogenizing order of the functional grid, what Deleuze and Guattari call "striated space", "divisible, homogeneous space striated in all directions".[23] On Greek sites, to the contrary, the Smithsons found "a beautiful grasp of topography", "a coming together of a building and its site", where a site, unbound from the horizontal plane of gridded space, is "capable of rising to an occasion".[24] This observation brings landscape into the Brutalist undoing of the distinction between figure and ground that is so key to Paolozzi and Dubuffet. In Paolozzi's bronzes, formed through casts of objects as found, the sculptural work at once forms and is unformed by the "unabsorbed and unresolved" component parts, thus troubling "the false divide between the material and the representational", the ground and the figure, as Ben Highmore puts it.[25] And in Dubuffet's painting, the artist does not place the work on top of the medium; "One no longer covers over".[26] Rather, "one raises, accumulates, piles up, goes through, stirs up, folds", in Deleuze and Guattari's words, the "ascent of the ground with Dubuffet".[27]

With this ascent of the ground I turn to the final built form of Robin Hood Gardens, a form between architecture and nature – the garden's extraordinary mound, a "territorial imprint" to confirm the charged void.[28]

The Brutalist Mound

"Hills are a great formal idea", the Smithsons declared, "ever various, expressive of mood, expectant of weather" (Figure 7.6).[29] These words accompany a double-page colour photograph of Robin Hood Gardens in the scheme's publication in *Architectural Design*. Shot from up high in nearby Balfron Tower, the photograph shows the two slab blocks pushed to the edges of the wide expanse of garden, and at its centre the estate's mound. As the accompanying text makes plain, the architects understood that inserted in this traffic-bound, ex-industrial setting, the bucolic quality of the mound was a remarkable asset. In Wayne Alison's words, "It is something you see in the countryside, not in the middle of East London!"[30]

Originally only grass-planted, and once accompanied by a smaller partner, over time the mound became abundant with shrubs and trees (Figure 7.7).[31] Its height of two storeys was enough to have a commanding presence in the green, where it extended the kinetic quality of the scheme, hiding and revealing parts and wholes of the two buildings as one walked

Figure 7.6 The Brutalist mound at inception. (Peter Smithson, 1972. Smithson Family Collection)

Figure 7.7 Mother and daughter, summer Fun Day, with the mound in the background. (Kois Miah, August 2014)

along the green's edges or around and over the summit.[32] The mound features prominently too within the apartments themselves, so much a part of the sight lines that in many of the bedrooms and kitchens it appears to *lean in* to the building.

For all the pleasures of landscape, it is important to appreciate the estate's mound as an artificial or constructed form. If the mound and green brought a little of the countryside into working-class Poplar, and if, in the Smithsons' imagination, there was something of an English landscape in play here, it was a complex and contradictory formation, not a means to ground a *nativist* working class. Architecturally, the green's interplay with the sheer concrete blocks could scarcely suggest an English idyll. And the mound itself had a deliberately constructed quality. It references ancient earthworks like Silbury Hill, 1960s Land Art and the slag heaps familiar to the coal-mining regions of the Smithsons' youth, picking up the unhomely atmospheres of these forms in its intervention in the classed conditions of industry and nature, as I show now.

"Today we might make contour relief by means of the same earth shifting equipment that opencasts coal", the Smithsons continue in their appraisal of

Figure 7.8 The mound of rubble. (Tony Ray-Jones, 1972. RIBA Library Photographs Collection)

the formal idea of the mound, as if productive industry could be repurposed for the anti-utilitarian pleasures of the charged void. It is a reasonable aim, but the formulation appears beholden to the industrial paradigm, the site as tabula rasa. On closer inspection, however, this "opencast" intervention in landscape is nudged aside by Brutalism's more immanent relation to matter, for the mound is an extraordinary work of matter as found. The mound was not a *natural* feature of East London topography, clearly. It was a great assembling of existent *rubble*, rubble from the demolished Grosvenor Buildings tenements that preceded the estate, the two streets that were demolished for the build, Manisty Street and Mackrow Street, and other spoil from the construction (Figure 7.8). The Smithsons were keen to convey this, and it is well known among residents. Two I spoke with who witnessed the assembling of the mound recalled with pleasure, and what I took to be knowing participation in the estate's mythology, the sight of old prams, bicycles, bathtubs and cookers piled up amid the rubble.

It is an unusual architectural move, where the industrial paradigm and its assumed tabula rasa is displaced, and the awkward, pre-existent and unproductive matter that this paradigm denigrates and disavows instead takes a leading role. This point is made by David Gissen, who shows also how nature, as it is conceived in today's development industry, is problematized through this use of rubble.[33] Damaged and unproductive rubble – a form of *subnature*, in Gissen's account – presents a far more ethical relation to the natural world as found, nature thoroughly threaded through with the social, and damaged by it, than does so-called *green* development. For the latter is imbued with a vitalist ideology of fecund and inclusive nature which, "in the name of mending a natural relationship", actually "enhances the power of urban wealth".[34] The cynicism of this green ideology is something to behold, where nature's putative vitality serves as cover for environment-*degrading* demolition and replacement, and the concomitant exclusion of working-class populations from their liveable territories. In Gissen's example, "one only has to consider the recent green building booms in New York's Times Square and Battery Park City, and the corresponding production of a homogenous and elite social sphere, to understand how the restoration of nature is used to re-establish a specific class-based idea of the city".[35]

My point is not that the mound at Robin Hood Gardens *resolves* these destructive forces of industry – "Subnature will not *save* us from our inequities" – so much as it *faces up* to them, modulates them in its form, makes industrial nature felt but also liveable.[36] Amid the concatenating crises of climate, ecology and social reproduction that convulse the world today, one might say that the mound approaches the problem of a landscape adequate to "life in capitalist ruins", life otherwise, to borrow from Anna Tsing.[37] In the same vein, the mound adds to the scheme's articulation of the environmental quality of *light*. For only by grappling with the denigrated material of rubble can the estate's articulation of light, a socially valorized form of nature, be sure to escape a "neo-Victorian" urban vision, as Gissen puts it, "the utilization of nature as an instrument that cleans the world" while "advancing the social sphere as it exists" in this dereliction.[38]

A complex of ruined matter, the mound is also an assemblage of *time*. It is a burial of sorts, holding traces of the site's recent past present in the new. Fragments of matter are carried forward but unresolved, held together in the slow time of the charged void. In the mix is also a sense of *deep* time, insofar as the mound projects the form, and with it the *mythic* quality, of prehistoric earthworks. It is a quality the Smithsons were attentive to already in the 1950s, drawing on ancient Egyptian symbolism to evoke a "primeval mound", which in *Ordinariness and Light* is accompanied by an image, from the Theban *Book of the Dead*, of the scribe Ani as a swallow, perched on a

Figure 7.9 Completion of the maze from St Catherine's Hill atop the mound in Poplar. (Eve Lear with anon., 2017)

steep hill. As the caption has it, "the creator was said to have emerged out of the waters of chaos and to have made a mound on which he could stand".[39]

These temporal and mythic features give an unmistakable totemic quality to the mound. It is a quality that must have enticed the person or persons who, in spring 2017, marked up its summit with the seventeenth-century maze from St Catherine's Hill, Winchester.[40] Rendered on site in chalk and touched-up in the photographic record with a spray-paint effect, it is all the more appealing for its quality of fleeting presence (Figure 7.9). A more

Figure 7.10 Sundial on the mound. Designed by David Bratby of SPLASH Arts and children from Woolmore Primary School; built by Maud Milton of Artyface. (David Bratby, 2000)

enduring addition to the summit came with a refurbishment at the turn of the millennium, when the mound gained a large sundial. The summit was slightly flattened with a concrete circle and set with coloured enamel tiles in the shape of a bow and arrow, after the estate's Sherwood Forest namesake (Figure 7.10). A sundial of the analemmatic type, it told the solar time when a person acting as gnomon to cast the shadow stood on the correct month sequenced in the arrow's feather. The hand-made tiles in the bow were glazed with designs by children from the adjacent Woolmore Primary School – the Egyptian sun god Ra, a flying fish with clock, seagulls and other creatures, following the theme "time flies".[41]

In the same millennium refurbishment, a staircase ascent was added to the mound and a spiral path to its summit. Wittingly or not, the spiral echoes the Smithsons' Tees Pudding (1977) proposal for a gorse- and wildflower-covered slag mound at a bend in the River Tees at Middlesbrough, where two spiral paths lead to a summit viewing-circle (Figure 7.11).[42] Tees Pudding was part of a minor theme of *mound work*, we might call it, that included also Slaggie Eleven: Heroes of the Slag Heap (1977), a proposal for a Spennymoor slag heap, populated by conglomerate clinker fashioned into figurative, Dubuffet-style sculptures and painted in the colours of seven local football teams.[43]

The totemic quality of the Poplar mound also travelled, finding its way to Venice, at the exhibition *A Clockwork Jerusalem* in the 2014 Architecture

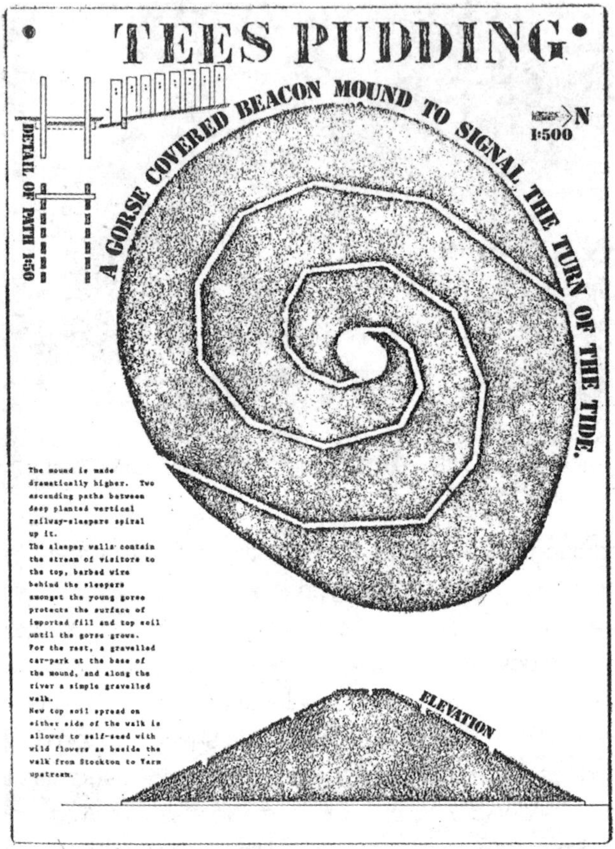

Figure 7.11 Tees Pudding, plan and elevation. (Alison and Peter Smithson, 1977. Smithson Family Collection)

Biennale. The exhibition explored the curious qualities of British modernism, where Brutalism was framed as a constellation of the mythic, the pastoral, the urban and the modern, all figured by a large viewing mound placed at the centre of the pavilion, bright pink and covered in soil – including soil sourced from the mound at Robin Hood Gardens. “Over the course of the research that we undertook”, commented one of the curators, “it became apparent that the strange, perhaps unique feature of British architecture, is the mound”.[44] One should be wary of affirming anything especially *English* or *British*, for national characterizations are never fully separable from the violent and debasing visions of race and nation. But it is a *conflictual* and *classed* terrain that informed this exhibition's splicing of William Blake, *A Clockwork Orange* and Brutalist council estates, wherein the mound expressed something altogether deeper, and more anomalous, than national heritage. As the curators understood it, the installation "represents a burial mound (a kind of end) but, at the same time, the construction site – the place where things can begin". I have considered this deep time already, but it is framed here in an enticing way, where the mound is "also perhaps 'unarchitecture': a state either before or after architecture. It has a kind of destabilising quality."[45]

It is instructive to reflect a little on this formulation of unarchitecture. To be "before or after architecture" is to be *before or after human agency*. This is the domain of the *eerie*, as Mark Fisher identifies it in his book *The Weird and the Eerie*. For Fisher, the eerie is an affect particular to landscape, engendered when the agent that produced a notable presence or an absence remains partially obscure. As he writes, "A sense of the eerie seldom clings to enclosed and inhabited domestic spaces; we find the eerie more readily in landscapes partially emptied of the human. What happened to produce these ruins, this disappearance? ... What kind of agent is acting here? Is there an agent at all? ... *Why is there something here when there should be nothing?*"[46] I raise the eerie here because, in Fisher's formulation, it is an affect that pertains specifically to *capitalist* social relations, surprising though that may seem. The eerie at once evokes and unsettles the peculiar kind of agency that is capital. "Capital is at every level an eerie entity", Fisher writes, "conjured out of nothing, capital nevertheless exerts more influence than any allegedly substantial entity".[47] That is to say, in Marx's terms, capital is an *impersonal* agency, operative behind our backs, where individual agents, the capitalist and the worker, are not agents at all, but merely functional personifications of the impersonal dynamics of commodity production and exchange.[48] Evoking this obscured and ungraspable agency, the eerie makes it strange, an enticing and unnerving discombobulation, and makes it liveable too. Unmoored from a grasp of agency – and from agency's grasp – the eerie affect of the mound is one of calm disengagement, the impersonal force of the outside as a *serenity* that comes with "detachment from the urgencies of the everyday".[49] Interpreted this way, as eerie, the mound at Robin Hood Gardens is not only a space without determined use and economy, but it raises and troubles the command of capitalist society also in its *affective* state.

No doubt I am engaging in flights of imagination here, reverie about the mound from my own experience. But in writing this book, and I hope in its reading, I have sought to allow Robin Hood Gardens to provoke moments of imaginative flight, flight incited by immersion in the estate's material and social forms as found. All the same, I will close this discussion of Brutalist landscape with a more direct and decisive critique of developer capitalism, as shared with me in the charged void of the estate's green.

I had been sitting at the mound's summit on a sun-drenched afternoon in September 2015, tuning into the atmosphere. Two children were clambering up and running down the mound. "Joseph, hold my hand!" gleefully yelled the little girl to her younger friend or sibling as they ran. I descended the spiral path to the long, uncut grass of the garden, observing small groups of adults and children walking along the desire path carved diagonally across the green and around the mound's eastern edge – it was the end of the school day at the adjacent Woolmore Primary School. I noticed a man entering the garden and striding towards me along the same path. He was tall, Black, dressed in a navy-coloured suit, a little shabby, not the style of a Canary Wharf office worker. My camera gave me away as a party interested in the estate's architecture, a social type familiar here, so as I greeted him with a nod and a smile he volunteered a spontaneous critique of the redevelopment, with barely a pause in his stride: "They're demolishing them you know. There's nothing wrong with them. It's capitalism. They're sharks."

On that warm September afternoon, the green held a dream-like quality. Enveloped in the space between, its sense impressions were so palpable it was as if it would last forever, a present reaching back and forward in time. Yet the threat of impending demolition loomed over the estate throughout our research, and two years after this encounter half the homes of Robin Hood Gardens had been lost to the wrecker's ball, the other half soon to follow. The early plans for Blackwall Reach included laying waste to the mound too – though it is now set to remain, buffed and domesticated into corporate banality.

Notes

1 Fitzgerald, interview, 12 September 2014.
2 Manfredo Tafuri, *The Sphere and the Labyrinth: Avant-Gardes and Architecture from Piranesi to the 1970s*, trans. Pellegrino d'Acierno and Robert Connolly (Cambridge, MA and London: MIT Press, 1987), 270.
3 *Ibid.*, 269.
4 Peter Smithson, "Simple Thoughts on Repetition", *Architectural Design* 41 (1971): 481. Alison and Peter Smithson, *Without Rhetoric: An Architectural Aesthetic 1955–1972* (London: Latimer, 1973), 36.
5 Alison and Peter Smithson, *Ordinariness and Light: Urban Theories 1952–1960 and their Application in a Building Project 1963–1970* (London: Faber and Faber, 1970), 189.
6 *The Smithsons on Housing*, dir. B. S. Johnson (BBC, 1970), available on YouTube.
7 Dheraj Shamoo, interview, 7 September 2014.
8 Motiur Rahman, interview, 4 December 2015.
9 It is not that there were no anti-social uses of the garden, but these were rarely remarked upon in our conversations with residents. Furse reports teenagers rolling lorry tyres down the mound, aimed at residents' front doors and causing damage, as well as motorbikes being ridden on the mound and green. John Furse, *The Smithsons at Robin Hood Gardens*, unpublished PhD thesis (University of Sussex, 1982), 232. For my part, as the estate became progressively more neglected in its last years, on two occasions I witnessed the remains of cars that had somehow been driven to the top of the mound and set alight.
10 Wayne Alison, interview, 18 January 2016.
11 Alison and Peter Smithson, *Italian Thoughts* (privately published, 1993), 32–33.
12 *Ibid.*, 62.
13 Khaled Elgohari, interview, 1 February 2015.
14 Alison and Peter Smithson, *Without Rhetoric: An Architectural Aesthetic 1955–1972* (London: Latimer, 1973), 36.
15 Peter Smithson, "Intention", in Alison and Peter Smithson, *The Charged Void: Architecture* (New York: The Monacelli Press, 2001), 11.
16 Max Risselada, "The Space Between", in Alison and Peter Smithson, *The Space Between*, ed. Max Risselada (Köln: Walther König, 2017), 262.
17 *Ibid.*, 260.
18 Peter Smithson, "Empooling", *Re-Envisioning Landscape / Architecture*, ed. Catherine Spellman (Barcelona: Actar, 2003), 77, 73.
19 Alison and Peter Smithson, "The Space Between", *Oppositions* 4 (1974): 75–78, 77.
20 *Ibid.*, 78.
21 Smithson and Smithson, *Without Rhetoric*, 55, emphasis added.
22 *Ibid.*, 55–56.
23 Gilles Deleuze and Félix Guattari, *A Thousand Plateaus: Capitalism and Schizophrenia Volume 2*, trans. Brian Massumi (Minneapolis: University of Minnesota Press, 1987), 223.
24 Smithson and Smithson, *Without Rhetoric*, 56, 55.
25 Ben Highmore, *The Art of Brutalism: Rescuing Hope from Catastrophe in 1950s Britain* (New Haven, CT and London: Yale University Press, 2017), 179, 182.

26 Gilles Deleuze and Félix Guattari, *What Is Philosophy?*, trans. Hugh Tomlinson and Graham Burchell (London: Verso, 1994), 194.

27 *Ibid.*, 194.

28 Peter Smithson, "Territorial Imprint", in Alison and Peter Smithson, *The Space Between*, ed. Max Risselada (Köln: Walther König, 2017), 161.

29 Alison and Peter Smithson, "Robin Hood Gardens London E14", *Architectural Design* 42 no. 9 (1972): 562.

30 Wayne Alison, interview, 18 January 2016.

31 The second mound, large enough to have had a children's slide installed down its length, was, I understand, flattened at the time the stairwell and spiral path were added to the main mound. The green's four circular sunken play-pits for younger children were removed at the same time, replaced by a new and larger play area in the north-west of the green. For a time there was also a play area outside of the protected green, built into the estate's boundary at the south-east corner where Robin Hood Lane meets Poplar High Street, a photograph of which is included in Alison and Peter Smithson, *The Shift* (London: Academy Editions, 1982), 54.

32 This point about the kinetic quality of the scheme is one of the many insights in Alan Powers' essay "A Critical Narrative", in *Robin Hood Gardens: Re-Visions,* ed. Alan Powers (London: Twentieth Century Society, 2010).

33 David Gissen, "Thoughts on a Heap of Rubble", *Kerb: Journal of Landscape Architecture* 19 (2011): 50–51.

34 David Gissen, *Subnature: Architecture's Other Environments* (New York: Princeton Architectural Press, 2009), 23.

35 *Ibid.*, 24.

36 *Ibid.*, 25.

37 Anna Lowenhaupt Tsing, *The Mushroom at the End of the World: On the Possibility of Life in Capitalist Ruins* (Princeton, NJ: Princeton University Press, 2015), vii.

38 Gissen, *Subnature*, 23.

39 Smithson and Smithson, *Ordinariness and Light*, 21.

40 "Completion of the Mis-Maze Atop the Sacred Mounds of St Catherine's Hill / Robin Hood Gardens", saladofpearls, 7 March 2012, https://saladofpearls.wordpress.com/2017/03/07/completion-of-the-mis-maze-on-the-sacred-mounds-of-st-catherines-robin-hood-gardens/. For discussion of the maze at St Catherine's Hill, see London Psychogeographical Association and the Archaeogeodetic Association, *The Great Conjunction: The Symbols of a College, the Death of a King and the Maze on the Hill* (London: Unpopular Books, no date).

41 Photographs of the complete work and some of the individual tiles can be seen on the Artyface website: www.artyface.co.uk/projects-archive/arty_robin.php.

42 Alison and Peter Smithson, "Tees Pudding, Middlesbrough, Spring 1977", *The Charged Void: Architecture* (New York: The Monacelli Press, 2001), 414.

43 Alison and Peter Smithson, "The Slaggie Eleven of the Spenymoor Slag Heaps, Spring 1977", *The Charged Void: Architecture* (New York: The Monacelli Press, 2001), 415.

44 Sam Jacob, in James Taylor-Foster, "Sam Jacob and Wouter Vanstiphout on Curating 'A Clockwork Jerusalem'", *ArchDaily*, 24 June 2014, www.archdaily.com/517501/interview-sam-jacob-and-wouter-vanstiphout-curators-of-a-clockwork-jerusalem-at-the-2014-venice-biennale.

45 *Ibid.*

46 Mark Fisher, *The Weird and the Eerie* (London: Repeater Books, 2016), 11–12.

47 *Ibid.*, 11.

48 "The *functions* fulfilled by the capitalist are no more than the functions of capital – viz. the valorization of value by absorbing living labour – executed *consciously* and *willingly.* The capitalist functions only as personified capital, capital as a person, just as the worker is no more than labour personified." Karl Marx, *Capital: A Critical Analysis of Capitalist Production*, vol. 1, trans. Ben Fowkes (London: Penguin, 1976), 989.

49 Fisher, *The Weird and the Eerie*, 13.

8

Robin Hood in Reverse: Culture as Dispossession in the V&A's Fragment of Robin Hood Gardens

[Demolition] is a waste of many things – a waste of energy, a waste of material, and a waste of history. Moreover, it has a very negative social impact. For us, it is an act of violence.

Anne Lacaton

The logic of using art to heal social wounds while at the same time worsening them.

Josephine Berry, *Art and (Bare) Life*

Demolition came for Robin Hood Gardens in December 2017. It was a slow, drawn-out process as the estate's west block was torn down along its length, but no less violent for it. As images of the initial deep breach in the building circulated in the press and social media, a tweet by the Twentieth Century Society encapsulated the mood of many: "Feels like seeing an old friend having their teeth knocked out" (Figure 8.1).[1] By April 2018, the block had been ground to fine rubble, the remaining building, inhabited increasingly by residents on temporary tenancies, awaiting the same fate. The concrete monstrosity had been dispatched. And yet, no sooner had this stigmatizing trope fulfilled its promise in demolition, than it ceded its hold on Robin Hood Gardens to the symbolism of beautiful Brutalism, under the agency, no less, of the Victoria and Albert Museum (V&A). Announced with much fanfare a few weeks before demolition commenced, the V&A salvaged from the destruction a three-storey section of the estate for permanent exhibition, the building now described as "a New Brutalist masterwork", the fragment a "small segment of a masterpiece".[2]

Figure 8.1 West block of Robin Hood Gardens under demolition. (Kois Miah, December 2017)

It is an unprecedented acquisition, where front and back façades of two apartments, each measuring 8.8 metres high and 5.5 metres wide, are to be reconstructed, potentially as one whole apartment, complete with a portion of the scheme's streets in the sky and interior fittings.[3] The fragment is destined for the V&A East, a new museum and a collections and research centre on the former Olympic site in Stratford, East London, part of a vast state- and culture-led regeneration three miles north of Robin Hood Lane. The V&A East is not due to open until 2024, but a scaled-down version of the fragment was exhibited at the 2018 Venice Architecture Biennale, the showpiece of an exhibition titled *Robin Hood Gardens: A Ruin in Reverse*.

The V&A's fragment of Brutalist council housing is the object of this chapter, where we see the afterlife of Robin Hood Gardens taking shape, through the culture and regeneration industries, as something entirely different to its prior form. The fragment appears to be a seamless artefact of modern architectural heritage. But this appearance is part of the *destructive* valence of what is actually a fraught and class-ridden artefact, implicated in the dispossession and demolition of working-class housing. Given that it is likely to take a lead in how that the estate is represented into the future – represented *against itself* – the fragment warrants consideration in some depth. It is significant too for understanding how Brutalism and representations of council housing can be arrogated to culture- and state-led regeneration.

In broad terms, the V&A's fragment is an articulation of beautiful Brutalism, the usurping of working-class housing for middle-class consumption – though with a twist. Robin Hood Gardens is not being handed to developers and middle-class homebuyers *directly* as housing, but as *symbolic* and *cultural* consumption, as a museum artefact. Yet in this form it will no doubt contribute to the aesthetic elevation and stabilization of ex-council housing in the market for private purchase. The twist, and this is where I focus, is that the fragment's impact on working-class housing is also in estate *demolition* – counterintuitive though that sounds. Rather than inviting the social violence of estate demolition, as does the rival trope of the concrete monstrosity, this artefact *obscures* demolition and *contains* opposition. For it lifts Robin Hood Gardens – and with it the social form of the post-war council estate – out of the conflictual terrain of housing in the present and into the sealed and sanitized past of a museum artefact, a past to ground a future ever evacuated of the conflictual present.

Unpacking this complex formation through the features of the V&A's fragment, I first take its partial exhibition in Venice as opportunity to investigate how it bears certain *museum effects* that obscure and contain the crisis of social housing – effects of cultural history, the public, neutrality and civic exchange. My focus here is on the V&A's exhibition literature and the response of its director, Tristram Hunt, to housing-movement opposition. In a second move, the chapter considers the fragment's direct implication in the state- and culture-led regeneration of East Bank, the planned site of its full and permanent exhibition. I attend to the regeneration's effects of working-class dispossession and displacement, before considering how the fragment shapes and is shaped by these class processes. To understand the fragment's features and effects here, I locate it within a trend in the aesthetics of regeneration where council housing *becomes public art*, a framework I use to appraise the exhibition film, by the artist Do Ho Suh, and the physical exhibit's likely form at the V&A East.

As is apparent from this outline, the chapter zooms in and out through artefactual features of the V&A's fragment and issues of class, museums, housing crisis, public art and urban development. It is key to my methodology that these wider issues are engaged not as *context* for the V&A's fragment, but as *constitutive features*, no less part of the fragment than are its salvaged blocks of concrete. To understand the fragment in this way is to grasp it as a complex and moving assemblage of artefactual, institutional, discursive and symbolic parts, variously manifest in different sites of instantiation and reception, sites which in today's multi-platform media environment are not limited to its physical exhibition.

A Ruin in Reverse: Brutalism in the Circuit of Global Culture

It could scarcely be more telling of the delivery of Robin Hood Gardens from working-class housing to middle-class cultural consumption that the first public outing of the V&A's fragment was a major stop on the global circuit of art and culture. In 2008, the V&A had declined a request from the journal *Building Design* to support its petition against demolition. But now, with the estate half-demolished, the museum championed this "small segment of a masterpiece", in the words of Christopher Turner, co-curator with Olivia Horsfall Turner of the Biennale exhibition. Considerably reduced in scale to that proposed for the V&A East, the Venice exhibit comprised a section of street deck and balustrade, supported by a façade fashioned from eight of the scheme's protruding mullions, all assembled together with scaffolding and plywood (Figure 8.2). Set outside on the Venetian Arsenal, the construction, it was claimed, allowed visitors "to stand on an original section of a 'street in the sky' – the elevated access deck designed by the Smithsons to foster interaction between neighbours and promote community".[4] Inside the pavilion was an accompanying text and image panel display, presenting a version of the vision, history and fate of Robin Hood Gardens, and filmed interviews with critics and residents (Figure 8.3). The exhibition's third feature was a specially commissioned 34-minute panoramic film, by the artist Do Ho Suh, of the estate's interiors, architecture and demolition, which was later shown at the V&A in London, projected at spectacular scale over the course of five weeks in 2019 – a work I consider later.

The exhibition's subtitle, *A Ruin in Reverse*, referenced the estate's earlier Biennale appearance, part of an installation by the Smithsons in the *Europa/America* exhibition in 1976. Titled "Sticks and Stones", it comprised a billboard-sized photograph of Robin Hood Gardens and a bench in the

Figure 8.2 Part of the V&A's fragment of Robin Hood Gardens at the Venice Architecture Biennale. (V&A, 2018)

style of a concrete mullion, accompanied by image-boards of fragments of Greek temples and ruins of classical architecture.[5] Borrowing a phrase from the artist Robert Smithson, the Smithsons' accompanying text drew associations between construction and ruination, where "A building under assembly is like a ruin in reverse", two states of incompletion that accentuate architecture's materiality and potential.[6] It would have been remiss of the curators of the 2018 exhibition to let this formulation pass by, for along with the pathos it confers on the ruined fragment it facilitates the exhibit's

Figure 8.3 Panel displays at *Robin Hood Gardens: A Ruin in Reverse*, Venice Architecture Biennale, screen-capture from promotional film. (V&A, 2018)

harnessing to a progressive cause – a future for social housing. Both are integral to the exhibition's framing, apparent, for example, in the following passage from a V&A blog post by Turner.

There is a photo of Alison Smithson at the 1976 Venice Biennale, where the couple curated an exhibition of their work called "Sticks and Stones." Shot from behind, she sits on a bench that is a 50 per cent enlargement of one of the concrete fins from Robin Hood Gardens, and is shown admiring a large construction photograph of the Smithsons' only council estate – a site still pregnant with possibility. "A building under assembly is like a ruin in reverse," the architects wrote in the accompanying catalogue. As the bulldozers move in, it seems appropriate to return a fragment of Robin Hood Gardens to Venice, where the V&A will assess the building's successes and failures and, from the vantage point of a "street in the sky," look to the future of social housing.[7]

Contrary to the seamlessness of this picture, however, and its progressive trajectory, the V&A's fragment is a fraught and class-ridden artefact. It is less a ruin in reverse than a work of *ongoing ruination*, obscuring and facilitating the programme of council-estate demolition and regeneration that provided the V&A with its fragment in the first place. Granted, as the museum was quick to point out, the salvage plan arrived late on the scene, long after the estate's fate was sealed.[8] But the acquisition is not so disconnected from demolition as the V&A likes to suggest. Or rather, this disconnection is a key *effect* of the fragment, its destructive valence bound up with its ability to appear not so, as I consider first through its form as a museum exhibit.

Museum Effects: The Public, Neutrality and Civic Exchange

As a museum exhibit, the fragment of Robin Hood Gardens takes shape in the mode of representation that Walter Benjamin calls "cultural history", the features of which I will unpack before pursuing their articulation in the V&A's response to housing-movement opposition.[9]

Cultural history, Benjamin writes, frames the museum audience as "a 'public' rather than a class".[10] That is to say, its presupposition and consequence is a representation of the social as cohesive and unified – a representation that substitutes for the reality of class society, where working-class experience is characterized not by coherence but by *crisis*, a condition of exploitation, insecurity and dispossession, ever pulled out of shape by the conflictual social relations that condition and course through it. The working class, as fraught social experience and critical standpoint, is in this way obscured and delegitimized – and sometimes, as we will see at the end of this chapter, reified against itself for the public's self-consolidation.

As with the *subject* of cultural history, so with its *objects*. For Benjamin, the artefacts of cultural history are "completed" and "reified", mere "sediment" wrested from the crisis-ridden flux of the social world.[11] They are treated "independently both of the material conditions of their own epoch and of those of the present", as Douglas Crimp puts it, and placed "in a reified historical continuum", an integrated narrative of progress upon which class society – or its avatar, the public – legitimates, flatters and propels itself.[12]

The museum achieves these reifying effects while declaring its manoeuvre to be *neutral* or non-political, so pulling off the trick of being simultaneously highly political and casting politicization as an illegitimate incursion. Evacuated of politics, of crisis and conflict, the declared function of the museum and its artefacts is to entertain – "to *stimulate*, to *offer variety*, to *arouse interest* ... to relieve monotony", in Benjamin's words.[13] Entertainment might seem harmless enough, but it serves here to close down the potential of an artefact to reveal and challenge social crisis, to antagonize rather than consolidate, to bear "a consciousness of the present that shatters the continuum of history".[14]

It is on imperial terrain that cultural history's role in obscuring and containing conflict and crisis is most acutely revealed, and this brings the V&A into the discussion. The historical continuum of European modernity has served to consolidate and enshrine not only a public delineated against the working class, but a *national* public delineated against the colonized and racially abjected (within which sectors of the working class were progressively incorporated in the public's own chauvinist image, as patriarchal, industrious and white). In the V&A's founding, as Tim Barringer puts it, the "representations of the world which it offered were deeply imbedded in the developing culture of Victorian Imperialism".[15] Its collection of artefacts, drawn from the colonial peripheries into the imperial centre, were ordered and re-ordered to produce "a fantasy of knowledge made into power", "a three-dimensional imperial archive", propagating colonial order, civic nationalism and the hierarchies and abjections of race science.[16] It is a past that carries into the present, as today's movement for museum decolonization asserts, a point forcefully made by Sumaya Kassim: "To many white people, the [museum] collections are an enjoyable diversion, a nostalgic visit which conjures up a romanticised version of Empire. For many people of colour, collections symbolise historic and ongoing trauma and theft. Behind every beautiful object and historically important building or monument is trauma."[17]

This is an order of culture but also of economy. The putative neutrality of cultural history is established in part through the vaunted autonomy of art and culture from the economic, but the modern museum was in fact thoroughly integrated with the colonial economy. The V&A is a quintessential example. Founded as the South Kensington Museum, it was a lynchpin of the surrounding Albertopolis complex of museums, colleges and institutions, where colonial research, trade and plunder in art, design, science and technology were harnessed for industrial development.[18] And cultural history continues to take an economic role, as I show later, now that museums are repositioned on the *internal* frontier of urban development, accompanied by a reconfigured structure of nation, racialization and, as is my focus here, class.

Turning now to the V&A's fragment, these museum effects are fulsomely articulated, and another added, in Tristram Hunt's attempt to fend off criticism of the acquisition. I focus on a short article he penned for *The Art Newspaper*, a response to dissenting voices and coordinated demonstrations held simultaneously at the opening of the Biennale in Venice and at the V&A in South Kensington on 24 May 2018, in which I took part.[19] As explained in a bilingual leaflet distributed at the demonstrations, they sought to expose and challenge how the V&A's "butchered chunk" of Robin Hood Gardens provided aesthetic cover for the social vandalism of estate demolition, making it a macabre "monument to London's social cleansing".[20] The Venice demonstration also took the opportunity to challenge the damage to social fabrics and housing affordability consequent on the city's transformation by the circuits of tourism and global culture.

Hunt's response in *The Art Newspaper* a few days later is a textbook illustration of cultural history. First, Hunt lifts the acquisition out of its fraught social conditions in the present and integrates it within the historical continuum of the museum's collection of reified artefacts: "Since its foundation, the V&A has preserved and exhibited large fragments of architecture – from the 17th-century timber facade of Sir Paul Pindar's House in Bishopsgate, London, to the gilded Music Room salvaged from Norfolk House in St. James's Square, London. The three-storey section of Robin Hood Gardens joins the Museum's world-renowned architecture collections, ensuring that a part of the building will remain in a public collection for future generations" (Figure 8.4).[21]

The fragment thus safely ensconced in the public collection, Hunt then turns to the question of politics. He starts with a broadly accurate presentation of the case against, "that acquiring and exhibiting a section of the estate validates the so-called 'social cleansing' taking place in east London. Better that the architecture is lost forever, they assert, than to be involved in 'art-washing' gentrification and the dispersal of local communities."[22] But Hunt then pivots, avoiding these terms of opposition to instead address what lies "behind this critique", as he sees it, which he sketches and attempts to discredit in an ever more fanciful and dismissive fashion as the article proceeds. The museum effect of neutrality is his ground, which readers of his thought-pieces against museum decolonization will find he wields with regularity. Here neutrality is asserted against "the increasingly popular conviction that not only can museums not be neutral sites, but that they also have a duty to be vehicles for social justice. Rather than chronicling, challenging and interpreting, we should be organising demonstrations and signing

Figure 8.4 Dismantling housing for heritage at Robin Hood Gardens. (Nicholas Thoburn, 2018)

petitions."[23] And this "conviction" is in turn indexed to a pluralism-denying "era of absolutist, righteous identity politics", as he puts it, deploying a framework dear to centrist and right-wing pundits for dismissing criticism of the racialized and gendered identity of the national public. Having thus raised the stakes, at the close of the article Hunt allows his prized dispassion to slip, dispelling critics as mere fly-by-night indignants: "the V&A has been active in east London since the opening of our Bethnal Green museum in 1872. And we will still be there long after the keyboard warriors and 'art-wash' agitators have moved on to their next bout of indignation."[24]

For all of Hunt's opposition to the fragment's critics, he knows not to reject the question of social housing, neither as context for the fragment nor as social issue: "Where critics are right to caution us is to ensure that our focus on design does not preclude context, and that we avoid fetishising architecture devoid of its social prehistory. That is why our pavilion in Venice forms part of a broader engagement with the question of social housing, which includes further debate at this year's London Design Festival and continued work with our near neighbours in North Kensington."[25] The choice of words here is revealing, where the "social" of Robin Hood Gardens is framed in terms of its "prehistory" not its present, concordant with the museum effect of confining it to the past. Still, we saw in Venice that the fragment was harnessed to a "future of social housing", a framing which is repeated so often in the fragment's publicity as to make it an integral feature of the work. Hunt, for example, notes the urgency of "the contemporary challenge around social housing", and another promotional text registers "unprecedented urban pressures and the redevelopment of numerous post-war housing projects".[26] Since the fragment serves to obscure the crisis of social housing, as I am arguing, why does social housing feature so integrally and in this seemingly positive way?

In part, this framing serves as a *palliative*, a virtuous gesture with which visitors can identify, should the social realities of estate demolition disturb their pleasure in this fragment of Brutalist council housing. But there is more to it, involving an additional museum effect, that of *civic exchange*, an effect encapsulated by this remark from Hunt: "I see the role of the museum not as a political force, but as a civic exchange: curating shared space for unsafe ideas."[27] In the fragment's curated space of civic exchange, *conflict is rendered into conversation*, so overlaying estate demolition and the affordability crisis with a veneer of polite debate, debate fixed on a nebulous future and unhurried by, without impact upon, the pressing realities of today. The content of this public conversation can be sympathetic to critical ("unsafe") ideas, but it severs itself from and disdains political action, not only through its civic standpoint but also in its favoured *style* – as Hunt's article, again, perfectly illustrates.

As we have seen, Hunt's cultivated objectivity and dispassionate rationalism is posited against the "indignant" righteousness and emotionality imputed to standpoints that contest the grounds of civic debate, whose illegitimacy is in this way exposed. This is not incidental. In Hunt's style is the very essence and function of the modern aesthetic, which, as David Lloyd has shown, "arises out of the necessity to forestall the revolutionary claims of its epoch and to substitute for the immediacy of political demands and practices an aesthetic formation of the disinterested and 'liberal' subject".[28] Conversely, the conflict that is disdained when it informs critical standpoints and interventions *empowers* the standpoint of the public. For the capacity to hold conflict in a shared community of dispassionate discourse is a foundational value of civic nationalism, "a secularised guarantor of the sacred cohesion of the body politic", in Jacopo Galimberti's phrase.[29] And so, in the V&A's civic exchange about social housing, the crisis of housing affordability, which risks scuppering the exhibit and its integrated public, is instead sublimated for the latter's health.

Some comment is warranted, nonetheless, on the specific *content* of this civic exchange. If the destructive effects of regeneration are obscured by museum neutrality, it is inevitable that regeneration's discourses will feed into the conversation, since they *are* the neutral commonsense, the doxa, of contemporary urbanism. For instance, describing the tenure composition of Blackwall Reach in favourable terms, Turner leaves unchallenged the government's notoriously dissembling category of affordable housing, and credulously repeats the council's discredited partial poll of residents that was used to claim consent for demolition.[30] He also fashions the terms of dispute into a polarity that once again casts council housing into the past, as heritage, while positing council-estate demolition and private rebuild on the side of progressive housing policy. "Some critics complain", Turner writes, "that the architectural infrastructure and heritage of the welfare state is rapidly being obliterated. Others argue that the loss of such derelict and inefficient housing is a worthwhile sacrifice for urgently needed new homes."[31] There is a third position, but this has no place in Turner's dissimulating polarity: the demolition of council estates for private rebuild at much-inflated prices, and the consequent uplift in adjacent land values, *creates* the housing crisis that it claims to solve. It is, however, a passing remark from Hunt that I will pick up for further analysis, what he calls "the constructive role that cultural institutions can have in promoting much-needed urban regeneration".[32]

The V&A East, the Olympic Legacy and the Social Cleansing of East London

With Hunt's commonsense advocacy of culture-led regeneration I commence the second move of this chapter. Thus far, we have traced the fragment's museum effects in the realm of cultural consumption, effects which obscure and contain council-estate demolition in the forms of the public, cultural history, neutrality and civic exchange. I turn in what follows to unpack additional features of the fragment, but now as an artefact *embedded in and fashioned by a site of regeneration*, that of East Bank.

The V&A East – comprising the V&A East Storehouse, where the fragment will be the centerpiece, and the V&A East Museum – is a key institution in the £1.1-billion (and rising) cultural mega-hub that is East Bank, which includes also new sites for the BBC, Sadler's Wells dance theatre, University College London and London College of Fashion. This is the culture-industry component of the vast state-led regeneration that is the legacy project of the London 2012 Olympics, overlapping with Newham council's 1,412-hectare Arc of Opportunity, a self-declared "regeneration supernova" that sweeps through a borough which includes 60% of the Olympics host site.[33] It is fitting that the V&A has a place here, since in the legacy project's initial conceptualization as Olympicopolis it sought inspiration from the Albertopolis complex, now with colonial extraction and manufacturing swapped out for cultural and knowledge industries, a "new powerhouse for innovation, creativity and learning".[34] But it is the effect of this regeneration on social housing that is my focus here, discussion of which requires first some consideration of the socio-economic conditions of the locale and their discursive appropriation by the V&A.

The V&A East will sit at the nexus of four of London's poorest boroughs, or what the museum's marketing describes as "four of the city's fastest-growing and most diverse boroughs".[35] In discursive framings such as this, the class and racial composition of the site is appropriated and retold as a culture of "hybridity and cosmopolitanism", to use Hunt's characterization of the V&A's civic mission.[36] It is a characterization cast backwards and forwards in time, validating the museum in a seamless duration that at once absolves and primes. Facing backwards, Hunt's characterization rewrites the imperial identities and hierarchies of race and nation, and the museum's role therein, as a hybrid scene of "the mongrel lineages of global culture" (and imputes the problem of racial and cultural identity instead to the movement for decolonization – a jaw-dropping instance of gaslighting).[37] Then, facing forwards, my interest here, this characterization of hybridity and cosmopolitanism gears the museum to urban social conditions in postcolonial and neoliberal times, where the economic role of museums has partially shifted from the external to the internal periphery.[38] Though well-sounding and apparently inclusive, such phrasing engages *in order to dispel*, substituting a marketing image of culture for the site's social realities, so as to usher it into the dispossession of redevelopment.

Since this image of hybridity and cosmopolitanism is disseminated primarily through the V&A's self-presentation and marketing, there is little requirement for it to reflect directly on extant communities. The moments when it does so, however, are revealing. For instance, though much of the declared "diversity" of the area is due to its large Bangladeshi and Somali Muslim population, a question at a public talk prompted Hunt to brandish the V&A's cosmopolitan civic vision *in opposition* to the welcoming provision of a dedicated prayer room at the new museum.[39] More revealing still, he bolstered his case with a barely concealed stereotype of the easily offended Muslim, a racializing trope by which Muslim populations are today figured as the backward and dangerous object for the self-demarcation and intervention of liberal cosmopolitanism, in both its neo-imperial and civic nationalist modes.[40] Hunt's cosmopolitan civic vision can also be seen reacting against the new museum's site in ways that draw from the repertoire of *class* hostility, in this comment, for example, made at the opening of the V&A Dundee: "before we get too romantic about what Stratford was like before the Olympics, there were a lot of mountains of fridges and burnt out double-decker buses in this part of London".[41]

In reality, East London suffers not from a surfeit of derelict fridges and burnt-out buses but from dire housing poverty. The new museum's host borough, Newham, has London's highest rate of homelessness, with 14,535 households living in temporary accommodation, as of November 2018, often in grim conditions of repair and overcrowding.[42] Newham also has the highest number of households placed in temporary accommodation outside of the borough, 3,292 between 2012 and 2017, through a provision of the 2011 Localism Act.[43] This pernicious and punitive piece of social-cleansing legislation, eagerly seized upon by Newham's Labour council, allows councils to discharge their duty to temporarily house the unintentionally homeless by placing them in cheaper private accommodation across the country, with often devastating effects on support networks, employment and mental and physical health.[44] To this situation, Hunt's "much-needed urban regeneration" is not the solution that it presumes to be – quite the opposite. Newham's crisis of housing affordability and security has been *exacerbated* by the massive residential building programme of the Olympics legacy, which is "high on hyperbole but low in terms of genuinely tackling the manifold housing problems of East London", as Paul Watt and Penny Bernstock have shown. Here "the living circumstances of those at the bottom of East London's broken housing system are even worse than they were before the Games".[45]

This dire situation was confronted with considerable effect by the Focus E15 Campaign, which I sketch briefly here as illustration of local conditions and to foreground resistance to regeneration. In September 2013, when 29 young women and their children were faced with eviction by the closure of Newham's Focus E15 homeless hostel, the Labour council informed them that Housing Benefit cuts and the scarcity of council homes could see them rehoused in temporary accommodation as far as 70 to 200 miles away.[46] Campaigning against their eviction and displacement, the women sought support from Newham's mayor, Robin Wales, only to be told, "if you can't afford to live in Newham, you can't afford to live in Newham".[47] Indifferent and dismissive, Wales' declaration also belies the fact that increasing property values and the expulsion of working-class residents have long been the council's *active pursuit*. As council leader in 1997, Wales made his priorities clear: "There are too many people, those currently living in Newham and those attracted from other London boroughs, who survive on low incomes or who present themselves as homeless. Whilst we will offer support and carry out our legislative duties, our aim will be to increase Newham's property values."[48]

Taking direct action against their dispossession, in September 2014 the Focus E15 mothers and supporters held a two-week occupation of two empty council flats on the Carpenters Estate, just a mile from the future V&A East, where some two-thirds of 700 council units had been emptied of residents and boarded up in readiness for post-Olympics demolition and regeneration (Figure 8.5).[49] It was a galvanizing moment in a campaign that, under the slogan *Social Housing Not Social Cleansing!*, opposes welfare retrenchment and the crisis of housing affordability, and the uneven distribution of these conditions by gender, racialization, ability and age. The campaign continues today, nine years on, while East Bank rises and the Carpenters Estate remains half-empty, awaiting demolition.

Council Housing as Art: Community, Spectacle and Regeneration

Viewed in relation to East Bank, the V&A's fragment of Robin Hood Gardens is not, then, a salvage work after the fact of demolition, but a showcase exhibit for a key institution in a major regeneration. Implicated in this process of working-class dispossession and displacement, the fragment also

Figure 8.5 Focus E15 occupation of flats in the Carpenters Estate. (Paul Watt, 2014)

shapes and is shaped by it. To understand how requires consideration of the place of class and council housing in the heritage component and public art of regeneration.

It is well documented that regeneration schemes like to corral class-contoured local heritage for their placemaking and legitimation, refashioning it accordingly. The broad features are well put by Malcolm James, regarding Newham's mega-regeneration: "The Arc of Opportunity's clean facades, cultural zones, warehouse educational establishments are predicated on the obliteration of the working population and their histories. All that is left are nostalgic adornments and clichéd branding. The refurbished quay cranes and lighter vessels provide packages of working-class 'community' and 'spirit' – sold to those investing in dehistoricised places."[50]

When class-contoured local heritage shifts from adornment to a major exhibit in a culture-led regeneration, one has reason to expect it to continue this placemaking and legitimation function. But can *council housing* play this role? At first it seems unlikely. When the role is taken by historical industry, as is typical, it is usually on sites long vacated by industry's conflictual class conditions, whereas here, the heritage fashioning of the working class must occur in the place *and time* of its displacement, raw with the housing crisis and "still warm", as Ana Vilenica puts it, "from the bodies of those who used to call it home".[51] Yet it is precisely this proximity that elects council housing for the role, a means of legitimation through the aesthetic repurposing of, and pseudo-identification with, that which is being destroyed – made all the more useful by the swarm of emotions and meanings, positive and negative, that are attached to home and council estates. These are the conditions for the curious regeneration practice of turning council housing *into public art*, of which the V&A's fragment is an example.

The features of this council-house art can be drawn from Josephine Berry's *Art and (Bare) Life* and her book with Anthony Iles, *No Room to Move: Art and the Regenerate City*. Berry and Iles identify a mode of public art on sites of demolition and displacement, council estates in particular, that emerged with the embrace of culture-led regeneration by the UK's New Labour administrations from 1997. Tending towards the participatory and dematerialized form of *relational* or *socially engaged* art, it provides a measure of participation and social inclusion for existent residents *at the moment of their imminent displacement*. As Berry puts it, such participatory art is "a way to include the so-called socially excluded into fields of action or theaters of meaning whose horizon", and here's the rub, "is retained as art".[52] This is the "logic of using art to heal social wounds while at the same time worsening them".[53]

A much-espoused value of such public art is *community*. Community serves as a localized version of Benjamin's class-excising unity of the public, though now amid the conflictual social terrain that it masks. Artists "fabricate totemic symbols of integrated communities" for populations undergoing "traumatic transformation and disintegration at the hands of the very parties who are funding the art work".[54] Indeed, such is the prominence of community, and the extent of its instrumentalization, that "a community's inclusion in art has today even come to betoken their imminent displacement".[55] This is not to say that this community inclusion must be especially successful, for it serves developers primarily as public relations, a *representation* of local consent. The group Southwark Notes encapsulates the function thus: "the artists claim to be engaged in a process of making the community visible, while the developer uses this process to demonstrate that the community is visibly engaged with the process of regeneration".[56]

Though typically dematerialized, the public art of regeneration can also take *artefactual* form, generally at the next phase, demolition itself, wherein "a localized artistic aura" is leveraged for placemaking with a now broader and more moneyed constituency, potential residents in waiting.[57] Notions of community often remain in these works, but as a negative image, its destruction turned into a haunting aesthetic of absence, a meditative, pacifying and readily marketable aesthetic value. And it combines with a new feature, that of *spectacle*, where works of extravagant scale, often incorporating the process of demolition itself, institute and symbolize the breach with a site's past and constitute the first act of placemaking. Now the physical form of council housing takes a role.

A forerunner is Rachel Whiteread's *House* (1993), her freestanding concrete cast of the inside space of a demolished terraced house in Bow, East London. More recent is Roger Hiorns' *Seizure* (2008, 2009–2010), an installation fashioned from a council flat in Southwark, South-East London, part of a post-war block being readied for demolition. Here the interior of a three-room flat was sealed and filled with 75,000 litres of copper sulphate solution, which solidified over three weeks to generate startling surfaces of encrusted, vivid blue crystal. Hiorns initially had Robin Hood Gardens in mind for the work.[58]

Both *House* and *Seizure* were commissions by Artangel, a major arts organization specializing in spectacular site-specific public art, whose board of trustees includes property developers, fund managers and founders of private equity firms, the drivers and beneficiaries of regeneration.[59] So too was the 2013 commission, ultimately unrealized due to opposition from residents and campaign groups, to construct an enormous pyramid or ziggurat from the demolished homes of Southwark's Heygate estate, the site of a notorious regeneration where 1,212 council homes were replaced by a development of 2,689 units, of which just 92 were for social rent.[60]

As to the social meaning of these artworks, it is as compromised by regeneration as is their institutional support. In his dissection of the planned Heygate pyramid, Christopher Jones shows the extraordinary degree of insensitivity, cack-handedness and regeneration boosterism that arises when artists and sponsors endeavour to explain and validate these works with reference to their social form and setting.[61] To take *Seizure* as example, in Artangel's contextualizing interview Hiorns presents an homology between the claustrophobia of its crystalline grotto – "forever growing inwards, an unrelenting, unknowing chemical activity going deeper inwards" – and the supposed stifling effects of council housing, which "provided no room for movement, zero mobility to move further, they are completely static materially and emotionally".[62] It is the integral meaning of this socially engaged work, which visitors were invited to experience and coproduce in their cramped shuffle through the flat (25,000 of them in the first three months alone, some queuing for hours to enter).[63] The problem here is not that *Seizure* misses the nature of the crisis facing council housing. Worse than that, it perpetuates a truism of regeneration – that of council housing as a bar to individuality and social mobility – and thus *legitimizes* demolition, a major cause of the housing inequality and crisis that *Seizure* purports to expose.

Do Ho Suh's Haunting Abstraction

The features and effects of this council-house art – pseudo-community, haunting absence and spectacular scale – supply means to grasp the different but complementary aesthetic forms of Suh's exhibition film, as I consider now, and the physical artefact, discussed subsequently.

As Turner sees it, Suh's film, titled *Robin Hood Gardens, Woolmore Street, London E14 0HG* (2018), "brings ... to life" the architectural fragment.[64] But the life it brings is one of haunting absence, its defining quality. The film includes drone footage of the exterior and demolition of the estate's west block, but mostly it concentrates on the interiors of the yet-to-be demolished east block. A disembodied camera-eye tracks languidly up and across through four apartments, passing seamlessly through floors and walls – Suh used time-lapse photography and photogrammetry to achieve the effect, stitching together hundreds of images in fine-grained detail. The few residents that feature, in the film's final scenes, sit silent and still in their homes, bearing a ghostly affect that is accentuated as they fade into absence. In some of the scenes the photography is superimposed with images from 3D scans, glitches included. The effect confers an uncanny quality to the film that resonates with the artist's previous sculptural works, consideration of which assists analysis of the film and its reception.

Suh is well known for engaging with the form, memory and affect of home and displacement, of which one example is illuminating.[65] *Seoul Home / L.A. Home / New York Home / Baltimore Home* (1999) is a scaled replica of the traditional Korean Hanok house that was Suh's childhood home, taking form as a suspended, diaphanous canopy of green silk organza, its physical details exactingly reproduced in stitched seams. As much as the representation and detailing situate the home in time, place and biography, the work's insubstantial materiality also renders it an *abstract emblem*, lifted out of particularity and made *universal*. As Frances Richard writes, "Premised in autobiography yet dematerialized to a lyrical husk, *Seoul Home* ... appears as a scrim onto which anybody may project his or her reveries about any absent home."[66]

In this universalizing effect, mobility and translatability are key. "I experience space through, and as, the movement of displacement", writes Suh, and this is encoded in the title of the work, which accumulates city names as it travels to each new site of exhibition.[67] This is, however, a *particular form* of movement and translatability, that of a privileged international class, *masquerading* as universal. "Suh's vision of 'intrinsically transportable and translatable space' takes for granted a world in which the peregrination of an artist who commutes between Seoul and New York while preparing for exhibitions in Venice and LA makes perfect sense."[68] In this the work shares in a trend for contemporary art to channel, uncritically, the dynamics of capitalist circulation and equivalence, if we shift from Suh's universally mobile class to its constituting and enabling conditions. The trend is isolated by Berry and Iles: "As with the piazzas, statuary and symbology of old, the public art of today likewise bears the insignia of its master – capital. Its universalizing force of equivalence leaves an indelible impression on contemporary art as openness and interchangeability become some of its defining characteristics."[69]

By stark contrast, this is not at all the experience of ex-residents of Robin Hood Gardens, Newham's Focus E15 hostel and all those subject to the crisis of housing affordability, whose social lives do not accord with, but are *made fraught and insecure by*, the movement and translatability of capital. Their housing displacement is not chosen but imposed, their homes are pulled out of shape and security by class society. Granted, Suh's *Robin Hood Gardens* registers this difference in part; it features not an individual private house but a council estate, in a scene of destruction not portability; the interiors are coded as working-class; and the homes, in their mundane detail, are evidently long-inhabited, not interchangeable, a situatedness conferred also by the film's title. Yet there is little here to puncture the film's languid, disembodied, haunting affect, which neutralizes this conflictual site of displacement while delivering it to the transportable aesthetic of contemporary global art. Indeed, insofar as class and crisis register in Suh's image, they are better seen as a *part* of its haunting abstraction, an instance of today's "spectacle of the abject", in Christoph Lindner's phrase, where interruptions and class contradictions in the neoliberal urban landscape are eagerly aestheticized into "a combination of sensation, indulgence, ambiance, delirium, and distraction in which human suffering becomes decorative, nostalgic, spectral".[70]

This aesthetic form and its subject are encapsulated in a widely used promotional photograph for *A Ruin in Reverse*.[71] Its mise-en-scène resembles the "Sticks and Stones" image of Alison Smithson on her bench, though not so its meaning. Two people, the curators perhaps, are seated in the Biennale warehouse-cum-gallery watching Suh's film in a relaxed manner, their gaze soaking up an expansive panorama of housing destruction. The estate's exterior is ripped off, yet it is rendered to them – and to the class that this image indulges and interpolates – as beautiful, serene and haunting, framed by a glorious urban sunset.

A Ruin Made Whole in Dispossession

Turning now to the physical fragment at the planned V&A East, the spectacular scale of previous council-house art is a patent feature. Taking a huge chunk of Brutalist housing into a museum interior shares in the *wow* effect of *House* and *Seizure*, as already evident in the acquisition's announcement and media reception. Unlike these time-limited works, however, the fragment at the V&A East will *endure*, enabling the site-cleansing effects of spectacle and placemaking to repeat into the future. What will be the specific features of these effects at the V&A East? One cannot know if the initial ambition and scale will be fully realized, as one whole apartment, or what precisely the exhibition features will be.[72] But since this is to be the fragment's permanent instantiation, to which its setting in the East Bank regeneration is integral, it warrants risking some speculation, drawing on features of the exhibited fragment thus far.

To continue in speculative mode, then, as the fragment moves into the future I contend that it will work *on the past*. *House* and *Seizure* opened to the future by spectacularizing and then demolishing the present, rendering it past. At the V&A East, the fragment will usher in the future, legitimating and flattering the regeneration, by *reconstructing* the past – a spectacular experience and representation of a council-house ruin *made whole*.

Components of this representation can be foreseen, centering on working-class *community*. Recall that the pseudo-community created in relational-art approaches to regeneration has binding and legitimating effects that precede demolition, after which it has no credible role. In contrast, at the V&A East, pseudo-community can endure, or endure as representation. The comforting quality of *home* presents a ready ground for this community, realizing the opportunity to assemble the apartment, with its meticulously salvaged original fittings, as a complete domestic unit. The exhibition panels of *A Ruin in Reverse* indicate that the *sociality* of estate life will also feature, in archival images of interaction on the streets in the sky and children playing on the estate's green, images that in Venice were weighted heavily on the estate's early years.

In a broader frame, the V&A's remit necessitates that the exhibit will focus on issues in design, Brutalism and the Smithsons, but the programme of post-war council housing will not be left aside. *A Ruin in Reverse* showed some circumspection about the viability of council housing – a panel in the section "The Road to Ruin" carried an enlarged quotation of an unfortunate remark by the Smithsons in order to imply that mistreatment by residents had a role in the estate's demise, and another featured Charles Jencks' damming appraisal of the estate.[73] This is no surprise, given current discursive and policy assaults on council estates and their residents. But I expect, on balance, that the exhibit will make a sympathetic appraisal of historical council housing. Doing so will enable it to bind council housing with home and street life to produce a positive representation of a unified, working-class, council-estate community, all held together in the reconstructed apartment. While Suh's film provides the haunting absence of working-class community in the present, I suggest that the fragment will furnish a community *made whole in the past*.

This is the reification of class, an image of the working class turned against itself. It fits with a dominant culture-industry representation of class today, which helps us understand the features and function of this reification. As I have said, the working-class condition is not one of coherent identity and community, but of crisis, ever produced anew as such. This is a *contemporary* condition, as true today as throughout capitalist modernity – or *more* so, given that deindustrialization and economic stagnation have ushered precarity, under-employment and personal debt into the heart of the wage relation.[74] However, in today's culture industries, as Steph Lawler has argued, the working class is commonly represented as an *identity* in crisis, in crisis and collapse *for having outlived its time*. The working class is discursively produced as an "anachronistic space", deemed to be "suffering from a political, social and cultural atavism: *in* the present, but not *of* it".[75] This representation of the working class as anachronistic in the present is bolstered if it can be found *vital and whole in the past*. If a set of images and signifiers of working-class experience (council estates, industrial labour, traditional markets, local pubs etc.) can be excavated from the past, assembled together and made whole in a nostalgic image of working-class community, then this serves all the better to render class to the past, revealed to be its proper place.

As to the V&A East, I am suggesting, then, that its fragment of Robin Hood Gardens will endure into the future as a reified and nostalgic representation of working-class housing and community in the past, its physical quality of a reconstructed ruin further establishing its distance from the present.[76] The site calls out for it. For if the fragment bears this representation, its affectionate image of the working class thus configured will flatter and legitimate the museum, while obscuring and substituting for the *crisis* of class and social housing that is the site's regeneration reality – a past to ground a future ever evacuated of the conflictual present.[77]

The different steps taken in this chapter bear repeating, for the V&A's fragment of Robin Hood Gardens is indeed multi-faceted. We have seen that the V&A's fragment is a fraught and class-ridden artefact, reflective of, and implicated in, the dispossession and demolition of working-class housing. It confounds this interpretation, however. For the fragment's destructive valence is bound up with its ability to appear *not* so, but rather as a seamless item of modern architectural heritage, a museum exhibit inserted neatly into the historical continuum of cultural history. Hence, I began unpacking the features of this acquisition by showing how it generates certain museum effects that serve to obscure and contain the crisis of social housing. Key here is the fragment's presupposition and consequence in the social form of the public, constituted as cohesive and unified through disavowal of the *class* conditions of society. This is not to say that the fraught social conditions of class are made entirely mute – indeed, conversation on matters of social housing is a prominently declared feature of the acquisition. But this conversation sublimates social conflict and political intervention into polite and indefinite civic exchange, a self-consolidating feature of the public form.

Though I teased out these museum effects in relation to *A Ruin in Reverse*, they are not tethered to this Biennale exhibition but manifest in various combinations and degrees of prominence in the fragment's different discursive and artefactual instantiations, including its emerging instantiation at the V&A East. However, I investigated the fragment's relation to the V&A East through a second set of concerns, shifting from its museum effects to consider how it shapes and is shaped by the state- and culture-led regeneration of East Bank. Here the fragment is a version of what I called *council-house art*, with the latter's regeneration aesthetics of pseudo-community, haunting absence and placemaking spectacle. In Do Ho Suh's exhibition film, Robin Hood Gardens is emptied of social content and made haunting and translatable, the aesthetic of high-end global culture masquerading as a universal experience. By contrast, the physical artefact, I speculated, will take a different but complementary form, where the working class that the film renders *absent in the present* will be found *whole in the past*, a reified representation of class community upon which the class-*cleansing* of Newham can be obscured, flattered and propelled.

Notes

1 Twentieth Century Society, tweet (December 14, 2017), https://twitter.com/c20society/status/941414874244055041?lang=ca.

2 Tristram Hunt, "Displaying the Ruins of Demolished Social Sousing at the Venice Architecture Biennale is not 'Art-Washing'", *The Art Newspaper*, 28 May 2018, www.theartnewspaper.com/comment/displaying-the-ruins-of-demolished-social-housing-is-not-art-washing-the-v-and-a-is-a-place-for-unsafe-ideas; Christopher Turner, "A Small Segment of a Masterpiece", *V&A Blog*, 6 March 2018, www.vam.ac.uk/blog/museum-life/a-small-segment-of-a-masterpiece-2.

3 The acquisition included 232 items of internal joinery and 67 façade elements, including two interior concrete staircases. Details obtained by a Freedom of Information request by Tom Keene,

www.whatdotheyknow.com/request/information_on_robin_hood_garden#incoming-1187565.

4 "The V&A at the 2018 Architecture Biennale", no date, www.vam.ac.uk/articles/la-biennale-di-venezia-2018.

5 Nelson Mota, *An Archaeology of the Ordinary: Rethinking the Architecture of Dwelling from CIAM to Siza*, unpublished PhD thesis (Delft University of Technology, 2014).

6 Alison and Peter Smithson, "'Sticks and Stones" Exhibition", *The Charged Void: Architecture* (New York: The Monacelli Press, 2001), 393.

7 Christopher Turner, "A Small Segment of a Masterpiece", *V&A Blog*, 6 March 2018, www.vam.ac.uk/blog/museum-life/a-small-segment-of-a-masterpiece-2.

8 The idea for the acquisition came from Lisa Fiore, of muf architecture, at the time she held a residency at the V&A.

9 Walter Benjamin, "Eduard Fuchs: Collector and Historian", trans. Knut Tarnowski, *New German Critique* no. 5 (Spring 1975): 27–58, 32.

10 *Ibid.*

11 *Ibid.*, 35, 36.

12 Douglas Crimp, *On the Museum's Ruins* (Cambridge, MA: MIT Press), 204.

13 Benjamin, cited in *ibid.*

14 Benjamin, cited in *ibid.*, 204–205.

15 Tim Barringer, "The South Kensington Museum and the Colonial Project", in *Colonialism and the Object: Empire, Material Culture and the Museum*, ed. Tom Flynn and Tim Barringer (London: Routledge, 1998), 11.

16 *Ibid.* Dan Hicks, *The Brutish Museums: The Benin Bronzes, Colonial Violence, and Cultural Restitution* (London: Pluto Press, 2020), 4.

17 Sumaya Kassim, "The Museum will not be Decolonised", *Media Diversified*, 15 November 2017, https://mediadiversified.org/2017/11/15/the-museum-will-not-be-decolonised/.

18 Greame Evans, "From Albertopolis to Olympicopolis: Back to the Future?" in *Mega-Events: Placemaking, Regeneration and City-Regional Development*, ed. Graeme Evans (London: Routledge, 2020).

19 Hunt, "Displaying the Ruins".

20 Vile&Arrogant, *No al monumento alla gentrificazione del museo V&A di Londra / No to V&A's Monument to London's Social Cleansing*, two-sided A4 leaflet, no date [2018], https://southwarknotes.files.wordpress.com/2018/05/robin-hood-gardens-eng-ita.pdf.

21 Hunt, "Displaying the Ruins".

22 *Ibid.* The critical paradigm of artwashing – the use of art by government and corporations to disguise and facilitate revanchist urban development – has been advanced by Stephen Pritchard, including regarding the V&A's fragment. See Stephen Pritchard, "The Artwashing of Gentrification and Social Cleansing", in *The Handbook of Displacement*, ed. Peter Adey, Janet C. Bowstead, Katherine Brickell, Vandana Desai, Mike Dolton, Alasdair Pinkerton and Ayesha Siddiqi (London: Palgrave, 2020).

23 Hunt, "Displaying the Ruins".

24 *Ibid.*

25 *Ibid.*

26 "The V&A at the 2018 Architecture Biennale".

27 Hunt, "Displaying the Ruins".

28 David Lloyd, *Under Representation: The Racial Regime of Aesthetics* (New York: Fordham University Press, 2018), 3.
29 Jacopo Galimberti, *Images of Class: Operaismo, Autonomia and the Visual Arts (1962–1988)* (London: Verso, 2022).
30 Turner, "A Small Segment of a Masterpiece".
31 *Ibid.*
32 Hunt, "Displaying the Ruins".
33 Aaron Morby, "1bn Stratford East Bank Scheme Clears Final Planning", *Construction Enquirer* (2019), www.constructionenquirer.com/2019/06/12/1bn-stratford-east-bank-scheme-clears-final-planning/.
34 "East Bank", no date, www.queenelizabetholympicpark.co.uk/east-bank; Evans, "From Albertopolis to Olympicopolis".
35 "The V&A East Project", no date, www.vam.ac.uk/info/va-east-project.
36 Tristram Hunt, "Museums Must Confront the Big Issues", *The Art Newspaper*, 20 December 2018, www.theartnewspaper.com/comment/museums-must-confront-the-big-issues.
37 *Ibid.*
38 Sometimes museums operate on external and internal peripheries simultaneously, as Saree Makdisi shows in his devastating critique of the Jerusalem Museum of Tolerance. Saree Makdisi, *Tolerance Is a Wasteland: Palestine and the Culture of Denial* (Oakland, CA: University of California Press, 2022).
39 Jonathan Knott, "Tristram Hunt 'Not Interested' in V&A Prayer Room", *Arts Professional*, 27 June 2019, www.artsprofessional.co.uk/news/tristram-hunt-not-interested-va-prayer-room.
40 *Ibid.* Hunt's words: "Because we live in a discourse where notions of being offended by culture and being offended by imagery is so prevalent, you want to hold the ring quite firmly about the civic function of an organisation." For discussion of how Hunt's anti-Muslim sentiment here combines with the museum's civic mission to both exclude and justify that exclusion, see Sumaya Kassim, "The Museum Is the Master's House: An Open Letter to Tristram Hunt", 26 July 2019, https://medium.com/@sumayakassim/the-museum-is-the-masters-house-an-open-letter-to-tristram-hunt-e72d75a891c8. For the wider role of *cosmopolitanism* in the dynamics of class appropriation, see Beverley Skeggs, *Class, Self, Culture* (London and New York: Routledge, 2004), 155–166.
41 Jonathan Knott, "Three Comments that Reveal Tristram Hunt's Approach to Cultural Inclusion", *Arts Professional*, 5 July 2019, www.artsprofessional.co.uk/news/three-comments-reveal-tristram-hunts-approach-cultural-inclusion.
42 "Housing Reaffirmed as Biggest Priority for Mayor of Newham as Shelter confirms East London Borough has Homeless Crisis", www.newham.gov.uk/Pages/News/Housing-reaffirmed-as-biggest-priority-for-Mayor-of-Newham-as-Shelter-confirms-east-London-borough-has-homeless-crisis.aspx.
43 Emma Youle, "The Great Housing Postcode Lottery: Ex-Newham Mayor Slammed over 3,000 Homeless Moved Out of Borough", *Newham Recorder*, 25 July 2018, www.newhamrecorder.co.uk/news/ex-newham-mayor-slammed-over-3-000-homeless-households-moved-out-of-borough-1-5607150.
44 Tom Gillespie, Kate Hardy and Paul Watt, "Surplus to the City: Austerity Urbanism, Displacement and 'Letting Die'", *Environment and Planning A: Economy and Space* 53 no. 7 (October 2021): 1713–1729.

45 Paul Watt and Penny Bernstock, "Legacy for Whom? Housing in Post-Olympic East London", in *London 2012 and the Post-Olympics City: A Hollow Legacy?*, ed. Phil Cohen and Paul Watt (London: Palgrave, 2017), 130, 132. See also the damming appraisal of the legacy development by the Greater London Authority's Budget and Performance Committee, in January 2021. It reveals that up to then only 22% of the 10,111 new homes were "affordable" – of which only half, at most, were at social rent – and concludes that the development "doesn't even begin to help address the capital's crippling affordable housing issue, despite having the means". Budget and Performance Committee, *LLDC's Finances During the COVID-19 Crisis* (January 2021), 5.

46 Patrick Butler, "Young Mothers Evicted from London Hostel May be Rehoused 200 Miles Away", *The Guardian*, 14 October 2013, www.theguardian.com/society/2013/oct/14/young-single-mothers-focus-e15-newham-rehoused.

47 Robin Wales, cited in Tom Gillespie, Kate Hardy and Paul Watt, "Austerity Urbanism and Olympic Counter-Legacies: Gendering, Defending and Expanding the Urban Commons in East London", *Environment and Planning D: Society and Space* 36 no. 5 (2018): 812–830, 818.

48 Focus E15 Campaign, "Sara and Her Children Must Stay in Newham!" 8 December 2017, https://focuse15.org/2017/12/08/sara-and-her-children-must-stay-in-newham/.

49 Gillespie et al., "Austerity Urbanism".

50 Malcolm James, "Authoritarian Populism / Populist Authoritarianism"', in *Regeneration Songs: Sounds of Investment and Loss from East London*, ed. Alberto Duman, Dan Hancox, Malcolm James and Anna Minton (London: Repeater Books, 2018), 297.

51 Ana Vilenica, "Against Museumification of Social Housing", talk at Four Corners Gallery, London, 1 June 2019.

52 Josephine Berry, *Art and (Bare) Life: A Biopolitical Inquiry* (Berlin: Sternberg Press, 2018), 305.

53 *Ibid.*, 306.

54 Josephine Berry Slater and Anthony Iles, *No Room to Move: Art and the Regenerate City* (London: Mute Books, 2010), 33.

55 Berry, *Art and (Bare) Life*, 305.

56 Southwark Notes, "Empowerment for Surrender: People's Bureau, Engaged Art and the Elephant", 1 January 2017, https://southwarknotes.wordpress.com/art-and-regeneration/empowerment-for-surrender-peoples-bureau-engaged-art-the-elephant/.

57 Jen Harvie, "Democracy and Neoliberalism in Art's Social Turn and Roger Hiorns's *Seizure*", *Performance Research: A Journal of the Performing Arts* 16 no. 2 (2011): 113–123, 119.

58 *Ibid.*

59 Christopher Jones, "Pyramid Dead – The Artangel of History", *Mute*, 17 April 2014, www.metamute.org/editorial/articles/pyramid-dead-artangel-history.

60 35% Campaign, "Elephant Park MP5 – the Final Chapter", 5 August 2019, http://35percent.org/2019-08-05-elephant-park-final-phase-affordable-housing/.

61 Jones, "Pyramid Dead".

62 Roger Hiorns and James Lingwood, "Writing: The Impregnation of an Object", *Artangel blog*, July 2008, www.artangel.org.uk/seizure/the-impregnation-of-an-object/.

63 This meaning was widely assumed by critics. Take Gilda Williams in *Artforum*: "this tenement-housing apartment has not been rendered unlivable so much as exposed for how unlivable it always was, what with its oppressively low ceilings, poky rooms, minuscule

hallways and claustrophobic bathroom". Cited in Harvie, "Democracy and Neoliberalism in Art's Social Turn", 115.

64 Christopher Turner, "Poplar in Panorama", *V&A Magazine* 50 (2019): 48–55, 55.

65 Paul Laster, "Do Ho Suh: From Sculpture to Film", *Whitehot Magazine* (November 2019), https://whitehotmagazine.com/articles/ho-suh-from-sculpture-film/4436.

66 Frances Richard, "Home in the World: The Art of Do-Ho Suh", *Artforum* (January 2002), www.artforum.com/print/200201/home-in-the-world-the-art-of-do-ho-suh-2092.

67 Do Ho Suh, cited in *ibid*.

68 Richard, "Home in the World: The Art of Do-Ho Suh".

69 Berry Slater and Iles, *No Room to Move*, 33.

70 Christoph Lindner, "Brutalism, Ruins, and the Urban Imaginary of Gentrification", in *The Routledge Companion to Urban Imaginaries*, ed. Christoph Lindner and Miriam Meissner (London: Routledge, 2018), 285.

71 The photograph is included in Christopher Turner, "La Biennale di Venezia 2018", 25 May 2018, www.vam.ac.uk/blog/museum-life/la-biennale-di-venezia-2018.

72 In August 2017, muf architecture's preferred option was to display one whole apartment, including both façades and its lower-level access to and portion of street deck. The V&A's curator of contemporary architectural collections, Neil Bingham, hoped for reconstruction so visitors could walk in. See "5 RHG Options 20170823", www.whatdotheyknow.com/request/information_on_robin_hood_garden#incoming-1187565 and Mark Brown, "V&A Acquires Segment of Robin Hood Gardens Council Estate", *The Guardian*, 9 November 2017, www.theguardian.com/artanddesign/2017/nov/09/va-buys-three-storey-chunk-robin-hood-gardens-council-estate-alison-peter-smithson-brutalist-architecture.

73 Charles Jencks, *The Language of Post-Modern Architecture*, 2nd edn (London: Academy Editions, 1978).

74 Endnotes, "A History of Separation", *Endnotes* 4 (2015): 70–192.

75 Steph Lawler, "White Like Them: Whiteness and Anachronistic Space in Representations of the English White Working Class", *Ethnicities* 12 no. 4 (2012): 418.

76 This aspect of the acquisition was wryly observed in an anonymous agitprop that appeared in London Tube carriages in May 2018, an apparent advertisement for a V&A exhibition named *Prole Zoo*. Aside a cut-out section of Robin Hood Gardens placed behind bars, the text read: "The last working-class person left in London is to be displayed in a reconstruction of its natural environment in this exciting new immersive exhibition by the Victoria & Albert Museum."

77 This homely image of class past can also serve the middle-class market in ex-council housing, contributing to beautiful Brutalism the alienable qualities of welfare-state community, ideals and optimism that were seen in the marketing of the Balfron Tower private sale.

Epilogue: A Book Is a Small Building

Writing comes before and after *and is* architecture. This insight is of much significance to the Smithsons' practice, as Christine Boyer encapsulates: "All their works, including their children's stories, were in essence architectural – and architecture in turn was never just about buildings."[1] Prolific writers, the Smithsons' writing was the primary field of emergence of their concepts, concepts which grappled with social and architectural problems towards, in parallel with and often without built form. Writing did not function alone, though, but in association with the Smithsons' sketches, diagrams, photographs, installations, groups, meetings – the parts of a "not quite architecture", in Boyer's characterization, without which the architecture would not have taken shape.[2] My interest in this epilogue is not with these parts as such, however, but with the means by which they were assembled and circulated – that is, with the Smithsons' *books*, more precisely with the *form* of these books, and with what they illuminate about the form of *this* book, *Brutalism as Found*.

Though we often miss it, lost in the immersive flow of text, books have *material form*, to which the Smithsons gave an unusual degree of attention – not only to crafting the words, concepts and styles of their books, but also to how these were co-constituted with formats, page layouts, covers and typography.[3] For instance, one of their books appraises the Modern Movement through the form of a *scrapbook*, a great gathering of images with very little text.[4] Another, *AS in DS*, the most formally experimental, is a "sensibility primer" for the landscape experience of a passenger in a car.[5] Here different and layered levels of perception, movement and topography are expressed through text at once flowing and fragmented, typography that curves, fans out and zigzags, variously assembled on the pages with sketches, diagrams, maps and photographs of Alison Smithson's passenger journeys. The book itself is cut to the streamlined outline of a Citroën DS, the fabled car from whence the observations were made.

The Smithsons' publications, then, were "built" as much as they were written. "For us", wrote Alison, "a book *is a small building*".[6] If this is no casual comment nor simple metaphor, it prompts us to ask, how were these books built? What kind of buildings are they? How do they relate to the architectural projects themselves? In short, what is the Smithsons' Brutalism of publishing?

As a means of intuiting and working out architectural form, the Smithsons' books were not integrated wholes. Their textual content is typically brief, fragmentary and impressionistic, and was rarely written directly for books, only later assembled as such from prior publication as magazine articles, editorial interjections, group reports, lectures, letters, diary and scrapbook entries and other non-book textual forms. It is an approach, whether it was by preference or force of circumstance, that recalls Walter Benjamin's taste for the textual fragment over the finished work – the "prismatic fringes" and "inconspicuous forms" of publishing, flush with social antagonism, over the "pretentious, universal gesture of the book".[7] This is not to say that the Smithsons' books as such lacked formal qualities. Assembled into books, these fragments and inconspicuous forms *nudged aside* the self-enclosed and self-sated form of the book, in books that partially consolidated certain problems and forms, but just as much *set the fragments working again*. Their books are a looping field of ideas, collaged, juxtaposed, reworked, rediscovered, folded into and out of each other, a plane of publishing "characterized by a kind of connective association of interactive loops".[8]

The Smithsons' books were also criss-crossed and charged by voids – not for nothing did they name their mammoth two-volume retrospective *The Charged Void* or was the third volume, assembled after their deaths, titled *The Space Between*. Their ideas are set in relation to each other without synthesis, the "space between" ideas arousing curiosity, provoking interpretation, as Max Risselada describes it.[9] And so, for Alison Smithson, "a book about architectural ideas does not have to be completely logical. The creative impulse often springs from a sense of connection ... Idea-energies are sparked off one another; a well-timed sighting can be a recognition of something capable of bearing idea-seeds, or an informed word initiate quite other ideas."[10]

The space between is a feature also of the relation between their books and their architectural projects. As means of grappling with problems and forms, the Smithsons' books do not converge towards refined and completed projects, so serving as the projects' explanation or as brochure-like marketing for their office. Rather, they persist as parts of an experimental, unfinished and impressionistic plane: the Smithsons' "texts are largely independent constructions that come about parallel to their projects. There is always a 'distance' between text and project – a space open to one's own interpretation."[11]

In turn, their completed buildings provoked new writing, writing like *this* book. The space between is here no less significant, its qualities described wonderfully by Boyer: "Once a project is constructed, something arises from the walls, the voids, the site, is released into the air to speak an unspoken language", an unspoken language which the "Smithsons' writings navigate".[12] It is an affective, imagistic, imaginative language, "speaking into the void in full acknowledgement of the indeterminacy of words released into the air".[13] In *Brutalism as Found*, I have sought to tap into this unspoken quality of the architecture of Robin Hood Gardens. This book is a building, a building with a close relation to its architectural object – Chapters 3, 4, 6 and 7 discern, tease out, reconstruct and walk through Robin Hood Gardens as an arrangement of deforming forms, each distinct, overlapping and folding into and out of the others. But in seeking to understand the architecture, to bear it into a future after demolition, my aim in this book is also to convey the affective, imagistic and imaginative qualities of the estate and its lived experience, qualities that exceed the book and yet are carried with it.

Comprised of fragments, criss-crossed by voids, provoked by architecture, this is not to say that books do not stand up by themselves. If a book is a small building, it has a certain autonomy. Here Manfredo Tafuri is again illuminating. Given the "untranslatability of architecture in linguistic terms", he too finds a "void" between architecture and writing.[14] But in this distance between the two, writing gains "autonomy with respect to the given that provokes it", as Marco Biraghi puts it.[15] This is the space of criticism, the *book* of criticism, the book of *class architecture*. At once attuned to and disrupting the givens of an architectural work and its times, *putting into crisis* that which appears whole, criticism "rearranges the work's materials in a different order" – it fashions a building in its own right.[16] Such a book-building is generative, but only insofar as it turns its method back upon itself: "by putting crisis into the real", writes Tafuri, "criticism must be capable of constantly putting *itself* into crisis" – it "recognizes itself as an 'unsafe building'".[17]

Critical, such books are also emotional or affective, and in various tones. Attentive to this, an appendix to *The Space Between* by Simon Smithson gives an intimate and moving sketch of his parents' writing – its habits, styles, tools and affects. "Writing was a constant in the lives of A & P", Alison especially.[18] Writing "was a discipline within the discipline of being an architect. It was an act of construction in and of itself and hence the publication of any manuscripts gave them enormous pleasure."[19] Pleasure and love. Drafts were exchanged, "a game of pass the parcel with each unwrapping and rewrapping part of the ongoing task of honing the manuscript". These exchanges, he came to realize, "were also an act of love – small missives past back and forth between A & P".[20] Love and anger. Forced by encounters in the world, as I have shown, the posing of architectural problems takes place in "a range of affective tones: wonder, love", yes, but also "hatred, suffering".[21] Affects of this latter variety are strikingly evident in one of the Smithsons' encounters with demolition, where the affects of pain and indignation conditioned and coursed through an extraordinary book, *The Euston Arch*.

The Smithsons devoted only two books to single buildings, one of which was to the Euston Arch, architect Philip Hardwick's hulking Doric propylaeum, 21 metres tall, which fronted London's Euston train station from 1837 until 1962, when it was demolished in the face of considerable opposition, from the Smithsons included. Of all their books' different intensions, repertoires and styles, this was their only "engaged" book, as Peter Smithson later recalled – it was "absolutely political", "the one thing which was consciously political in our life".[22] A book of architecture, absolutely political, and engaged against the social violence of demolition – it is an apt book with which to invoke and draw out the affective tones and durational form of *Brutalism as Found*.

Titled in full *The Euston Arch and the Growth of the London, Midland and Scottish Railway*, it is a large landscape format of some 70 unpaginated pages, and deliberately experimental in form, a point Alison Smithson underscored by referring within to the experimental books of the Bauhaus.[23]

It bursts with a multitude of photographs, engravings, drawings, diagrams, plans and snippets of historical and contemporary text. They are fragments of the construction, life and demolition of the Euston Arch and the Railway Age – its locomotives, instruments, materials, workshops, landscapes, maps, regulations, affordances, navvies, operatives, engineers, inventors, obstacles, enmities, struggles etc. – of which the Arch was deeply symbolic, "the gateway to the first great railway to storm England's capital city".[24] The overall effect is of a maelstrom of impressions – a "wildly signalling assemblage", as Peter Smithson's postscript calls it.[25] But it is the affective tone of the book, and how this is carried through its form, that concerns me here.

The book's tone is encapsulated in the title of one of the opening texts, "The Euston Murder" – *Architectural Review*'s plotting of the path to demolition – and is up front also in the title of Alison Smithson's essay, "The Arch Criminals of the Euston Arch", which runs across a quarter-section of 17 of the early pages. Her title is set out on the page as a *spiral*, thus repeating in typography the format of the book's first edition, a spiral-bound paperback wrapped tightly around a stick and sealed in translucent purple plastic, reminiscent of a rocket firework.[26] The spiral also provides the essay's motif, standing for "indignation" at the wanton destruction, this "supreme act of delinquency of the whole society".[27] It is an indignation that spirals out through biographical, psychic, architectural and social dimensions of the railway, the Arch and its demolition.

"When a real catastrophe travels round and round in one's bones", Smithson begins in personal register, "it is time to invent the spiralling book – obviously enough spirally bound – each page an agonizing reflection or pang, all continuous, round and round and round".[28] "That I have to keep stopping – my indignation makes me shake so – justifies the spiral form". Round and round, the affective condition of indignation at the destruction is not a point in linear time, but an *excess*, a duration that *endures*. It spirals backwards and forwards in time, as does the event of destruction itself: "to a happening like the annihilation of the Euston Arch there is no beginning – and no end. Each would-be end goes far out of sight, either way." Hence the absence of page numbers – such a duration has no linear, numerical pacing.

While the duration of destruction and indignation is non-linear, it certainly had causes and agents, and Smithson's essay spirals through them with a lively contempt. The grey men of state and bureaucracy, "the dull, the operators of the machinery of modern existence". This "nation of dog lovers", seemingly unable to "prize inanimate objects": "Can we not commune with buildings, stones, views – despite Wordsworth and all our Romantic poets/painters?" "British corporate taste: nondescript house or ill-bred offices, a penchant for the shoddy." "England, spiritually spent, pulling down her sooty past." Plotting all this is seemingly a task greater than the book: "To study with the morbidity of a Gide the men who destroyed the Euston Arch", to study "How all decisions / actions / pending trays / commuters' journeys coagulated into a big destructive act." Smithson interrogates causes and effects closer to home too: those who fought with too "genteel sobriety", the people "who went to the Prime Minister and limply left without a promise – or a scene". "Can I only blame myself?" she writes, attending now to the complex affects of struggle and defeat: "Those who lost", the "terrible feeling of knowing they fight a losing battle", "The embarrassment of caring". Above all, the essay frames demolition as "a ritual act" of vengeful destruction, an "act of revenge by the south against the north", an "anti-north punch", for the Railway Age "was the first time for centuries the power which the court and the south control suddenly came to depend on the industrial energy of the north".[29]

Yet, just as much as the affect of the book's duration is indignant, it is also *joyful*, which again is encoded in its form. In place of the page numbers is the magical device of a *flipbook*. The bottom right-hand corners of the pages bear a series of incrementally different line drawings which animate the construction of the Arch as one flicks through, thus inviting a circular, continuous and playful engagement. The flipbook animation also evokes a sense that this book, in its small way, is a *reconstruction* of the Arch, a paper *monument* that bears the Arch into the future.[30] It is a reconstruction in fragments. The book's compositional method of multitudinous fragments bears joy in each sought-out detail, in the smallest of its minutiae as much as in the large, and joy in the process and form of assembly itself. Here the Arch, in its fullness and its destruction, is not the presence or absence of a single structure, but extends backwards and forwards in time through planes of social, technological, psychic and material culture.

The book registers the Arch's joyful duration also by its measure of the "magnitude" and "wonder" of what had been destroyed. Now the Doric takes over from the spiral as the guiding thread. Like the Doric temples planted in

Greek landscape, as if from nowhere, devoid of striating spatial plans, the Arch too was dropped down in the open terrain. They share a quality too of anomalous historical emergence. "Compared with other styles of architecture there is no sign of how the Doric temple developed: it sprang fully formed out of the dark ages." Likewise, the railways, whose locomotives and carriages often took names from the Greek revival, "must have appeared to spring forth, fully clad in all their gear and trappings". Such are "the supreme moments of creation of an era", the moments of invention, of the *event* of invention.

We see, then, that indignation, pain and anxiety at the destruction – the fraught conditions of the Smithsons' book – are also the route to a work of wonder and joy, which Alison gropes towards naming by comparing the book to a Boys' Own Encyclopaedia, a Christmas-present annual or even a lollipop, a "spiral on a stick; to lick at, rather than pore over".[31] The external appearance of the hardback edition is indeed suggestive of such children's annuals, or even an innocuous railway history – until one pays closer attention to the cover, where blood-red pooling around the negative image of the Arch starts to look a lot like a scene of murder.

The Euston Arch, much admired though it was, may seem an odd entity for modernist architects to devote such attention and emotion, but it is clear that the book's wonder and joy are not contained in this one entity but reach out through a maelstrom of material, social and technological parts, forms and processes. And the book's concern with destruction, extending backwards and forwards in time, is a trenchant stand against architectural destruction *in general*, as Peter Smithson's postscript underscores. The book did not arise from a nostalgic impulse, but rather "Its concern is with why society does not value its good buildings, to try and think out why good buildings, even when they – like new housing – are something society needs, are subject to senseless destruction."[32] And that, of course, is an insistent question for *this* book too, concerning society's wanton destruction of council housing. *Brutalism as Found* is not a spiral book, a lollipop or an annual – its formal inventions are of a more methodological and textual kind. But it shares with *The Euston Arch* the affect of indignation, and joy in architectural form.

The indignation that informs this book's research, writing and presentation was generated by and directed at numerous concatenated features of class society, which bear naming, in an open-ended list: the demolition and privatization of council housing under the guise of regeneration; the desperate crisis of housing affordability, security and safety, amid and produced by vast surpluses of property and wealth; the conversion of London land and housing into a basin of financial speculation and accumulation; the rapacious property industry and its investors, agents and apologists in government and the press; the Brutalist revival as vector and palliative for the middle-class appropriation of working-class housing; social cleansing disguised as art and heritage; the museum as means and mask for dispossession; the stigmatization and marginalization of working-class estates and their residents, delivered with faux solidarity by those who reap rewards from demolition; and the razing of Robin Hood Gardens, as both a singular loss and an egregious example of all of the above.

Indignation fuelled the book's grappling of these features into the problem and concept of class architecture, and my reconstruction of the deforming forms by which class architecture took shape as Robin Hood Gardens. Simultaneously, this reconstruction courses with joy – a joy spiralling in and out of the forms, lived experience and theory of this extraordinary estate. The indignation and joy of class architecture are, in this book, coarticulated. One cannot exist without the other, for the condition of class architecture as experimental, critical and unfinished form is the crisis of class society, crisis that it at once bears, confronts and deforms.

As the deforming forms and lived experiences of Robin Hood Gardens are fashioned and expressed in this book, I think of it as having a *duration*. It is a duration that exceeds and counters the linear time of the estate's demolition and the V&A's butchered chunk of Brutalism, wherein Robin Hood Gardens is confined to the past. As a duration, the book extends backwards and forwards in time, bearing between its covers a manifold of component parts, forms, materials, concepts, diagrams, myths, atmospheres and narratives of the estate's living architecture and its demolition. In this is a final feature of the book's form. As a duration, *Brutalism as Found* is a small, unfinished fragment of a *monument*. Here, as Deleuze and Guattari have it, a "monument is not something commemorating a past" – or not only that; "it is a bloc of present sensations ... that provide the event with the compound that celebrates it".[33] A monument is not a work of nostalgia; indeed nostalgia, the post-war class settlement bundled up into a marketable image of Brutalism, is one of the book's targets. Rather, this book as monument is a *continuation* of the estate's engaged architecture. It "confides to the ear of the future" the deforming forms and lived experiences, the indignation and joy, the rough poetry that is Robin Hood Gardens as found. And in this the book stands, awkward and wrenching, against the crisis of the present.

Notes

1 M. Christine Boyer, *Not Quite Architecture: Writing around Alison and Peter Smithson* (Cambridge, MA and London: MIT Press, 2017), 389.

2 This phrase, which titles Boyer's book, named a series of articles in *The Architects' Journal* to which Alison Smithson occasionally contributed under the pen name Margaret Gill, her middle and maiden names. *Ibid.*, 397. See Boyer for discussion of the Smithsons' children's stories, Alison's novels and other of their less directly architectural writings.

3 They describe this at one point as seeking a "fit between text, format, invention and book-as-object". Alison and Peter Smithson, *The Shift* (London: Academy Editions, 1982), 62. For discussion of experimental publishing, see Nicholas Thoburn, *Anti-Book: On the Art and Politics of Radical Publishing* (Minneapolis and London: Minnesota University Press, 2016) and Nicholas Thoburn, "Twitter, Book, Riot: Post-Digital Publishing against Race", *Theory, Culture and Society* 37 No. 3 (2020): 97–121.

4 Alison and Peter Smithson, *The Heroic Period of Modern Architecture* (London: Thames and Hudson, 1981).

5 Alison Smithson, *AS in DS: An Eye on the Road* (Delft: Lars Müller Publishers, 2001 [orig. 1983]).

6 Alison Smithson, in Smithson and Smithson, *The Charged Void: Urbanism* (New York: The Monacelli Press, 2005), 15, emphasis added. This undated text is one of the prefatory snippets assembled to describe the evolution and structure of their two-volume retrospective, *The Charged Void*, books which Peter Smithson characterizes as having been "built". *Ibid.*, 17. Jane Rendell has made a similar point, underscoring its significance for architectural practice today: "In writing we might think of the patterning of words on a page or the design of a page itself – its edges, boundaries, thresholds, surfaces and the relation of one page to another – as the distribution of objects in space. So it is possible to consider criticism as a form of architecture, and it is also desirable, because in so doing, in thinking one in terms of another, we are able to see more clearly what the differences between the two might be, and what is at stake in the binary and often hierarchical definition of those differences." Jane Rendell, "Introduction: Architecture Writing", in *Critical Architecture*, ed. Jane Rendell, Jonathan Hill, Murray Fraser and Mark Dorrian (New York: Routledge, 2007), 89. Rendell has pioneered here, her methodology of *site-writing* building books-as-architecture across a range of textual, spatial, sensory, psychic, social and imaginative planes, where the book is immanent to the object of criticism at hand. See Jane Rendell, *Site-Writing: The Architecture of Art Criticism* (London and New York: I.B. Tauris, 2010) and, the more formally inventive, Jane Rendell, *The Architecture of Psychoanalysis: Spaces of Transition* (London and New York: I.B. Tauris, 2017).

7 Walter Benjamin, "Unpacking My Library", in *Illuminations*, ed. Hannah Arendt, trans. Harry Zohn (New York: Schocken Books, 2007), 68. Walter Benjamin, *One-Way Street*, ed. Michael

W. Jennings, trans. Edmund Jephcott (Cambridge, MA and London: Harvard University Press, 2016), 21. It was sometimes a struggle for the Smithsons to find publishers for their books, and at least one, *Italian Thoughts*, was self-published – though I say that not at all to diminish it; quite the opposite.

8 Boyer, *Not Quite Architecture*, xii.

9 Max Risselada, "The Space Between", in Alison and Peter Smithson, *The Space Between*, ed. Max Risselada (Köln: Walther König, 2017), 262.

10 Alison Smithson, "Transmissions and Connections", in Alison and Peter Smithson, *The Charged Void: Architecture* (New York: The Monacelli Press, 2001), 37.

11 Risselada, "The Space Between", 261. That the Smithsons break with the office-brochure approach to architectural monographs is a point made by Dirk van den Heuvel in his review of *The Charged Void: Architecture*, *AA Files* No. 49 (Spring 2003): 97–100.

12 Boyer, *Not Quite Architecture*, xiv.

13 *Ibid.*

14 Tafuri, cited in Marco Biraghi, *Project of Crisis: Manfredo Tafuri and Contemporary Architecture*, trans. Alta Price (Cambridge, MA and London: MIT Press, 2013), 8.

15 Biraghi, *Project of Crisis*, 8.

16 *Ibid.*, 6.

17 Manfredo Tafuri, *The Sphere and the Labyrinth: Avant-Gardes and Architecture from Piranesi to the 1970s*, trans. Pellegrino d'Acierno and Robert Connolly (Cambridge, MA and London: MIT Press, 1987), 9, 12, emphasis added.

18 Simon J. B. Smithson, "A Few Words about A & P Writing", in Alison and Peter Smithson, *The Space Between*, ed. Max Risselada (Köln: Walther König, 2017), 243.

19 *Ibid.*

20 *Ibid.*

21 Gilles Deleuze, *Difference and Repetition*, trans. Paul Patton (New York: Columbia University Press, 1994), 139.

22 Peter Smithson, "Think of it as a Farm! Exhibitions, Books, Buildings. An Interview with Peter Smithson", in *This Is Not Architecture*, ed. Kester Rattenbury (London: Routledge, 2002), 96.

23 Though not entirely true, she writes here that "there hasn't been any proclamation in book form worth opening and not reading to get the visual message since the Bauhaus books". Alison Smithson, "The Arch Criminals of the Euston Arch", in Alison and Peter Smithson, *The Euston Arch and the Growth of the London, Midland and Scottish Railway* (London: Thames and Hudson, 1968), unpaginated.

24 L. T. C. Rolt, *George and Robert Stephenson*, cited in *ibid.*

25 Peter Smithson, "Postscript", in Alison and Peter Smithson, *The Euston Arch and the Growth of the London, Midland and Scottish Railway* (London: Thames and Hudson, 1968).

26 The spiral edition (very limited) can be spotted in a photograph of the Smithsons' books in Smithson and Smithson, *The Shift*, 62.

27 Alison Smithson, "The Arch Criminals of the Euston Arch". Subsequent references are to this essay unless otherwise stated.

28 The spiral reaches back to childhood: "It starts for me with railways as part of the blood stream", "the first tubular chrome furniture and wide windows I ever saw were in the dining car on the Harrogate run: these were Modern".

29 I will not get carried away and claim that this is a *class* analysis of causes. The uncritical romance of the railway that runs through Smithson's essay is problematic, for steam power

and rail transportation must, at the very least, be considered dialectically in relation to their extension of capitalist extraction and exploitation, the transatlantic slave trade and imperialism. Using formal features of *The Euston Arch* to illuminate the affective and durational form of *Brutalism as Found* is not to concur with all of its analysis.

30 "This book is both a memorial and a protest", the back-cover description begins, though I prefer monument to memorial, a form that has a more political and dynamic quality, as I show shortly.

31 *Ibid.*

32 Peter Smithson, "Postscript". He remarks also that *The Euston Arch* was assembled in the period following the cancellation of their commission to design the British Embassy in Brasilia, after a good deal of work. It was "a profoundly disturbing gap in our lives, a gap which was filled by the preparation of this book", "the ritual destruction of the Euston Arch ... felt by us at such a time in a specially painful way". This suggests some displacement in their object of indignation, the British government having been a leading party in both decisions.

33 Gilles Deleuze and Félix Guattari, *What Is Philosophy?*, trans. Hugh Tomlinson and Graham Burchell (London: Verso, 1994), 167–168, 176.

Acknowledgements

My gratitude above all goes to the residents of Robin Hood Gardens, who welcomed us into their homes and generously gave their time to be interviewed and photographed, teaching us about the social life and architecture of their extraordinary estate.

The book issues from a collaborative research and photography project with my friend and colleague Kois Miah, who has been a joy to work with. Kois taught me the pleasures of photography as a research and exhibition medium, as we teased out together how to bring photography and sociology to bear upon each other. I owe a huge thank you to Aklima Begum and Runa Khalique for their assistance and critical insight in interviewing residents.

The ideas in this book have benefitted greatly from the opportunity to air and discuss them at talks and conferences. I would like to thank Saree Makdisi and Dana Cuff for a wonderful visit to UCLA Architecture and Urban Design; Mark Crinson for a talk at Birkbeck's Architecture, Space and Society Centre; and Jacopo Galimberti for a seminar on Brutalism at the University of Bologna. Mark also provided valuable insight and guidance at the proposal stage of the book, and discussions with Saree and Jacopo about architecture, urbanism, art and politics over recent years have been most rewarding.

For the photography exhibitions of our project, many thanks to Nizam Uddin, Docklands Outreach, and SPLASH at St Matthias Community Centre; to Four Corners gallery, especially Ruby Rees-Sheridan and Howard Francis; and to Anna Weaver for her design of the online exhibition. Sister Christine Frost has been a campaigning force for social housing in Poplar and around since Canary Wharf, uninvited, first dropped itself down on the Isle of Dogs, and was a great help in the early stages of the research.

Many thanks indeed to Soraya and Simon Smithson for permission to reproduce material from the Smithson Family Collection, and to Soraya, Lucas Wilson and Maria Prieto Moris for all their help sourcing the images.

The project was enabled by a British Academy/Leverhulme Small Grant, for which I am thankful. The School of Social Sciences at the University of Manchester generously supported the project's three exhibitions, with a Small Grant, a Social Responsibility Award and a Research Support Grant.

I am grateful to Atau Tanaka for encouraging me to submit the book proposal to Goldsmiths Press. Discussion about Brutalism, urbanism and public art with series editors Josie Berry, Dubravka Sekulić and Atau during the writing has been a pleasure. Ellen Parnavelas was supportive and accommodating throughout the sometimes rocky path of completing a book during the Covid pandemic. Many thanks to the two anonymous readers of the manuscript.

The book was first sketched out in the last year of the Centre for Research on Socio-Cultural Change, where conversation about materials and infrastructure with Eleanor Casella, Jeanette Edwards, Gillian Evans, Penny Harvey, Hannah Knox, Chris McLean, Damian O'Doherty, Madeleine Reeves and Kath Woodward sparked many ideas.

My first encounter with Brutalism was Denys Lasdun's campus at the University of East Anglia. As boys my brother Alan and I would wander and play around its elevated walkways, student-dorm ziggurats and open grounds while our parents, academics, would look in from time to time, take us to lunch in the canteen and otherwise usher us into a world where certain built forms and spaces are special. It is a terribly fond memory, for which, and for much else besides, I am grateful to June and John.

Friends and colleagues assisted the writing of this book with discussion and guidance, reading of drafts, image-sourcing, transcription, introductions, a home from home and event-organizing – thank you to Les Back, Bridget Byrne, Darsavini, Alberto Duman, Ben Highmore, Anthony Iles, Jakob Jakobsen, Chris Jones, Vanessa May, Khalid Nadvi, Sara and Sami Nadvi-Byrne, Jackie O'Callaghan, Simon O'Sullivan, Motiur Rahman, Dheraj Shamoo, Ana Vilenica and Paul Watt. As well as his friendship, Stephen Zepke's ever-acute insight has been invaluable at various stages of the writing.

While the book was being researched, my sons Ilan and Noah had to put up with some Saturday-afternoon absences from *both* their parents, since Runa was part of the research group. Occasional trips to the estate's mound may have made up for it, where some historic hill-rolling sessions took place. It is to Runa and our boys that I dedicate the book, with much love.

An early version of parts of the book was published as "Concrete and Council Housing: The Class Architecture of Brutalism 'as Found' at Robin Hood Gardens", *City* 22 no. 5–6 (2018). A version of Chapter 8 was published as "Salvage Brutalism: Class, Culture and Dispossession in the Victoria and Albert Museum's Fragment of Robin Hood Gardens", *Oxford Art Journal* 45 no. 2 (2022).

Bibliography

Adonis, Andrew and Bill Davies, eds. *City Villages: More Homes, Better Communities*. London: Institute for Public Policy Research, 2015.

Albuerne, Alejandra. "Robin Hood Gardens: Reinforced Concrete Design and Construction of a Museum Artefact in Reinforced Concrete." Unpublished conference paper, April 2020.

Archer, Tom and Ian Cole. *Profits before Volume? Major Housebuilders and the Crisis of Housing Supply*. October 2016, www4.shu.ac.uk/research/cresr/sites/shu.ac.uk/files/profits-before-volume-housebuilders-crisis-housing-supply.pdf.

Architects for Social Housing. "Embodied Carbon Estimation for Central Hill Estate: Report by Model Environments". February 2017, https://architectsforsocialhousing.co.uk/2017/02/02/embodied-carbon-estimation-for-central-hill-estate-report-by-model-environments/.

Back, Les and Michael Keith. "Reflections: Writing Cities". In *Stories of Cosmopolitan Belonging: Emotion and Location*. Hannah Jones and Emma Jackson, eds. London and New York: Routledge, 2014.

Baillieu, Amanda. "To the Rescue of Robin Hood". *Building Design* 1807. 22 February 2008, 2.

Balfron Social Club. "Balfron Tower Redevelopment Video by Hawkins\Brown". 20 July 2015, http://balfronsocialclub.org/2015/07/20/balfron-tower-redevelopment-video-by-hawki nsbrown/.

Banham, Rayner. "The New Brutalism". *October* 136 (2011 [orig. December 1955]): 19–28.

Barringer, Tim. "The South Kensington Museum and the Colonial Project". In *Colonialism and the Object: Empire, Material Culture and the Museum*. Tom Flynn and Tim Barringer, eds. London: Routledge, 1998.

Baudrillard, Jean. "Symbolic Exchange and Death". In *Selected Writings*. 2nd edn. Mark Poster, ed. Stanford, CA: Stanford University Press, 2002.

Bell, Jonathan. "London's Brutalist Balfron Tower Is Brought Back to Life". *Wallpaper*. 2 July 2018, www.wallpaper.com/architecture/balfron-tower-brutalism-london-londonewcastle-stu dio-egret-west-brody-associates.

Benanav, Aaron. *Automation and the Future of Work*. London: Verso, 2020.

Benjamin, Walter. "Eduard Fuchs: Collector and Historian". Trans. Knut Tarnowski. *New German Critique* 5 (Spring 1975): 27–58.

Benjamin, Walter. "Unpacking My Library". In *Illuminations*. Hannah Arendt, ed. Harry Zohn, trans. New York: Schocken Books, 2007.

Benjamin, Walter. *One-Way Street*. Michael W. Jennings, ed. Edmund Jephcott, trans. Cambridge, MA and London: Harvard University Press, 2016.

Berry, Josephine. *Art and (Bare) Life: A Biopolitical Inquiry*. Berlin: Sternberg Press, 2018.

Berry Slater, Iles, Josephine and Anthony Iles. *No Room to Move: Art and the Regenerate City*. London: Mute Books, 2010.

Biraghi, Marco. *Project of Crisis: Manfredo Tafuri and Contemporary Architecture*. Alta Price, trans. Cambridge, MA and London: MIT Press, 2013.

Birmingham, Elizabeth. “Refraining the Ruins: Pruitt-Igoe, Structural Racism, and African American Rhetoric as a Space for Cultural Critique”. *Western Journal of Communication* 63 no. 3 (1999): 291–309.

Blackwall Reach, London E14, marketing brochure, https://blackwallreach.co.uk/application/files/9615/6163/6074/Blackwall_Reach_Brochure_-_HOST.pdf.

Boughton, John. *Municipal Dreams: The Rise and Fall of Council Housing*. London: Verso, 2018.

Boyer, M. Christine. *Not Quite Architecture: Writing around Alison and Peter Smithson*. Cambridge, MA and London: MIT Press, 2017.

Boys Smith, Nicholas and Alex Morton. *Create Streets*. London: Policy Exchange, 2013, https://policyexchange.org.uk/wp-content/uploads/2016/09/create-streets.pdf.

Brennan, Jessie. *Regeneration! Conversations, Drawings, Archives and Photographs from Robin Hood Gardens*. London: Silent Grid, 2015.

Brown, Mark. “V&A Acquires Segment of Robin Hood Gardens Council Estate”. *The Guardian*. 9 November 2017, www.theguardian.com/artanddesign/2017/nov/09/va-buys-three-storey-chunk-robin-hood-gardens-council-estate-alison-peter-smithson-brutalist-architecture.

Buchli, Victor. “Moisei Ginzburg’s Narkomfin Communal House in Moscow: Contesting the Social and Material World”. *Journal of the Society of Architectural Historians* 57 no. 2 (1998): 160–181.

Budget and Performance Committee. *LLDC’s Finances During the COVID-19 Crisis*. January 2021.

Building Design. “Council Drafts in Smithson”. *Building Design* 1239. 20 October 1995.

Building Design. “EH Fails to Support Robin Hood Gardens”. *Building Design* 1818. 9 May 2008.

Building Design. “Hodge Refusal to List Snubs Profession”. *Building Design* 1826. 4 July 2008.

Building Design. “Timeline of BD’s Campaign to List the Estate”. *Building Design* 1826. 4 July 2008.

Bulley, Dan, Jenny Edkins and Nadine El-Enany, eds. *After Grenfell: Violence, Resistance and Response*. London: Pluto Press, 2019.

Butler, Patrick. “Young Mothers Evicted from London Hostel May be Rehoused 200 Miles Away”. *The Guardian*. 14 October 2013, www.theguardian.com/society/2013/oct/14/young-single-mothers-focus-e15-newham-rehoused.

Calder, Barnabas. *Raw Concrete: The Beauty of Brutalism*. London: William Heinemann, 2016.

Cameron, David. “I’ve Put the Bulldozing of Sink Estates at the Heart of Turnaround Britain”. *The Times*. 10 January 2016, www.thetimes.co.uk/article/ive-put-the-bulldozing-of-sink-estates-at-the-heart-of-turnaround-britain-rtcgg2gnb6h.

Chan, Carson. "Lacaton and Vassal: Game Changer". *032c*. 4 March 2013, https://032c.com/o-architects-where-art-thou-game-changer-lacaton-vassal.

Châtelet, Gilles. *Figuring Space: Philosophy, Mathematics, and Physics*. Robert Shore and Muriel Zagha, trans. Dordrecht: Kluwer Academic, 2000.

Coe, Jonathan. *Like a Fiery Elephant: The Story of B. S. Johnson.* London: Piacador, 2004.

Coleman, Alice. *Utopia on Trial: Vision and Reality in Planned Housing*. London: Hilary Shipman, 1985.

Colenutt, Bob. *The Property Lobby: The Hidden Reality Behind the Housing Crisis*. Bristol: Policy Press, 2020.

Colomina, Beatriz. "Unbreathed Air 1956". *Grey Room* 15 (2004): 28–59.

Colomina, Beatriz and Peter Smithson. "Friends of the Future: A Conversation with Peter Smithson". *October* 94 (Autumn 2000): 3–30.

Commission for Racial Equality. *Homelessness and Discrimination: Report of a Formal Investigation into the London Borough of Tower Hamlets*. London: Commission for Racial Inequality, 1988.

Cook, Peter. "Regarding the Smithsons". In *Alison and Peter Smithson: A Critical Anthology*. Max Risselada, ed. Barcelona: Ediciones Polígrafa, 2011.

Copley, Tom. "Right to Buy: Wrong for London". London Labour Assembly. January 2019, www.london.gov.uk/sites/default/files/rtb_report_feb_update.pdf.

Create Streets. "Alice in Wonderland". 2014, www.createstreets.com/wp-content/uploads/2017/12/Interview-with-Alice-Coleman.pdf.

Crimp, Douglas. *On the Museum's Ruins*. Cambridge, MA: MIT Press.

Crinson, Mark. "Brutalism: From New to Neo". Talk at Birkbeck, University of London. 19 May 2016, https://backdoorbroadcasting.net/2016/05/mark-crinson-brutalism-from-new-to-neo/.

Crinson, Mark. Talk at "Forgotten Estates". Royal Academy of Arts. 3 October 2016, www.youtube.com/watch?v=K-xktCBOd70.

Crinson, Mark. "Eye Wandering the Ceiling: Ornament and New Brutalism". *Art History* 41 no. 2 (April 2018): 318–343.

Crinson, Mark. *Alison and Peter Smithson*. Swindon: Historic England, 2018.

Crinson, Mark. "Neo Brutalism". *London Art History Society Review* (2021): 6–7.

Crosby, Theo, Alison Smithson and Peter Smithson. "The New Brutalism". *Architectural Design* (January 1955): 1.

Davies, Caroline. "David Cameron Vows to 'Blitz' Poverty by Demolishing UK's worst Sink Estates". *The Guardian*. 10 January 2016, www.theguardian.com/society/2016/jan/09/david-cameron-vows-to-blitz-poverty-by-demolishing-uks-worst-sink-estates.

Davis II, Charles L. *Building Character: The Racial Politics of Modern Architectural Style.* Pittsburgh, PA: The University of Pittsburgh Press, 2019.

Day, Gail. "Manfredo Tafuri, Fredric Jameson and the Contestations of Political Memory". *Historical Materialism* 20 no. 1 (2012): 31–77.

Deleuze, Gilles. *Cinema 1: The Movement-Image*. Hugh Tomlinson and Barbara Habberjam, trans. London: Athlone, 1986.

Deleuze, Gilles. *Foucault*. Seán Hand, trans. Minneapolis, MN: University of Minnesota Press, 1986.

Deleuze, Gilles. *Bergsonism*. Hugh Tomlinson and Barbara Habberjam, trans. New York: Zone Books, 1988.

Deleuze, Gilles. *Difference and Repetition*. Paul Patton, trans. New York: Columbia University Press, 1994.

Deleuze, Gilles. *Negotiations 1972–1990*. Martin Joughin, trans. New York: Columbia University Press, 1995.

Deleuze, Gilles. *Francis Bacon: The Logic of Sensation*. Daniel W. Smith, trans. London and New York: Continuum, 2003.

Deleuze, Gilles and Félix Guattari, *Kafka: Toward a Minor Literature*. Dana Polan, trans. Minneapolis: University of Minnesota Press, 1986.

Deleuze, Gilles and Félix Guattari. *A Thousand Plateaus: Capitalism and Schizophrenia Volume 2*. Brian Massumi, trans. Minneapolis: University of Minnesota Press, 1987.

Deleuze, Gilles and Félix Guattari. *What Is Philosophy?* Hugh Tomlinson and Graham Burchell, trans. London: Verso, 1994.

Depani, Alpa. "Gone in Forty Seconds". *CLOG: Brutalism* (2013): 162–163.

Dubuffet, Jean. "Art Brut in Preference to the Cultural Arts". Orig. 1949, https://cornpone.tumblr.com/post/8698135872/art-brut-in-preference-to-the-cultural-arts-jean.

Edelman, Lee. *No Future: Queer Theory and the Death Drive*. Durham, NC and London: Duke University Press, 2004.

Eisenman, Peter. "From Golden Lane to Robin Hood Gardens: Or If You Follow the Yellow Brick Road, It May not Lead to Golders Green". In *Alison and Peter Smithson: A Critical Anthology*. Max Risselada, ed. Barcelona: Ediciones Polígrafa, 2011.

Elmer, Simon and Geraldine Dening. "The London Clearances". *City* 20 no. 2 (2016): 271–277.

Endnotes. "Afterword". *Endnotes* 1 (2008): 208–216.

Endnotes. "A History of Separation". *Endnotes* 4 (2015): 70–192.

Engels, Frederick. *The Housing Question*. London: Lawrence and Wishart Ltd, 1942.

Evans, Greame. "From Albertopolis to Olympicopolis: Back to the Future?" In *Mega-Events: Placemaking, Regeneration and City-Regional Development*. Graeme Evans, ed. London: Routledge, 2020.

Fairness Commission. *Who Lives in Tower Hamlets? Where Do They Live? Communities and Housing Evidence Pack*. No date, www.towerhamlets.gov.uk/Documents/One-TH/Communities-and-Housing-Evidence-Pack.pdf.

Femi, Caleb. *Poor*. London: Penguin, 2020.

Fisher, Mark. *The Weird and the Eerie*. London: Repeater Books, 2016.

Focus E15 Campaign. "Sara and Her Children Must Stay in Newham!" 8 December 2017, https://focuse15.org/2017/12/08/sara-and-her-children-must-stay-in-newham/.

Forty, Adrian. *Concrete and Culture: A Materialist History*. London: Reaktion Books, 2012.

Forty, Adrian. "Paean to Brutalism". *RIBA Journal*. 8 August 2016, www.ribaj.com/culture/the-beauty-of-brutalism.

Furse, John. *The Smithsons at Robin Hood Gardens*. Unpublished PhD thesis, University of Sussex, 1982.

Galimberti, Jacopo. *Images of Class: Operaismo, Autonomia and the Visual Arts (1962–1988)*. London: Verso, 2022.

Gillespie, Tom, Kate Hardy and Paul Watt. "Austerity Urbanism and Olympic Counter-Legacies: Gendering, Defending and Expanding the Urban Commons in East London". *Environment and Planning D: Society and Space* 36 no. 5 (2018): 812–830.

Gillespie, Tom, Kate Hardy and Paul Watt. "Surplus to the City: Austerity Urbanism, Displacement and 'Letting Die'". *Environment and Planning A: Economy and Space* 53 no. 7 (October 2021): 1713–1729.

Ginsburg, Norman. "Institutional Racism and Local Authority Housing". *Critical Social Policy* 8 no. 24 (1988): 4–19.

Gissen, David. *Subnature: Architecture's Other Environments*. New York: Princeton Architectural Press, 2009.

Gissen, David. "Thoughts on a Heap of Rubble". *Kerb: Journal of Landscape Architecture* 19 (2011): 50–51.

Glinert, Ed. *East End Chronicles: Three Hundred Years of Mystery and Mayhem*. London: Penguin Books, 2006.

Gray, Neil, ed. *Rent and Its Discontents: A Century of Housing Struggles*. London: Rowman and Littlefield, 2018.

Glancey, Jonathan. "This Frog Could Become a Prince". *Building Design*. 29 February 2008.

Glendinning, Miles. *Mass Housing: Modern Architecture and State Power – A Global History*. London: Bloomsbury, 2021.

Grindrod, John. *Concretopia: A Journey around the Rebuilding of Postwar Britain*. London: Old Street Publishing, 2014.

The Guardian Editorial. "Building Blocks". *The Guardian*. 16 June 2008, www.theguardian.com/commentisfree/2008/jun/16/architecture.art.

Hall, Gary. *A Stubborn Fury: How Writing Works in Elitist Britain*. London: Open Humanities Press, 2021.

Hall, Stuart, Chas Critcher, Tony Jefferson, John Clarke and Brian Roberts. *Policing the Crisis: Mugging, the State and Law and Order*. London: Macmillan, 1978.

Hanley, Lynsey. "Britain Needs Decent New Council Houses – Not Just Musicals about Them". *The Guardian*. 3 April 2019, www.theguardian.com/commentisfree/2019/apr/03/britain-needs-new-council-houses-sheffield.

Harrabin, Roger. "Don't Demolish Old Buildings, Urge Architects". BBC News. 5 August 2020, www.bbc.co.uk/news/business-53642581.

Harvie, Jen. "Democracy and Neoliberalism in Art's Social Turn and Roger Hiorns's *Seizure*". *Performance Research: A Journal of the Performing Arts* 16 no. 2. (2011): 113–123.

Hatherley, Owen. *Militant Modernism*. London: Zero Books, 2009.

Hatherley, Owen. *A New Kind of Bleak: Journeys through Urban Britain*. London: Verso, 2012.

Hatherley, Owen. "Not the Same as Building for the Socialist State: Robin Hood Gardens in and Against the Architecture of the Welfare State". In Jessie Brennan, *Regeneration! Conversations, Drawings, Archives and Photographs from Robin Hood Gardens*. London: Silent Grid, 2015.

Hatherley, Owen. *Red Metropolis: Socialism and the Government of London*. London: Repeater Books, 2020.

Hicks, Dan. *The Brutish Museums: The Benin Bronzes, Colonial Violence, and Cultural Restitution*. London: Pluto Press, 2020.

Highmore, Ben. "Rough Poetry: *Patio and Pavilion* Revisited". *Oxford Art Journal* 29 no. 2 (2006): 269–290.

Highmore, Ben. *The Art of Brutalism: Rescuing Hope from Catastrophe in 1950s Britain*. New Haven, CT and London: Yale University Press, 2017.

Hill, Jonathan. *Weather Architecture*. London and New York: Routledge, 2012.

Hiorns Roger and James Lingwood. "Writing: The Impregnation of an Object". Artangel blog. July 2008, www.artangel.org.uk/seizure/the-impregnation-of-an-object/.

Hodkinson, Stuart. *Safe as Houses: Private Greed, Political Negligence and Housing Policy after Grenfell*. Manchester: University of Manchester Press, 2019.

Hunt, Tristram. "Displaying the Ruins of Demolished Social Sousing at the Venice Architecture Biennale is not 'Art-Washing'". *The Art Newspaper*. 28 May 2018, www.theartnewspaper.com/comment/displaying-the-ruins-of-demolished-social-housing-is-not-art-washing-the-v-and-a-is-a-place-for-unsafe-ideas.

Hunt, Tristram. "Museums Must Confront the Big Issues". *The Art Newspaper*. 20 December 2018, www.theartnewspaper.com/comment/museums-must-confront-the-big-issues.

The Irish Times. "Architecture Save Our Scheme... Architects Turn to Public". *The Irish Times*. 15 May 2008, www.irishtimes.com/life-and-style/homes-and-property/architecture-save-our-scheme-architects-turn-to-public-1.1264941.

Jacobs, Sidney. "Race, Empire and the Welfare State: Council Housing and Racism." *Critical Social Policy* 5 no. 13 (1985): 6–28.

James, Malcolm. "Authoritarian Populism / Populist Authoritarianism"'. In Alberto Duman, Dan Hancox, Malcolm James and Anna Minton, eds. *Regeneration Songs: Sounds of Investment and Loss from East London*. London: Repeater Books, 2018.

Jameson, Fredric. *Postmodernism: Or, the Cultural Logic of Late Capitalism.* London: Verso, 1991.

Jameson, Fredric. *Archaeologies of the Future: The Desire Called Utopia and Other Science Fictions*. London and New York: Verso, 2005.

Jameson, Fredric. "Architecture and the Critique of Ideology". In *The Ideologies of Theory*. London and New York: Verso, 2008.

Jameson, Fredric. "From Metaphor to Allegory". In Cynthia Davidson, ed. *Anything*. New York: Anyone Corporation, 2001.

Jappe, Anselm. *Béton: Arme de construction massive du capitalisme*. Paris: L'Echappée, 2020.

Jappe, Anselm. "Can We Cure Our Addiction to Concrete?" *Signe*. 29 May 2021, www.pavillon-arsenal.com/en/signe/11989-can-we-cure-our-addiction-to-concrete.html.

Jencks, Charles. *The Language of Post-Modern Architecture*. 2nd edn. London: Academy Editions, 1978.

Jencks, Charles. *The New Paradigm in Architecture*. New Haven, CT and London: Yale University Press, 2002.

Jenkins, Simon. "This Icon of 60s New Brutalism has Its Champions. So Let them Restore It". *The Guardian*. 20 June 2008, www.theguardian.com/commentisfree/2008/jun/20/architecture.

Johnson, B. S., dir. *The Smithsons on Housing*. BBC Television, 1970.

Jones, Christopher. "Pyramid Dead – The Artangel of History". *Mute*. 17 April 2014, www.metamute.org/editorial/articles/pyramid-dead-artangel-history.

Jones, Edward and Christopher Woodward. *Guide to the Architecture of London*. London: Phoenix, 2013.

Jorn, Asger. "Image and Form: Against Eclectic Empiricism". In *Fraternité Avant Tout: Asger Jorn's Writing's on Art and Architecture, 1938–1958*. Ruth Baumeister, ed. Paul Larkin, trans. Rotterdam: 010 Publishers, 2011.

Kallin, Hamish and Tom Slater. "Activating Territorial Stigma: Gentrifying Marginality on Edinburgh's Periphery". *Environment and Planning A* 46 (2014): 1351–1368.

Kassim, Sumaya. "The Museum Will Not Be Decolonised". *Media Diversified*. 15 November 2017, https://mediadiversified.org/2017/11/15/the-museum-will-not-be-decolonised/.

Kassim, Sumaya. "The Museum Is the Master's House: An Open Letter to Tristram Hunt". 26 July 2019, https://medium.com/@sumayakassim/the-museum-is-the-masters-house-an-open-letter-to-tristram-hunt-e72d75a891c8.

Kitnick, Alex. "Introduction". *October* 136 (2011): 3–6.

Kitnick, Alex. "The Brutalism of Life and Art". *October* 136 (2011): 63–86.

Klee, Paul. *Pedagogical Sketchbook*. Sibyl Moholy-Nagy, intro. and trans. London: Faber and Faber, 1968.

Knott, Jonathan. "Tristram Hunt 'Not Interested' in V&A Prayer Room". *Arts Professional*. 27 June 2019, www.artsprofessional.co.uk/news/tristram-hunt-not-interested-va-prayer-room.

Knott, Jonathan. "Three Comments that Reveal Tristram Hunt's Approach to Cultural Inclusion". *Arts Professional*. 5 July 2019, www.artsprofessional.co.uk/news/three-comme nts-reveal-tristram-hunts-approach-cultural-inclusion.

Kornbluh, Anna. *The Order of Forms: Realism, Formalism and Social Space*. Chicago, IL: Chicago University Press.

Laster, Paul. "Do Ho Suh: From Sculpture to Film". *Whitehot Magazine*. November 2019, https:// whitehotmagazine.com/articles/ho-suh-from-sculpture-film/4436.

Lawler, Steph. "White Like Them: Whiteness and Anachronistic Space in Representations of the English White Working Class". *Ethnicities* 12 no. 4 (2012): 409–426.

Lawrence, Felicity, Niamh McIntyre and Patrick Butler. "Labour Councils in England Hit Harder by Austerity than Tory Areas". *The Guardian*. 21 June 2020, www.theguardian.com/business/ 2020/jun/21/exclusive-labour-councils-in-england-hit-harder-by-austerity-than-tory-areas.

Lees, Loretta and Hannah White. "The Social Cleansing of London Council Estates: Everyday Experiences of 'Accumulative Dispossession'". *Housing Studies* 35 no. 10 (2020): 1701–1722.

Li, Ang. "Raised by Association: Robin Hood Gardens and Its Interpretations", *Thresholds* 43 (2015): 110–119.

Lindner, Christoph. "Brutalism, Ruins, and the Urban Imaginary of Gentrification". In *The Routledge Companion to Urban Imaginaries*. Christoph Lindner and Miriam Meissner, eds. London: Routledge, 2018.

Lloyd Thomas, Katie. "Rendered Plastic by Preparation: Concrete as Constant Material". *Parallax* 21 no. 3 (2015): 277–287.

The London Borough of Tower Hamlets (Blackwall Reach) Compulsory Purchase Order 2013: Statement of Reasons. London: London Borough of Tower Hamlets, 2013.

London Dockland Study Team. *Docklands Redevelopment Proposal for East London*. London: Department of the Environment, 1973.

London Psychogeographical Association and the Archaeogeodetic Association. *The Great Conjunction: The Symbols of a College, the Death of a King and the Maze on the Hill*. London: Unpopular Books, no date.

Londonewcastle. *Balfron Tower*. 2019. https://londonewcastle.com/content/4-for-sale/balf ron-tower/balfron-tower-brochure.pdf.

Lowe, Jennifer Maureen. *Social Justice and Localities: The Allocation of Council Housing in Tower Hamlets*. Unpublished PhD thesis, Queen Mary, University of London, 2004.

Madden, David and Peter Marcuse. *In Defense of Housing: The Politics of Crisis*. London and New York: Verso, 2016.

Makdisi, Saree. *Tolerance Is a Wasteland: Palestine and the Culture of Denial*. Oakland, CA: University of California Press, 2022.

Martin, Alice and Josh Ryan-Collins. "The Financialisation of UK Homes". *New Economics Foundation: The Housing Crisis, Land and the Banks*. 21 April 2016, https://neweconomics.org/2016/04/the-financialisation-of-uk-homes.

Marx, Karl. "A Contribution to Hegel's Philosophy of Right". In *Early Writings*. Rodney Livingstone and Gregor Benton, trans. Harmondsworth: Penguin, 1975.

Marx, Karl. "On the Jewish Question". In *Early Writings*. Rodney Livingstone and Gregor Benton, trans. Harmondsworth: Penguin, 1975.

Marx, Karl. *Capital: A Critical Analysis of Capitalist Production*, vol. 1. Ben Fowkes, trans. London: Penguin, 1976.

Marx, Karl and Friedrich Engels. "The Holy Family; or Critique of Critical Criticism". In *Collected Works*, vol. 4. London: Lawrence and Wishart, 1975.

Massumi, Brian. "Sensing the Virtual, Building the Insensible". In *Couplets: Travels in Speculative Pragmatism*. Durham, NC and London: Duke University Press, 2021.

May, Vanessa and Camilla Lewis. "Researching Embodied Relationships with Place: Rehabilitating the Sit-Down Interview". *Qualitative Research* 20 no. 2 (2020): 127–142.

McKay, Claude. *A Long Way from Home: An Autobiography*. London: Pluto Press, 1985.

Meek, James. *Private Island: Why Britain Now Belongs to Someone Else*. London: Verso, 2015.

Mellor, Joe. "Over 31,000 London Residents Losing Homes as Council Estates to be Demolished". *The London Economic*. 3 September 2018, www.thelondoneconomic.com/news/over-31000-london-residents-losing-homes-as-council-estates-to-be-demolished/03/09/.

Michael, Andrew and Laura Howard. "UK House Prices – Latest News". *Forbes Advisor*. 1 December 2021, www.forbes.com/uk/advisor/personal-finance/2021/12/01/house-prices-updates/.

Minton, Anna. *Scaring the Living Daylights out of People: The Local Lobby and the Failure of Democracy*. Spinwatch. March 2013.

Minton, Anna. *Big Capital: Who Is London For?* London: Penguin, 2017.

Minton, Anna. "Setting the Scene: Thirty Years of Regeneration in East London". In *Regeneration Songs: Sounds of Investment and Loss from East London*. Alberto Duman, Anna Minton, Dan Hancox and Malcolm James, eds. London: Repeater Books, 2018.

The Modern House. "A to Z of Modern Living: Ab Robers on Balfron Tower, Sensitive Architecture and Community-Focused Design". *The Modern House Journal*. 15 October 2019, www.themodernhouse.com/journal/ab-rogers-design-balfron/.

Morby, Aaron. "1bn Stratford East Bank Scheme Clears Final Planning". *Construction Enquirer*. 2019, www.constructionenquirer.com/2019/06/12/1bn-stratford-east-bank-scheme-cle ars-final-planning/.

Mota, Nelson. *An Archaeology of the Ordinary: Rethinking the Architecture of Dwelling from CIAM to Siza*. Unpublished PhD thesis, Delft University of Technology, 2014.

Muir, Hugh. "Diary". *The Guardian*. 19 February 2008, www.theguardian.com/politics/2008/ feb/19/1.

Newbury, Darren. "Photography and the Visualization of Working Class Lives in Britain". *Visual Anthropology Review* 15 no. 1 (Spring-Summer 1999): 21–44.

Newham local authority. "Housing Reaffirmed as Biggest Priority for Mayor of Newham as Shelter confirms East London Borough has Homeless Crisis". www.newham.gov.uk/news/ article/179/housing-reaffirmed-as-biggest-priority-for-mayor-of-newham-as-shelter-confi rms-east-london-borough-has-homeless-crisis.

Newsinger, John. "War, Empire and the Attlee Government 1945–1951". *Race and Class* 60 no. 1: 67–76.

Norfield, Tony. "Origins of the UK Welfare State". *Economics of Imperialism* blog. 8 October 2015, https://economicsofimperialism.blogspot.com/2015/10/origins-of-uk-welfare-state.html.

Olcayto, Rory. "Robin Hood Gardens Will Not Be Listed". *Building Design*. 1 July 2008, https:// architexturez.net/pst/az-cf-31331-1214927181.

Pauling, Darren. "I'm Sick of Concrete Jungle Creeping Up on Robin Hood Gardens". *The Docklands and East London Advertiser*. 6 December 2010, www.eastlondonadvertiser.co.uk/ news/i-m-sick-of-concrete-jungle-creeping-up-on-robin-3415390.

Pedret, Annie. "Dismantling the CIAM Grid: New Values for Modern Architecture". In *Team 10 1953–81: In Search of a Utopia of the Present*. Max Risselada and Dirk van den Heuvel, eds. Rotterdam: NAi Publishers, 2005.

Pedret, Annie. *Team 10: An Archival History*. London and New York: Routledge, 2013.

Phipps, Simon. *Finding Brutalism: A Photographic Survey of Post-War British Architecture*. Hilar Stadler and Andreas Hertach, ed. Zurich: Park Books, 2017.

Popham, Peter. "Brutalist, Original, But a Slum". *The Independent*. 1 October 1995, www.inde pendent.co.uk/arts-entertainment/art/news/brutalist-original-but-a-slum-1575542.html.

Powers, Alan. "A Critical Narrative". In *Robin Hood Gardens: Re-Visions*. Alan Powers, ed. London: Twentieth Century Society, 2010.

Prestsæter, Ellef, ed. *These Are Situationist Times! An Inventory of Reproductions, Deformations, Modifications, Derivations, and Transformations*. Oslo: Torpedo Press, 2019.

Price, Derrick. "Photographing the Poor and the Working Class". *Framework: The Journal of Cinema and Media* 22/23 (Autumn 1983): 20–25.

Pritchard, Stephen. "The Artwashing of Gentrification and Social Cleansing". In *The Handbook of Displacement*. Peter Adey, Janet C. Bowstead, Katherine Brickell, Vandana Desai, Mike Dolton, Alasdair Pinkerton and Ayesha Siddiqi, eds. London: Palgrave, 2020.

Reinders, Robert C. "Racialism on the Left: E. D. Morel and the 'Black Horror in the Rhine'". *International Review of Social History* 13 no. 1 (1968): 1–28.

Rendell, Jane. "Introduction: Architecture Writing". In *Critical Architecture*. Jane Rendell, Jonathan Hill, Murray Fraser and Mark Dorrian eds. New York: Routledge, 2007.

Rendell, Jane. *Site-Writing: The Architecture of Art Criticism*. London and New York: I.B. Tauris, 2010.

Rendell, Jane. *The Architecture of Psychoanalysis: Spaces of Transition*. London and New York: I.B. Tauris, 2017.

Richard, Frances. "Home in the World: The Art of Do-Ho Suh". *Artforum*. January 2002, www.artforum.com/print/200201/home-in-the-world-the-art-of-do-ho-suh-2092.

Risselada, Max. "The Space Between". In Alison and Peter Smithson, *The Space Between*. Max Risselada, ed. Köln: Walther König, 2017.

Roberts, David. "Making Public: Performing Public Housing in Ernő Goldfinger's Balfron Tower". *The Journal of Architecture* 22 no. 1 (2017): 123–150.

Rogers, David. "Hodge Scoffs at Latest Attempt to List Robin Hood Gardens". *Building Design*. 18 March 2015, www.bdonline.co.uk/hodge-scoffs-at-latest-attempt-to-list-robin-hood-gardens/5074417.

Rossall Valentine, Daniel. *Housing Crisis: An Analysis of the Investment Demand Behind the UK's Housing Affordability Crisis*. The Bow Group. 2015, https://paperzz.com/doc/9214114/daniel-rossall-valentine.

Salad of Pearls. "Completion of the Mis-Maze atop the Sacred Mounds of St Catherine's Hill / Robin Hood Gardens". saladofpearls. 7 March 2017. https://saladofpearls.wordpress.com/2017/03/07/completion-of-the-mis-maze-on-the-sacred-mounds-of-st-catherines-robin-hood-gardens/.

Savills. *Completing London's Streets: Savills Research Report to the Cabinet Office*. 7 January 2016, https://pdf.euro.savills.co.uk/uk/residential---other/completing-london-s-streets-080116.pdf.

Shilliam, Robbie. *Race and the Undeserving Poor*. Newcastle: Agenda Publishing, 2018.

Simondon, Gilbert. *Individuation in Light of Notions of Form and Information*. Taylor Adkins, trans. Minneapolis and London: University of Minnesota Press, 2020.

Skeggs, Beverley. *Class, Self, Culture*. London and New York: Routledge, 2004.

Skeggs, Beverley. "Introduction: Stratification or Exploitation, Domination, Dispossession and Devaluation?" *The Sociological Review* 63 no. 2 (2015): 205–222.

Slater, Tom. "The Invention of the 'Sink Estate': Consequential Categorisation and the UK Housing Crisis". *The Sociological Review Monographs* 66 no. 4 (2018): 877–897.

Smith, Neil. *The New Urban Frontier: Gentrification and the Revanchist City*. London: Routledge, 1996.

Smithson, Alison, ed. for Team 10. "Team 10 Primer". *Architectural Design* 32 (December 1962): 559–563.

Smithson, Alison. "The Arch Criminals of the Euston Arch". In Alison and Peter Smithson, *The Euston Arch and the Growth of the London, Midland and Scottish Railway*. London: Thames and Hudson, 1968.

Smithson, Alison. "The Violent Consumer, or Waiting for the Goodies". *Architectural Design* 5 (1974): 274–279.

Smithson, Alison. *AS in DS: An Eye on the Road*. Delft: Lars Müller Publishers, 2001 [orig. 1983].

Smithson, Alison. "Transmissions and Connections". In Alison and Peter Smithson, *The Charged Void: Architecture*. New York: The Monacelli Press, 2001.

Smithson, Alison. "Saint Jerome: The Desert ... The Study". In *Alison and Peter Smithson: From the House of the Future to a House of Today*. Max Risselada and Dirk van den Heuvel, eds. Rotterdam: 010 Publishers, 2004.

Smithson, Alison. "Into the Air". In Alison and Peter Smithson, *The Space Between*. Max Risselada, ed. Köln: Walther König, 2017.

Smithson, Alison and Peter. "House in Soho, London". *Architectural Design* 23 no. 12 (December 1953): 342.

Smithson, Alison and Peter. "Cluster City: A New Shape for the Community". *Architectural Review* 122 (1957): 332–336.

Smithson, Alison and Peter. "The New Brutalism: Alison and Peter Smithson Answer the Criticisms on the Opposite Page". *Architectural Design* (April 1957): 113.

Smithson, Alison and Peter. "Banham's Bumper Book on Brutalism". *The Architect's Journal* 144 no. 26 (1966): 1590–1591.

Smithson, Alison and Peter. "Contributions to a Fragmentary Utopia". In *Urban Structuring: Studies of Alison and Peter Smithson*. London: Studio Vista, 1967.

Smithson, Alison and Peter. *Urban Structuring: Studies of Alison and Peter Smithson*. London: Studio Vista, 1967.

Smithson, Alison and Peter. *The Euston Arch and the Growth of the London, Midland and Scottish Railway*. London: Thames and Hudson, 1968.

Smithson, Alison and Peter. *Ordinariness and Light: Urban Theories 1952–1960 and their Application in a Building Project 1963–1970*. London: Faber and Faber, 1970.

Smithson, Alison and Peter. "Signs of Occupancy". *Architectural Design* 42 no. 2 (1972): 91–97.

Smithson, Alison and Peter. "Robin Hood Gardens London E14". *Architectural Design* 42 no. 9 (1972): 559–572.

Smithson, Alison and Peter. *Without Rhetoric: An Architectural Aesthetic 1955–1972.* London: Latimer, 1973.

Smithson, Alison and Peter. "The Space Between". *Oppositions* 4 (1974): 75–78.

Smithson, Alison and Peter. *The Heroic Period of Modern Architecture.* London: Thames and Hudson, 1981.

Smithson, Alison and Peter. *The Shift.* London: Academy Editions, 1982.

Smithson, Alison and Peter. "Criteria for Mass Housing". In John Furse, *The Smithsons at Robin Hood Gardens.* Unpublished PhD thesis. University of Sussex, 1982.

Smithson, Alison and Peter. *Upper Lawn: Solar Pavilion Folly.* Barcelona: Edicions de la Universitat Politècnica Catalunya, 1986.

Smithson, Alison and Peter. "The 'As Found' and the 'Found'". In *The Independent Group: Postwar Britain and the Aesthetics of Plenty.* David Robbins, ed. Cambridge, MA: MIT Press, 1990.

Smithson, Alison and Peter. *Italian Thoughts.* Privately published, 1993.

Smithson, Alison and Peter. "Robin Hood Gardens, London". In *The Charged Void: Architecture.* New York: The Monacelli Press, 2001.

Smithson, Alison and Peter. "Sheffield University". In *The Charged Void: Architecture.* New York: The Monacelli Press, 2001.

Smithson, Alison and Peter. "'Sticks and Stones' Exhibition". In *The Charged Void: Architecture.* New York: The Monacelli Press, 2001.

Smithson, Alison and Peter. "Tees Pudding, Middlesbrough, Spring 1977". In *The Charged Void: Architecture.* New York: The Monacelli Press, 2001.

Smithson, Alison and Peter. "The Slaggie Eleven of the Spenymoor Slag Heaps, Spring 1977". In *The Charged Void: Architecture.* New York: The Monacelli Press, 2001.

Smithson, Alison and Peter. *The Charged Void: Urbanism.* New York: The Monacelli Press, 2005.

Smithson, Alison and Peter. "Aspect and Prospect Responsive". In *The Charged Void: Urbanism.* Chuihua Judy Chung, ed. New York: The Monacelli Press, 2005.

Smithson, Alison and Peter. "Sketch: Acoustic Boundary Wall". In *Robin Hood Gardens: Re-Visions*, Alan Powers, ed. London: Twentieth Century Society, 2010.

Smithson, Peter. "Postscript". In Alison and Peter Smithson, *The Euston Arch and the Growth of the London, Midland and Scottish Railway.* London: Thames and Hudson, 1968.

Smithson, Peter. "Simple Thoughts on Repetition". *Architectural Design* 41 (1971): 479–481.

Smithson, Peter. "On Le Corbusier". In Alison and Peter Smithson, *The Heroic Period of Modern Architecture.* London: Thames and Hudson, 1981.

Smithson, Peter. "National Life Story Collection: Architects Lives". Interview by Louise Brodie, 13 of 19 (1997), https://sounds.bl.uk/Oral-history/Architects-Lives/021M-C0467X0024XX-1300V0.

Smithson, Peter. "Think of it as a Farm! Exhibitions, Books, Buildings: An Interview with Peter Smithson". In *This Is Not Architecture*. Kester Rattenbury, ed. London: Routledge, 2002.

Smithson, Peter. "Intention". In Alison and Peter Smithson, *The Charged Void: Architecture*. New York: The Monacelli Press, 2001.

Smithson, Peter. "Empooling." In *Re-Envisioning Landscape / Architecture*. Catherine Spellman, ed. Barcelona: Actar, 2003.

Smithson, Peter. "Territorial Imprint". In Alison and Peter Smithson, *The Space Between*. Max Risselada, ed. Köln: Walther König, 2017.

Smithson, Peter and Hans Ulrich Obrist. *Smithson Time: A Dialogue*. Köln: Walter König, 2004.

Smithson, Alison, Peter Smithson, Jane B. Drew and E. Maxwell Fry. "Conversation on Brutalism". *October* 136 (2011 [orig. 1959]): 38–46.

Smithson, Simon. "Interview: Simon Smithson". *Building Design*. 21 February 2008, www.bdonline.co.uk/opinion/interview-simon-smithson/3107017.article.

Smithson, Simon. "We Called it 'Robin Hood Lane'". In *Robin Hood Gardens: Re-Visions*. Alan Powers, ed. London: Twentieth Century Society, 2010.

Smithson, Simon. "The Brutal Truth about the Destruction of Robin Hood Lane". In Jessica Mairs, "Robin Hood Gardens Demolition Is an 'Act of Vandalism' says Simon Smithson". *Dezeen*. 10 August 2017, www.dezeen.com/2017/08/10/robin-hood-gardens-demolition-simon-alison-peter-smithson-post-war-housing-estate-london-uk-news/.

Smithson, Simon J. B. "A Few Words about A & P Writing". In Alison and Peter Smithson, *The Space Between*. Max Risselada, ed. Köln: Walther König, 2017.

Southwark Notes. "Empowerment for Surrender: People's Bureau, Engaged Art and the Elephant". Southwark Notes. 1 January 2017, https://southwarknotes.wordpress.com/art-and-regeneration/empowerment-for-surrender-peoples-bureau-engaged-art-the-elephant/.

Stalder, Laurent. "'New Brutalism,' 'Topology' and 'Image': Some Remarks on the Architectural Debates in England around 1950". *The Journal of Architecture* 13 no. 3 (2008): 263–281.

Steiner, Hadas. "Life at the Threshold". *October* 136 (2011): 133–155.

Sylvester, David. "Klee – I". *About Modern Art: Critical Essays 1948–97*. London: Pimlico, 1997.

Sylvester, David. "Klee – II". *About Modern Art: Critical Essays 1948–97*. London: Pimlico, 1997.

Tafuri, Manfredo. *Architecture and Utopia: Design and Capitalist Development*. Barbara Luigia La Penta, trans. Cambridge, MA and London: MIT Press, 1976.

Tafuri, Manfredo. *The Sphere and the Labyrinth: Avant-Gardes and Architecture from Piranesi to the 1970s*. Pellegrino d'Acierno and Robert Connolly, trans. Cambridge, MA and London: MIT Press, 1987.

Tamás, G. M. "Telling the Truth about Class". *Socialist Register* 42 (2006): 1–41.

Taylor, David. "Smithson Excluded from Work on Estate he Designed". *Architects' Journal*. 10 August 1995.

Taylor-Foster, James. "Sam Jacob and Wouter Vanstiphout on Curating 'A Clockwork Jerusalem'". *ArchDaily*. 24 June 2014, www.archdaily.com/517501/interview-sam-jacob-and-wouter-vanstiphout-curators-of-a-clockwork-jerusalem-at-the-2014-venice-biennale.

Thoburn, Nicholas. "Do Not Be Afraid, Join Us, Come Back? On the 'Idea of Communism' in Our Time". *Cultural Critique* 84 (2013): 1–34.

Thoburn, Nicholas. "The People Are Missing: Cramped Space, Social Relations, and the Mediators of Politics". *International Journal of Politics, Culture and Society* 29 no. 4 (2016): 367–81.

Thoburn, Nicholas. *Anti-Book: On the Art and Politics of Radical Publishing*. Minneapolis and London: Minnesota University Press, 2016.

Thoburn, Nicholas. "Twitter, Book, Riot: Post-Digital Publishing against Race". *Theory, Culture and Society* 37 no. 3 (2020): 97–121.

Tower Hamlets. *Borough Profile 2020: Chapter 1. Population*. www.towerhamlets.gov.uk/lgnl/community_and_living/borough_statistics/Borough_profile.aspx.

Tsing, Anna Lowenhaupt. *The Mushroom at the End of the World: On the Possibility of Life in Capitalist Ruins*. Princeton, NJ: Princeton University Press, 2015.

Turner, Christopher. "A Small Segment of a Masterpiece". V&A Blog. 6 March 2018, www.vam.ac.uk/blog/museum-life/a-small-segment-of-a-masterpiece-2.

Turner, Christopher. "La Biennale di Venezia 2018". 25 May 2018, www.vam.ac.uk/blog/museum-life/la-biennale-di-venezia-2018.

Turner, Christopher. "Poplar in Panorama". *V&A Magazine* 50 (2019): 48–55.

Tyler, Imogen. "Classificatory Struggles: Class, Culture and Inequality in Neoliberal Times". *The Sociological Review* 63 no. 2 (2015): 493–511.

Urban Design London. *A New London Housing Vernacular*. 2018, www.urbandesignlondon.com/documents/24/ANEWLONDONVERNACULAR_-_COMP.pdf.

Van Berkel, Ben and Caroline Bos. "Diagrams: Interactive Instruments in Operation". In *This Is Not Architecture*. Kester Rattenbury, ed. London: Routledge, 2002.

Van den Heuvel, Dirk. *Alison and Peter Smithson: A Brutalist Story Involving the House, the City and the Everyday*. Unpublished PhD thesis, Delft University of Technology, 2003.

Van den Heuvel, Dirk. Review of Alison and Peter Smithson, *The Charged Void: Architecture*. *AA Files* no. 49 (Spring 2003): 97–100.

Van den Heuvel, Dirk. "Team 10 Riddles: A Few Notes on Mythopoesis, Discourse, and Epistemology". In *Team 10: Keeping the Language of Modern Architecture Alive*. Max Risselada, Dirk van den Heuvel and Gijs de Waal, eds. Delft: Delft University, 2006.

Van den Heuvel, Dirk. "Between Brutalists: The Banham Hypothesis and the Smithson Way of Life". *The Journal of Architecture* 20 no. 2 (2015): 293–308.

Victoria and Albert Museum. "The V&A East Project". No date, www.vam.ac.uk/info/va-east-project.

Victoria and Albert Museum. "The V&A at the 2018 Architecture Biennale". No date, www.vam.ac.uk/articles/la-biennale-di-venezia-2018.

Vidler, Anthony. "Another Brick in the Wall". *October* 136 (2011): 105–132.

Vile&Arrogant. *No al monumento alla gentrificazione del museo V&A di Londra / No to V&A's Monument to London's Social Cleansing*. Two-sided A4 leaflet. No date [2018], https://southwarknotes.files.wordpress.com/2018/05/robin-hood-gardens-eng-ita.pdf.

Vilenica, Ana. "Against Museumification of Social Housing". Talk at Four Corners Gallery, London. 1 June 2019.

Virdee, Satnam. *Racism, Class, and the Racialized Outsider*. London: Red Globe Press, 2014.

Wacquant, Loïc. "Territorial Stigmatization in the Age of Advanced Marginality". *Thesis Eleven* 91 no. 1 (2007): 66–77.

Wainwright, Oliver. "Wayne Hemingway's 'Pop Up' Plan Sounds the Death Knell for the Legendary Balfron Tower". *The Guardian*. 26 September 2014. www.theguardian.com/artanddesign/architecture-design-blog/2014/sep/26/wayne-hemingways-pop-up-plan-sounds-the-death-knell-for-the-legendary-balfron-tower.

Wainwright, Oliver. "The Case for... Never Demolishing Another Building". *The Guardian*. 13 January 2020, www.theguardian.com/cities/2020/jan/13/the-case-for-never-demolishing-another-building.

Wainwright, Oliver. "'Sometimes the Answer Is to Do Nothing': Unflashy French Duo Take Architecture's Top Prize". *The Guardian*. 16 March 2021, www.theguardian.com/artanddesign/2021/mar/16/lacaton-vassal-unflashy-french-architectures-pritzker-prize.

Watson, Joseph. "Towering Ambitions: Balfron Tower and the National Trust". 2014, www.balfrontower.org/document/93/flat-130-balfron-tower.

Watt, Paul. *Estate Regeneration and its Discontents: Public Housing, Place and Inequality in London*. London: Policy Press, 2021.

Watt, Paul and Penny Bernstock. "Legacy for Whom? Housing in Post-Olympic East London". In *London 2012 and the Post-Olympics City: A Hollow Legacy?* Phil Cohen and Paul Watt, eds. London: Palgrave, 2017.

Watts, Jonathan. "Concrete: The Most Destructive Material on Earth". 25 February 2019, www.theguardian.com/cities/2019/feb/25/concrete-the-most-destructive-material-on-earth.

Withagen, Rob and Simone R. Caljouw. "Aldo van Eyck's Playgrounds: Aesthetics, Affordances, and Creativity". *Frontiers in Psychology* 8 Article 1130 (4 July 2017): 1–9.

Youle, Emma. "The Great Housing Postcode Lottery: Ex-Newham Mayor Slammed over 3,000 Homeless Moved Out of Borough". *Newham Recorder*. 25 July 2018, www.newhamrecorder.co.uk/news/ex-newham-mayor-slammed-over-3-000-homeless-households-moved-out-of-borough-1-5607150.

Young, Michael and Peter Willmott. *Family and Kinship in East London*. London: Routledge and Kegan Paul, 1957.

Zepke, Stephen. "Modernism Forever: Towards a New 'New Brutalism'". Unpublished conference talk, no date.

Zepke, Stephen. *Art as Abstract Machine: Ontology and Aesthetics in Deleuze and Guatari.* New York and London: Routledge, 2005.

Zepke, Stephen. *Towards a New "New Brutalism": Wandering around of Robin Hood Gardens.* Bogotá: Universidad Nacional de Colombia, forthcoming.

35% Campaign, "Elephant Park MP5 – the Final Chapter". 5 August 2019, http://35percent.org/2019-08-05-elephant-park-final-phase-affordable-housing/.

35% Campaign. "Social Rent or Affordable Rent?" 16 January 2021, www.35percent.org/affordable-housing-monitoring-15000-homes/.

Index